The Red House on the Niobrara

Six months alone on a Panhandle cattle ranch

Alan Wilkinson

'The Nebraska Panhandle, huh? We-ell, I can tell you what it's like, feller.' He drew on his cigarette, paused, and exhaled. 'It's desolate.' Then he repeated the word, nice and slow, in case I hadn't caught it. 'De-so-late.'

Cowboy in diner, Bushnell, Nebraska, Sept. 1994

Contents

'I'll tell you what it's like out there'

I really wanted to start with Buffalo Bill, even though I can hear Mari Sandoz snorting her disapproval at the very mention of his name. She never thought much of him. But that's a great story, the one about my great-great-uncle. I mean the ship's captain, back in 1887, who ferried the old scout and his troupe of showmen, sharpshooters and Indians across the Atlantic on the *State of Nebraska* and introduced into my family the precious Wild West souvenirs that so fascinated me as a five-year-old. It always seemed to me that if I was going to tell a story about my time here on the Great Plains, that would be the place to begin, with Captain Wiltshire. Trouble is, it turned out that just because a story's been around for a hundred years it doesn't mean it's true.

So, if I'm going to explain what persuaded a sixty-two-year-old jobbing writer to spend six months alone in a semi-derelict hunting lodge in the remote and forbidding Sandhills of western Nebraska I'd better start with an earlier escapade, and a pretty foolhardy one at that. I mean the time I set off from the banks of the Missouri river on a borrowed bicycle, and pedalled west in my sandals until I was able to convince myself that the flickering whiteness I thought I saw on the far horizon might just be the Rocky Mountains.

Rulo to Kimball, and then some - the whole length of Nebraska, from its lowest point, 840 feet above sea level, to its highest, 5,424, just to get a sense of the place. It wasn't much more than 600 miles, but it was two weeks of hard going in a fierce September heatwave. I was on the last leg, shoveling breakfast down my throat in a tiny 'Mom and Pop' joint at Bushnell (population 124), the point where I would finally leave Highway 30 and make my way across country on graveled roads to Promontory Point, over a mile above sea level.

I can still see that cowboy at the next table, rubbing a calloused hand over his chin and looking out across the dusty yard at an endless vista of low hills, their bunch-grass overcoat ruffled by a brisk south-easterly. 'What exactly you say you're doin' out here?' he asked.

'Well,' I said, 'I'm pedaling my bike across Nebraska, east to west.' I wanted to tell him about my great-great uncle, about my interest in Mari Sandoz, biographer of Crazy Horse, who'd grown up just north of here but got the hell out as soon as she could, and the way she chose to paint it, years later, from the safety of the east: majestic, beautiful, haunting, calling to her from a thousand miles away. But out west you don't generally break into poetic abstraction unless you've earned the right, and that's the province of old-timers, drunks, or bona fide oddballs.

While I was thinking the cowboy lit a cigarette and said, 'Now what in the name o' tarnation made you do a damn fool thing like that?' He grinned at me through a veil of blue smoke. 'Lose a bet, did ya?'

It wasn't the first time I'd had to answer such questions in diners and bars along the way. By now I'd honed my response down to a single line and couched it in western idiom. 'Guess I wanted to see what Nebraska's really like,' I told him.

He stared out the window some more, watching the wind tug at the yellowing leaves of the old cottonwood against which I'd propped my bicycle. Then he turned towards me. 'We-ell, I can tell you what it's like, feller.' He drew on his cigarette, and exhaled slowly. 'It's desolate.' Then he repeated it, nice and slow, just in case I hadn't caught it. 'De-so-late.'

I'd used the very same word in my diary two days previously after I rode out of Ogallala and into a 55 mph head-wind, when a level sheet of cloud spread over the landscape like a huge grey tablecloth, compressing the space between earth and sky. The dirt was flying, the visibility dropped to fifty yards and I went down through the gears, click click click, until I just ground to a halt.

It wasn't the first time I'd felt like giving up. If I'm honest, there were moments along the undulations of the Republican river valley with its three, four, five hills per mile, later beside the railroad tracks that follow the Platte, when the temperature hit 97 and all I had to aim at was the next grain elevator hovering above a glassy horizon. Times like that I'd thought hard about giving up – except that there was nobody out there into whose arms a guy could surrender. No way back. The only option was to keep heading west.

I finished my breakfast in the little diner there under the cottonwood tree, said goodbye to the cowboy, got astride my bike and set off towards the sign on the highway bridge. PAVEMENT ENDS. Just fifteen miles on the dirt and my journey, which had started ten days earlier, on Labor Day, would be over. I headed south, then turned west, then south again, beside huge fields of sunflowers and bleached wheat stubble. Along the way I remember pausing to investigate an abandoned one-room schoolhouse, then braking to watch a herd of white-tail deer, twenty strong, arc across the road and slide from view, swiftly, silently, the way water sinks into sand. And all the time I kept thinking about what that guy had said, how he'd dismissed the entire area in a single word. I knew he was wrong. Had to be.

Even as I pedaled back to town that night, my quest completed, my name added to the register they keep in a tin box out at the highest point, a place barely distinguishable from any other in a huge expanse of grassland, I knew I'd have to come back and take another look. Had to find this magical Nebraska that Mari Sandoz writes about.

How many cowboys does it take to fix a few leaks?

Friday 8 April

It's 46 degrees (F), the sky is grey, and I'm wondering whether to walk down to the river for a wash. It's beginning to look as though I may have running water in the bathroom by evening time, but I'm a writer, for goodness' sake, and a romantic. I like a bit of drama.

There has been plenty of that around here lately. Matt is fortunate to be alive, and I'm damned lucky that this whole enterprise hasn't been strangled at birth. Barely a week before I flew in I received an email from Kitty to say that her husband had shot himself. My immediate thought was 'farm suicide'. I was thinking back to an elderly couple I stayed with in south-eastern Nebraska some years ago. They still farmed the old home place that had been in the family since the first wave of settlement, some time in the 1870s. They ran it on 'no-till' principles. That is to say, they didn't plough the soil between crops, just drilled straight into last year's litter. Saved on tractors, on fuel, and on labour. I always remember John laughing about his two hired hands. 'One has no teeth, the other has a pony-tail. They're grateful to be employed,' he said. This was but a few

5

short years after they'd hit hard times, in the mid-1980s - the era of Farm Aid. Then, they told me, they'd all sat around the kitchen table – John, his wife and their two boys - and discussed whether he should put a bullet through his head. It was his idea. Others they knew had gone down that road and their families had collected on the insurance.

What happened to Matt was more mundane. He was in the middle of calving, sleeping in a little room in the cattle-shed, right across the way from here. He has a TV, a fridge, a microwave and a bed in there. It's cosy enough – and that's what the skunk thought when it tried to move in under the floor. Matt spotted the guilty party outside, grabbed his rifle and gave chase on the ATV with the weapon laid across his knees. He chased it up the hill, turned to follow it down into a hollow, and that's where he hit the patch of mud and ice. Skidded down the slope, hit a rock and stopped dead. The rifle flew forward, the butt crashed against the dashboard, and off it went.

You have to be pretty unlucky for something like that to happen. You probably deserve every ounce of good fortune that follows. The X-rays they took, after Matt had crawled to his pick-up, driven up the hill and got a ride to hospital in Rapid City, gave a detailed picture of the bullet's course. Somehow it wove a path between several vital parts, missed his femoral artery by a whisker, then bumped into his hip bone and came to rest before it could do any more damage.

Matt still has the slug in there somewhere, but he's on the mend, probably doing more than the doctor would like, but hey, he's a cowboy. Drafted in his nephew to take over in the shed there until he's fit to be pulling on reluctant calves. And today he called in his buddy from up north to help him fix the plumbing down in my basement.

We turned on the main supply water and ducked for cover. Water was spurting out from fat pipes, thin pipes, vinyl, copper and steel, spraying in every direction, gathering on the cement floor and trickling towards the drain, which was blocked. I took a look, asked myself how many cowboys it takes to fix a few leaks, and splashed my way back to the stairs.

At least the electricity is on, so I have heat – narrow radiators that lie along the baseboards. I also have a vehicle. It's not pretty, but it goes. Mercy is a station wagon, a 1993 Chevy Blazer. It belongs to Kitty's father, who ranches on the far side of Highway 61. It used to be blue, and still is in places. It has two bald tyres, a couple of cracks right across the windscreen, 204,000 miles on the clock and blows thick black smoke out the rear end, but, as Matt said, squinting up at the steep grassy hills that surround me to the north and east, 'She'll git you up there no problem. Goes where most vehicles won't.'

'But I'll be using the trail,' I said.

He gave a short laugh. 'That two-track? Sure ya will, s'long as it's open.'

I've no complaints. I'd set aside a little money in case I had to go and buy an old jalopy. This one is free.

Saturday 9 April

This morning I have running water to the sink, can take my first shower since I left home seventy-two hours ago, and the toilet flushes, so no more forays to the woods armed with a stick. I can start settling in. It's going to take a little time. What troubles me most is being cut off from all the usual means of communication with the outside world. Yesterday I borrowed Kitty's truck and drove to Valentine, a 146-mile round trip. At around 18 to the gallon that's $32, but it had to be done. Mercy isn't legal yet. I've no insurance and we need a set of up-to-date licence tags. I bought a stack of groceries in town, and a phone. If I walk up to the high ground about six or eight hundred yards from here, and stand perfectly still, I can get a signal of sorts. I'll settle for that; the problem is… standing perfectly still. Despite the cold start yesterday, it warmed up nicely in the afternoon and out came the first of the insects. While I stood there a posse of small, dark flies hovered around me, growing in number and emitting something between a whine and a buzz. They're not unlike the ones we meet at home in the summertime, the ones that form a little halo around your head and follow you for mile after mile, and drive you nuts. Matt says once the weather warms up, which could be any day now, I can look forward to mosquitoes, gnats and deer flies – which he mentioned with a shudder, and a pitying smile, as in, 'Hey, whose idea was it to go live down by the river?' I am sending home for one of the veils we bought in the Highlands last year. If they can keep the Scottish midges out I should imagine they'll deal with whatever I find here.

Despite the warmth, everything around here still looks very wintry. The grass is all brown and crunchy underfoot, as are the remnants of last year's sunflowers. The cottonwoods are bare, their branches a ghostly pale grey; the cedars that mark the river's course and fill the canyons that branch off it are just about the only green thing in sight - apart from the soapweeds, and the cowshit that I've managed to get on my trouser legs.

8

Once everything comes to life I shall be studying my *Grassland Plants of South Dakota and the Northern Great Plains*. I like to know what it is I'm looking at.

Monday 11 April

Sun, sky and wind. I don't think I could imagine a nicer morning than we have today. There was a slight frost overnight, but by seven-thirty, when I set off for my walk, the thermometer registered forty-five degrees, the sky was blue from horizon to horizon, and – fortified by my porridge and safe in the knowledge that nobody would hear me - I was tempted to sing. Then I resisted. The meadowlarks were doing a far better job.

The landscape is mostly a dun colour, with splashes of white where the chalky rock shows through on the bluffs that overlook the river and pale yellow patches that mark the blow-outs, but there are plenty of signs that spring is happening. There's a hackberry tree at the front of the house, and one or two of its buds are starting to open. Up on the range I've found the odd shoot poking through the sand. These will be the cool season grasses. As soon as the soil starts to warm up to an appreciable degree they'll flower, make seed and ripen off, then give way to the warm season grasses, big blue stem, switch-grass and the like. Or so I read in my books.

My walk this morning took me down towards the river-bank where I found the cedar-trees full of flowers, readily yielding a puff of yellow pollen when I flicked them with the back of my hand. Down there, out of the wind, it was deliciously warm. Spring is really on the way, and I have time to enjoy it.

I'm free to walk where I wish. These 6,000 acres are

9

spread along several miles of the Niobrara, with some land to the south, some to the north. The fences – four strands of barbed wire - are easy enough for a long-legged guy like me to step over. Of the immediate neighbours – that is, those whose land abuts this place – one is a cousin, another is a friendly old geezer, they tell me, while a third needs to be treated with a little caution. 'But he won't shoot ya,' Matt said when he came through the yard this morning on his ATV, with Cinch the dog perched on the seat behind. 'Unless you have a gun with you, of course.' And with that he headed off, around the house and down to the river to check on a fence in the north pasture.

The calving is almost done. According to Matt's nephew, when I called in on him, there are no more than a couple of dozen heifers still to give birth. The new-borns and their mothers are confined in a small field, maybe eight or ten acres, beside the shed and along the river's edge. After a few days, if they're doing okay, they go out to pasture where they can browse on whatever they find – as well as a nightly spreading of hay.

Young Lightning is a quiet sort of guy. He wears glasses and chews tobacco. A lot of the guys here do, and when they're talking they'll pause, half turn away and spit on the ground - or in your kitchen waste-bin if they happen to be indoors. I'd guess Lightning is about twenty. There isn't a great deal of him. To look at him you wouldn't imagine him charging around a rodeo arena on the back of a half-ton bull, but that's what he does for fun. Brave feller. Makes money at it too.

Talking of brave fellers, I have caught my first mouse. Not something for a former exterminator of vermin to crow about, but it was the first trap I'd set. I've been hearing a lot of scampering and scuttling at night, and there are a fair few droppings scattered about every morning on the kitchen work-tops. As my old rat-catching mate Walter used to say, striding towards his van with a bucket of poison before setting off to some Lincolnshire farm-house, 'We'll educate the buggers!' Meanwhile I have put my flour, oats, nuts and raisins, etc. into stout plastic boxes. There are dozens of them in the cupboards.

This house is equipped to accommodate up to a dozen hunters, at a pinch. On the first floor there's a large living-room that runs from the front right through to the back of the house. That's on the eastern side and gets the morning sun. On the other side there's the kitchen, plus a small bedroom with two bunk-beds. The bathroom is between it and the living-room and has two basins, a toilet, a shower over the bath. Upstairs are two bedrooms which sleep four apiece. The basement houses a defunct kitchen and three other rooms. It's cold and dank down there, with bare cement floors, pressed tin ceilings, and a lot of overhead cables and pipes, plus several drips. I only go down to use the washing machine.

I am feeling a little more settled each day. The fact that I can walk up onto the ridge and get a good enough signal to talk with home is a huge comfort and a relief. I can receive, but not call out, so it's by appointment only. Even better is the fact that if I go up and park next to the ranch house, I can piggy-back on their wireless Internet signal. That's going to save me a heap of gas money, because the nearest library, where you can use the Internet for free, is fifteen miles north of town, at Martin, South Dakota; or I can go to Gordon, thirty miles west – but that one's not open every day.

Tuesday 12 April

The red house used to be someone's home, but that was a long time ago. It was abandoned by the original settlers in the 1940s. Since then it has been home to one or two temporary residents, a number of hunters, and a lot of wild animals. All that's left of the people who owned the place is a handful of photographs hanging on the walls and a few penciled notes on the staircase that leads down to the cellar where the bull-snake has taken up residence. The heights of various children, the count of heifers, calves and bulls, a telephone number or two. Back then, when eight blonde boys and girls lived here with their Danish parents, the place was full of life; now, you could be forgiven for thinking that its only role is to celebrate death. The people who come by, seasonal hunters who stay a few days in April for the turkeys, November for the deer, like to leave their trophies around the place. I wouldn't advise arriving here at dead of night, as I did, bumping and lurching down that sandy two-track under a full moon to see the eight-foot tall gate-posts wreathed in whitened deer antlers, the crux of the apple-tree piled high with bleached skulls, the shreds of polythene flapping against the naked windows, the bats darting to and fro to the accompaniment of the coyotes, holding their choir practice up on the bluffs.

Even now that I've got used to the place a night such as I've just had can be unnerving. With the wind whistling under the eaves and the rain lashing against the roof, I had to grab my torch and run up to empty the buckets that catch the drips in the attic. Back downstairs where I sleep, on the living-room floor, the lightning illuminated them all in turn, the whole damned menagerie: the elk's head, the raccoon, the badger on the coffee table with its tail held out behind it. Those are like old friends now, but the snarling lip and bared teeth of the coyote, high up there on the north wall and lit from below, that still bothers me, as does the bob-cat, languidly stretched out on a dead branch beside the door, right fore-leg dangling, its eyes seeming to follow you wherever you go. Throw in the rattle-snake skins stretched out over the window-frames, the severed feet of an eagle gathering dust on the little wooden shelf, the occasional mouse scampering back from the kitchen - sure, they have on occasion prompted me to pull the sheet over my head, close my eyes and turn my face towards the wall.

In daylight it's a different proposition. In an ocean of sunlit grass, twenty thousand square miles of it covering the largest dune complex in the western hemisphere, I have the rare luxury of shade, the shelter of broad-leaved trees. I have firewood aplenty, bluffs to steady the wind's progress, and I have the Niobrara river. It's a Native name, and means Running Water. It's spring-fed, constant, shallow, swift, serpentine, unpolluted. I have too the sky, limitless, always changing.

'It's not five-star, y'unnerstand'

People are already asking me why I'm here, and how I found the place. I give the abridged version. The whole story's too damned long. If I look for one particular incident that triggered all this I need to go back over half a century, to my uncle, who burst in on our uneventful lives with a whoop and a yell, picked up our mongrel bitch by the scruff of her neck and declared that she was 'just an old ham-bone.'

He was an American. I correct myself: he was a Yank – and by that I mean that he embodied everything we imagined an American ought to be. He was loud, cheerful, sun-tanned, friendly, generous. We assumed he was rich. He had no time for formalities, nor for that awful British restraint that held us so tight back then.

He'd met my father's sister in the 1930s, in India, where they were both missionaries, and whisked her off to the States, first to New Jersey, later California. When he rose to be director of the mission society he'd come by every two years or so on a round-the-world trip. This was the mid-1950s. I was still in primary school. He brought us gifts, none more exciting to my young imagination than a series of stereoscopic images from his native country. Those Viewmaster cards of Yosemite

National Park, the Grand Canyon, Niagara Falls, Mount Rushmore, the giant redwoods and such wonders, planted the notion in my mind that there was a magical land out there where everyone was bronzed, wealthy and contented, and every natural feature was huge, magnificent and accessible. They made England - the England I knew then - seem drab, cramped, unimportant. The seeds of fantasy he sowed in my head would soon be nourished by the westerns we watched, nightly, on the television which arrived in 1959.

My father wasn't fond of the Americans. Like many a veteran of the late war he felt aggrieved that they'd waited – just as they had in 1917 – to join a European conflict when the tide was about to turn, then taken all the credit for victory. His brother-in-law's gifts prompted him to show off his own collection of historical artifacts, items brought home by our sea-faring ancestors. There was a Chinese pagoda which we had to assemble by stacking successive pieces of pinkish stone on top of each other; and once it was up we had to be careful not to jump on the floorboards, lest we make it wobble and bring it crashing down again. There was a copy of the Bible in Chinese, a set of ivory elephants, the smallest no bigger than your thumb-nail, a brass rose-bowl from India which we had to polish with Duraglit whenever we had visitors. And then there were the autographed photos of Buffalo Bill and Annie Oakley. These, my father told us, were a gift to our great-great uncle, who captained the ship that brought the celebrated showman to England in 1887, the year of Queen Victoria's Golden Jubilee, when she came out of mourning and consented to attend the show at Earl's Court.

I'm going to resist the temptation to explain in minute detail the meandering paths along which my fascination with the West led me, and how, over thirty years and a dozen road trips, my interest started to focus on the Great Plains, then Nebraska, and finally this sparsely populated, western corner of the state. I dare say a few stories about that journey will percolate through in due course, because when you're in a place as remote as this there are days when very little happens – at least, nothing very noteworthy.

The fact is that over the last ten years or so I started to cast around for a place such as this. It was a simple enough idea, but it seemed an almost impossible dream: a little house in the middle of nowhere, uninhabited but weather-proof. It had to be slap-bang in the Sandhills, and it had to be one that a writer could afford. In the end it fell into my lap the way a thing that is meant to happen generally does. It came easily, suddenly, out of thin air, just when I was about to give up hoping. And it came at precisely the right time. After twenty years of struggle as a jobbing writer, I finally had enough money to allow myself six months away.

Before I go on, I need to put this all into some sort of context, so let's start with Cherry County, which embraces a chunk of the northern Sandhills to the south and borders South Dakota to the north. Each one of its 5,000 square miles is home to a single inhabitant, on average. So my neighbors are well scattered. The ranch-house where my hosts Matt and Kitty live is out of sight, about a mile and a half from me. It can take me as much as ten minutes to drive up there, depending on conditions along the sandy two-track.

16

There's another ranch about two miles further east, as the crow flies, but that's still a six-mile drive, four if you cut across the pasture. Up-river is a cousin's place, four miles west of here, but a twenty-five-mile drive. There are very few diagonal roads out here, just north-south or east-west, following the old survey lines.

Our county town, Valentine, is, by the standards of western Nebraska, large, having a population of 2800. It's seventy-five miles away to the east, so to go there and back you're looking at close to half a tank of fuel. It has grocery stores, diners, several gas stations, a few motels, a bookshop and a library. It has the only stop light along a 200-mile stretch of Highway 20 between Ainsworth and Chadron.

Our nearest town, Merriman, is fifteen miles. It has a post office, a ranch supplies store, a bank, a café that opens fourteen hours a day, a bar, a gas station with on-duty mechanic, a hair-dressing salon open one day a week, an elementary school, an air-strip… and 118 inhabitants, most of whom knew who I was before I even showed my face.

As to the ranch, it is modest in size. 6,100 acres. That's a shade under ten square miles, enough to feed roughly 350 head of black Angus cattle and a small family. There's one center-pivot which irrigates 130 acres where Matt raises a thousand bales of hay in a good year – alfalfa, millet, or triticale. There are no hired hands. If extra help is needed, at branding time, for example, or haying, everybody gets roped in: neighbors, friends, relatives, visiting British writers.

Now that I've got started on this, maybe I should introduce the woman whose life and work inspired me to come to this particular spot. I could try and weave her

17

into my narrative, artfully, but I'd rather lay some solid, expository foundations. I've traveled in these parts often enough to become wary of artifice. It just isn't the cowboy way.

When I first visited Nebraska, in 1991, I was most interested in Willa Cather, the novelist who grew up in Red Cloud in the 1880s and wrote so beautifully about the pioneer moment on the prairie, especially in *My Antonia*. In 1993 I was invited to give a paper at the annual Cather Conference, held that year in Hastings. I was at the time trying to get a foothold in the academic world. Fortunately, it didn't work out. Broke my heart at the time, but I know now that it wouldn't have worked for me. I just have to plough my own furrow.

By the time of the conference I had started reading more widely amongst writers from the Great Plains: Hamlin Garland, Bess Streeter Aldrich, Laura Ingalls Wilder - people like that. The one who was gripping my imagination – and speaking to something in me that I didn't quite understand yet - was Mari Sandoz, whose biography of her father catapulted her to fame and gave her the freedom she'd always craved, to write about the history of her region. She dedicated the rest of her life to that task, and produced some classics. I've brought with me a copy of *Crazy Horse*, also *Cheyenne Autumn*, and of course the one about her father, *Old Jules*, probably the book I like best of any I've ever read.

Mari grew up in the Sandhills region, moved away in her twenties, and is buried on a bare hillside, surrounded by grass, soapweed and sky, some thirty-five miles south-west of here. She was born in 1896, the first child of Jules Sandoz' fourth wife. He'd abandoned his medical studies in Switzerland back in 1881 after a fight with his family, sailed to the States and headed straight for the frontier, determined to go beyond the line of settlement. He was confident he could scrape a living with his gun. He was an excellent shot, and game back then was plentiful, even though the buffalo were already on the edge of extinction.

He fought with a first wife and left her, pregnant, in the town of Verdigre. That's in the north-eastern part of the state, not far at all from the point where the Niobrara empties into the Missouri. Heading upstream, he ventured into and through the remote and forbidding Sandhills. Settling on the flat lands beyond the north-western edge of the hills, he married again. This woman, Henriette, was soon in the insane asylum, a fate suffered by many a desperate, lonely, frontier wife - let alone one with a husband as violent and bad-tempered as Old Jules. So he sent for a third wife, Emelia, who came mail order from Switzerland. She stayed two weeks and slipped away when he was out hunting. She saw no resemblance in the dirty, bearded, lazy man, now crippled after a fall down a well-shaft, to the scholarly gentleman who had written her such elegant letters, boasting of his land holdings, education and status in the new community and admitting to one small failing, that of smoking a pipe.

Wife number four fell into his opportunist grasp when she arrived at the railroad depot at Hay Springs to meet her brother Jake, whose homestead wasn't too far from Jules' place. But Jake was busy at something and didn't show up – a woman, some say. On such accidents of fate whole histories revolve. Jules took her back to his place, and soon talked her into marrying him. He had, after all, a timber house, and fertile land. In no time he had her cleaning up, working in his fields, and carrying his baby.

We'll come back to Mari and her father – and her five siblings and overworked mother – in due course. Right now I want to recall the circumstances which led to me finding this place. I want to emphasize that for me, a Brit, America remains a land where anything is possible, and that I still find Americans, particularly westerners, positive enough in their outlook to respond to a person who demonstrates a spirit of enterprise. Show a sense of adventure and they will start cheering you on. As a great nation, their moment may be passing, but out West they still respect anyone who displays a bit of pioneer spirit, even if he is past his prime.

They have a Mari Sandoz conference each year up at Chadron. It's a town of just under 6,000 inhabitants, 10,000 when the college is in session. It's ninety miles or so from here by road. When you get that far west you're out of the Sandhills. You're seeing yellow sandstone bluffs, dark pine trees fringing the tops. Wyoming is just along the road. The first time I came by there I half expected to see Alan Ladd ride out from behind a boulder on horseback. That was in `93. In `96 I returned for an event to commemorate Mari's hundredth birthday, and somehow kept returning. In 2006 they inducted me as an Admiral in the Nebraska Navy. They tell me it's an honor doled out to all and sundry, but I'm proud to be on a list that includes Mari Sandoz. I still carry the laminated ID card they gave me, and have the scroll hanging on my study wall.

In 2010 I prepared to attend one more conference. It was time, as they say around here, to shit or get off the pot. If ever I was going to find my hideaway, I needed to put the word out. I stayed, along with a number of academics, in the Olde Main Street Inn. Never mind the cute spelling. This place, by U.S. standards, is ancient. The floors are crooked, the bedsteads are made of brass, the radiators of iron; when you turn on the shower in your room you wait a full three, four minutes for the water to run hot. The bar is long and straight, and out in the middle of the dining-room they have a stone-lined well. It's got a suitably exotic history to go with all that. At the time of the Wounded Knee trouble, in 1890, General Miles stayed there. Later it was home to itinerant railroad men. Under its current ownership it's found a place on the National Register of Historic Places.

The conference was over. It was Saturday morning and only a handful of us were left eating cinnamon rolls and coffee, down in the bar. The proprietor, the Olde Main Madam as she likes to call herself, had just finished cleaning her flintlock rifle and was squinting along the barrel. I was feeling as if I was on the brink of failure. Three more days and I'd be flying home with nothing to show for the entire trip but a great gaping hole in my bank account. And I was blaming myself. I had failed to be as pro-active as I'd intended. The fact is, I've got through life without ever learning to hustle. I've just been someone who has looked for opportunities and tried to make sure I'm in a position to grab them when they come along.

Over breakfast one of the academics asked the question. 'What exactly is it you're looking for?' I spelled it out. Solitude, peace, time. Me and the hills and the sky. A camp-fire at sundown. A chance to experience a bit of what Mari experienced, get to understand her attachment to that landscape out there and divine the spirit of the

21

place. A shack would do, so long as it was watertight –
and cheap.

She took out her cell phone. 'You need to talk to my
brother,' she said.

An hour later I was sitting in the coffee shop around
the corner. I was talking, not with Matt but his wife
Kitty, who was in town getting her hair seen to. 'We have
a place,' she said. 'It's not five-star, y'understand.'

Monday morning I drove east, turned south on
Highway 61, then west three miles on the dirt. Met her at
the ranch bungalow and did the final mile and a half in
her pick-up, down the dusty, rutted trail towards the
bend in the river. Half an hour later we were shaking
hands on a deal. So long as I paid for the utilities, I could
use it as long as I needed.

The yard is full of turkeys, the air is full of snow

Wednesday 13 April

Did I say spring was on the way? Just 44 degrees this morning, a forecast high of just 45, and there's talk of rain today, snow tomorrow. I got this off NPR, National Public Radio. It's the only station I can receive down here in daylight. They're having their spring membership push just now and are driving me nuts with their self-congratulatory messages, non-stop pleas for pledges and eulogies from Garrison Keillor. I already know all of their pitches by heart, and there are four more days to go.

Mice. The fight goes on. Having caught one of the little blighters two nights in a row, I set a second trap yesterday. Both had been triggered by midnight – and I heard more of them scampering around later on as I lay in bed.

There's actually a much larger crittur living somewhere in the woodwork. By the sound of its footsteps in the night – clomp clomp clomp right above my head – it's considerably bigger than a rat, and more ponderous in its movements.

I started reading up on Mari Sandoz last night. I suppose I mean revising, because I've read just about all her work, some of it more than once. I shoved a whole pile of related books in my suitcase when I was packing. I was surprised, however, to dig out a little book her sister published some years ago, about Mari's early career; surprised because I'd forgotten about it. Inside I found the inscription, "To Alan Wilkinson, who brought a bit of Britain into our lives, and who, I hope, took something of the Sandhills on his return." It's signed Caroline Sandoz Pifer and dated July 31, 1996. That was in fact my second visit with Mari's youngest sibling. The first was in 1993, two years after I became vaguely aware of this area and its most celebrated writer.

I made my first road trip on the Great Plains in 1991. I was teaching a course on the literature and history of the American West, and working on my PhD. This was back in the U.K. I wanted some material on the overland trails, and, after studying the maps, worked out a trip that would take me up the old Santa Fe Trail, travelling from New Mexico back east to its starting point in Missouri, then along the Oregon Trail, westward through the state of Nebraska.

All I'd heard about Nebraska was that it was flat, dusty and empty. No, let me correct myself. I'd heard more than that. Back in the 1980s I was living in Albuquerque as an exchange student. We had a neighbor, the daughter of a New England pastor. She was of that generation who had seen the Depression, the war and the staggering prosperity of the 1950s – the generation of Americans I have most enjoyed talking to over the years, because they have known hardship as well as good times, and lived though the sweeping changes of a tumultuous century. Harriet was well educated, articulate, provocative. She listened to NPR and took *The New York Times Review of Books*. Any morning, after about nine, you could walk out through the back door of our apartment into the communal yard and the chances were she'd be there, shorts and shirt, cigarette in one hand, first beer of the day in the other, taking the morning sun. And always willing to talk. After we came home in `87 I corresponded with her. I must have mentioned that I was taking a trip that would include a visit to Nebraska, adding that I had friends who had moved there – from New Mexico. The revelation that someone would leave the Southwest and head for the Cornhusker state ignited in her a blaze of indignation. 'How can anyone go there?' she stormed. 'It's a terrible place. Even the people who live there hate it. I can't name a single city in the entire state.'

My first impressions of Nebraska were somewhat at odds with Harriet's. I liked Lincoln from the get-go. I found it a clean, airy, attractive town where I could walk the tree-lined streets in safety, where people were polite and friendly. There was a beautiful university campus and a magnificent capitol building that seemed to me to celebrate the idealism and hope that was around when this nation was young. The significant moment for me, however, was when I visited the English Department of UNL and the late Susan Rosowski, a prominent Cather scholar, suggested I read Sandoz' story of her father's pioneering days in the Sandhills, *Old Jules*.

I did just that, and was mightily impressed. To this day I occasionally re-read the opening paragraph. It's up there with the beginning of *Moby-Dick* as one of those passages that thrills me every time I return to it. I have never found its equal in any piece of writing about the West.

Two years later, Professor Rosowski invited me to give a paper at the Cather conference in Hastings, Nebraska. There I met a marvelous white-haired old couple, Frank and Charlotte White, who pressed me to venture further west, into the Sandhills. They told me I should call on Mari's youngest sister, Caroline. She was a friend of theirs, still lived out there on her ranch. They even `phoned and told her I was coming.

I drove west the very next day, stopped for the night at Hyannis - barely an hour's drive south of where I am right now - and asked where I could camp. The guys in the Longhorn bar told me to pitch my tent on the lawn outside the American Legion. There was a fellow there who'd just finished sprinkling the grass. He wished me a good night and showed me how to turn on the water so that I could get washed next morning. I was up around six, back on Highway 2 not long after, and was soon heading north along 27, looking for the trail up to Caroline's place.

Picture me, a Tenderfoot in a shiny new rented sedan, nosing my way warily along a six-mile track defined by two wheel-ruts filled with talcum-fine dust, my path obstructed by knots of inquisitive cattle as I bounced across the occasional grid, or auto-gate as they call them out here. I found the house, eventually, and was feeling pretty pleased with myself, until my hostess greeted me. 'Where ya been all morning? It's eight thirty already.'

Caroline was in her early eighties at this time. She was leaning against the door-frame, and by her right hand was a .410 Winchester – 'To pepper those darned deer,' she explained. 'Keep eating my trees.'

Caroline fed me, then led me down into her basement where she kept a lot of her sister's effects and papers at that time. And so I was privileged to see, and read, the first typescript version of what was to become, after thirteen re-writes, the western classic that is *Old Jules*. Intemperate, self-centered, full of the indiscretions we make as young writers, *The Ungirt Runner* (I believe the title comes from a line of Walt Whitman's) is her honest attempt to get down the story of a girlhood spent on the farm frontier. I have extensive notes, somewhere in the suitcase full of papers I've brought with me, and I'll dig them out in due course.

Thursday 14 April

The yard is full of turkeys, the air is full of snow, and the temperature's 33 degrees. Welcome to the Great Plains in April. The snow's several inches deep and it's been driven by a high wind that's piled it up in drifts. I knew this was a possibility. Mari Sandoz writes about going out to round up the cattle after a blizzard in 1911. The dazzling May sun, reflected off the snow, cost her the sight in one eye, permanently. So, I'm going to put sun glasses on the shopping list, for whenever I finally make it to town – which could be quite soon. I have had confirmation that I am now insured. As to the licence tags, well, what are the chances of being stopped by the Highway Patrol?

I've taken a close look at the trail out of here. Instead of taking my usual short-cut, across the spur of rising ground, I bowed my head to the wind and followed the serpentine loop every foot of the way. As the track became steeper it became less and less defined. There was no way I was going to risk driving up there. I veered off up the hill and plowed along the low ridge, through two-foot drifts, towards the spot where I can get a phone signal. In the lee of a cedar I texted home, canceling this afternoon's phone conversation.

The fact that I can't get out yet is no great inconvenience. I've had a couple of spells of living way out in the country, and have learned about being well provisioned. I've enough grub, and beer, to keep me going another week or two – so long as I don't get sick of chile beans and spaghetti bolognese.

After checking the temperature once more – it had dropped to 30 - I brought the thermometer into the house. 47. I went down in the basement and turned the living room heaters on. Then I opened up my suitcase and pulled out the set of lightweight merino wool underwear that I almost didn't bring. With that on, plus my warmest clothes, down jacket and the hat with the ear- flaps, I'm pretty comfortable. Just a little bulky, that's all. There was an unnerving moment when I checked myself in the bathroom mirror. I haven't shaved since I left home, and the figure I saw staring back at me reminded me of none other than Old Jules himself.

Now, the mice. I am tempted to run up the flag and claim victory. I set all three traps last night and got not so much as a nibble. I'll leave them, with their tempting blobs of bacon grease. That's another tip from old Walter, my rat-catching tutor. 'Forget cheese,' he old me. 'That's for Tom `n` Jerry. Bacon grease is what you want.'

Sunday 17 April - morning

The temperature when I got up at 0600h this morning was a bracing 27 degrees. And that galvanized me. I may have balked at the prospect of driving up that trail yesterday, as the sun got to work on the drifts and sent rivulets of water to undermine the sand, but if it was frozen hard….

It was, and by 0730h I was on the road to Gordon, where I joined the library. They didn't give me a card: they'll recognise my face, they tell me. I checked out a volume I've been wanting to read but didn't want to pay $45 for. Dr Kimberli A. Lee's book, *I Do Not Apologize for the Length of This Letter*, is an edited collection of Mari Sandoz' written assaults on various agencies and individuals in which she promoted, aggressively, insistently, the rights and needs of the Native peoples she had known as a child. They were regular visitors to her father's first place, beside the Niobrara. They would gather around the kitchen table to smoke, to trade and tell stories. Young Mari would hunch herself up behind the stove, or at her attic door, and listen, and remember. Many years later she would go out to the South Dakota reservations to look up these people, some of them survivors of Wounded Knee or even The Little Bighorn. I have only just started reading, but have already been struck by one brief passage in the introduction: 'Understanding Mari's life or writing to any deep degree is well-nigh impossible without experiencing the land and environment of her childhood, which shaped her writing style and her sense of *being* in the world.' Maybe that's what I'm doing here.

I am now going to eat humble pie and confess that I have changed my mind about NPR. I still reserve the right to a minor rant at some stage, because some of their programming does drive me nuts. But for the moment, after a good night's sleep without any scuttling in the woodwork, and another two mice in the traps, I'm feeling a little better tempered, and have decided to succumb to their pestering and contribute to their funding drive. I shall brave the weather, trudge up that snow-bound hill, and call them toll-free.

Sunday 17 April - sundown

The great thing about having the sun go down over the bluffs, across the river there, is that any time after about 4.30 you can stake a claim for a sundowner. Depending where you've parked your chair, that is. And the great thing about a Great Plains spring is that just because you're trudging through a blizzard one day, and cut off from the world, it doesn't mean you won't be sitting outside enjoying a bottle of India Pale Ale in the sunshine a day or two later. This is a grown-up brew. 7 per cent. I bought it on impulse in a gas station on the way here from Rapid City last week. It's made by one of those small outfits that have sprung up all over the western states the past few years. It's having a soothing effect on me as I sit here with a bowl of corn chips and a jar of salsa, basking in 58 degrees as the last of the snow drifts shrink visibly around me, the buzzards drift in lazy circles, and the horses snort contentedly at the fresh bale of hay over by the cattle shed. Yes, sometimes life is truly blissful.

I have been thinking. You tend to do that when you're sitting all alone in the middle of nowhere and the sun's going down. I've been looking at the yard – or garden – that surrounds the red house, and thinking about the rather sad fresh produce I saw in the supermarket in Gordon yesterday. And the thought was born – well, resuscitated, because it had skittered across my mind some time ago. Could I raise a few green things here? Hell, we aren't short of natural fertilizer – and there's a river flowing right by the door. I reckon I could sow some lettuce, zucchini, tomato and so on indoors, then plant them out in about six weeks and be tucking in by the end of August.

Listen, they laughed at Old Jules Sandoz when he declared he could grow fruit in the Sandhills. And they flocked up to his place, not 30 miles from here, when they heard he was giving away baskets full of plums and cherries. Never mind the profit, the old son of a gun had made his point. Asparagus too. He may have been a tyrant, and a brute, but his kids ate pretty darned well.

We'll see. I need some netting against the cattle, the deer, the squirrels, the mice, and any turkeys that survive the hunters next month – and some protection against the insects. I've set myself a challenge. Guess I'm going to have to rise to it.

Monday 18 April

I believe the word is 'dreich'. It's a Scottish one, and, with a whole pint of Scottish blood in my veins (from my paternal grandmother's people), I am claiming the right to use it. It think it's the best word to describe the way it is out there this morning: grey, damp, drizzly, misty and cold. It was 37 degrees when I stuck my head out first thing, and here we are, ten o'clock, and still 37. As if to set the tone for a dismal day, there on the back of Lightning's pick-up are a pair of limp, dead calves, their feet dangling over the edge. Weaklings that never quite got the hang of feeding.

Yesterday I was watching Matt unload a bale of hay for the dozen or so animals that remain in the pen. Each bale is a substantial, drum-shaped thing, perhaps five feet in diameter, three or four thick. It's all grown right here on the ranch. This year it's millet. I know it is, because I can see the orange-brown seeds in the fresh cow-turds scattered around the hillsides; in other years it might be alfalfa, a crop that can be left in the ground for three or four years and will produce three cuttings annually, and a thousand bales. Millet has to be sown afresh each year, but the single crop yields just as well – 1,045 bales this last year.

Not far from the ranch house is the Center Pivot Irrigation rig (CPI) that makes the hay crop possible. When you fly over the western states you see great swathes of land patterned by these crop circles, each one watered by the long rotating arm, each one fed by the underground reserve, the Ogallala Aquifer. Matt's pivot waters 130 acres. Compare that with the standard acreage under the Homestead Act, which was 160. That was considered enough land to feed and support a family, back in the days when a brood of six or eight children was unexceptional. It probably was enough, back in the well-watered counties of eastern Nebraska, where the first homestead was claimed by one Daniel Freeman in 1862. There's a superb museum on the site, just outside of Beatrice, which I visited on my long bike-ride. But the further west the settlers pushed – and as the century progressed they homesteaded way up into Wyoming and Montana – the less viable the proposition was likely to be.

The often violent conflict between cattlemen and sod-busters, was, in part, caused by these land-hungry families from the east trying their hand at conventional farming on land that was better suited to cattle – and on farms that were way too small. Up in the Dakotas, and around here on the lower-lying land, some settlers did do okay for a year or two – if they avoided the locusts, drought or prairie fires – but the soils soon wore out, or blew away in a dry spell; or prices fell as more and more land came under cultivation. Why did Laura Ingalls Wilder's folk keep moving on from one Little House to the next? Because they failed, over and over. Re-reading those books some years ago, I was shocked at how much pain lay under their blithe tone. Each volume, more or less, represents a fresh start after another calamity.

Mari Sandoz' father, the irascible and obstinate Old Jules, fought the cattleman all his days – generally through the medium of the law, sometimes at the point of a gun. His own brother, Emile, was shot dead on his front porch by one of the cattlemen's hired killers, not so very far from here. Ironic, then, that his children – not Mari, of course - grew up and went into ranching. Ironic, but more or less inevitable.

I have finished reading the first section of my friend Kim's book, the collection of letters Mari wrote in support of Native peoples. I was particularly struck by a passage in which she talks about the changing ways in which people viewed the Indians: 'Once the Sioux and Cheyenne were a romantic, wondrous people, to be visited by foreign princes and lords and by sick and unhappy writers from Boston. Then came the time when the majority wanted their land, so they were made out as subhuman, as beasts; and men who killed them, or said they did, became heroes.' I would add that defeat and dispossession completed the work, rendering them poor, abject, dispirited and all the more despicable to a nation of people who saw prosperity as a sign of God's approval, poverty as personal failure. Read Mark Twain on the Utes of Utah, in *Roughing It*. He is shockingly harsh in his judgment of a beaten people.

Mice. I keep coming back to them. They have opened up a new front – or more probably they had that wee nest behind the bread-bin all along. Anyway, I've been setting a trap up there, and filled it two nights in a row.

Tuesday 19 April

It started snowing again as I left the red house at nine thirty this morning in search of a phone signal. It hasn't stopped, and here we are, approaching bedtime. At first it was just a typical springtime snow. Kind of picturesque. Hit the warm ground and disappeared as if into a sponge. Then around lunchtime there was this thin layer of slush outside the front door, and the merest hint of white on the straw that litters the yard. By mid-afternoon it was settling in earnest, and now there's three or four inches of it. Everything – trees, roofs, yard, the bluffs across the river, my venerable 4WD, the horses' backs – is white. The temperature has slumped from a perfectly reasonable 37 at dawn to 34, which seems a bit harsh on an April evening, especially on the day when my other half sent me a photo of the peas and broad beans we planted a fortnight ago poking up through a sun-kissed soil, back home in England.

So I haven't got out much. Instead I have, amongst other things, been listening to NPR, which, turncoat that I am, I am falling in love with. The thing is, there's very little else to listen to down here in this hollow, where radio signals hit the bluffs and are immediately deflected back into the ether. Except at night, that is, when they bring me a cacophony of baseball games, country music, ranting shock jocks and miscellaneous hissing noises.

Wednesday 20 April

It may be only 27 degrees, but the morning air is still, the sky is clear, the bluffs across the river are tinted pink by the rising sun, and the plink plink plink of water dripping into buckets has ceased.

This house is about ninety years old. It hasn't been used as a main dwelling in decades. So when you get snow piled on the roof and it starts melting, it finds little sneaky routes into the attic – and from there you can never tell where it's going to come out. Not that I'm complaining. It's snug in here, and peaceful; and with running water (from the taps, I mean) plus mains electricity, it's more than I hoped for when I first started looking for a Sandhills retreat. I would've settled for a wood stove, a well and oil lamps. Good enough for those old-timers, and good enough for me. Yesterday I had two plastic tubs collecting drips in my bedroom on the ground floor, one in the bathroom and another in the living room – until I investigated upstairs, found where it was getting in and put a couple of buckets up there. That solved it, and in any case by late afternoon, with the temperature nudging 50, the snow was all gone and the plinking had stopped.

As regards the roof, Matt keeps looking at it and wondering whether to cover it with tin when the summer comes. Sounds like a job I can help with. But right now he has other priorities. There are still fourteen cows left to calve, but little by little the herd is being turned out onto the range. They are wonderfully placid beasts, these black Angus. Back home, if we go hiking in cattle country in the spring, when the young have just been turned out to graze, they are more than curious. They are frisky, skittish. They will follow you. If you walk a little faster, so do they. I have more than once had to break into a fast trot to put a fence or hedge between myself and the pressing herd. But these guys here – they just stand and stare and then politely move aside.

It's the kind of day when I really would like to take to the hills with a picnic lunch. Instead, I plan a drive to Chadron. I'm hoping to visit the Sandoz Heritage Center, and call in on the Olde Main Street Madam.

Thursday 21 April

It's 41 degrees and heavily overcast, the wind is whistling through the timbers, and a large barbecue stand with gas bottle has just attempted a cartwheel across the yard. This is clearly destined to be a writing day, despite the fact that my legs are itching to get out and walk.

My trip to Chadron yesterday was good. I got a warm reception at the Center, and a fresh copy of the Sandoz Country Tour map. In theory this will take me to a number of sites that feature in Mari Sandoz' life. I don't trust it, however. I've tried it before and got lost every time.

From the Center I went to the Olde Main Street Inn to meet up with Jeannie. She is a remarkable individual, and a pretty sharp judge of character. She rode a large and noisy bike as a youngster and to this day accommodates a number of bikers who come each year for the Harley rally up at Sturges, South Dakota. These days she's a calm, self-possessed type; my guess is she's aiming for 'matronly' somewhere along the line. She put on a pot of coffee and filled me in on the goings-on around town. She showed me a four-page letter she had printed out and sent to the press and the city elders (I use the term loosely) in response to the activities of the police chief, whose HQ is right next door. It seems that he can't meet the needs of this small town with less than ten police cars. The previous incumbent managed with four. And the *modus operandi* seems to have changed too. Previously, a beat copper might call in at the bar from time to time, drink a coffee and chew the fat. He was considered an ally. The new tactic is for two officers to enter the bar, at night, pull out a video camera and film everybody at the bar. People are even filmed as they walk home, then questioned, breathalyzed and asked for ID. And it's driving custom away. 'My take is down 30%,' Jeannie told me, 'and it's the same at the other bars in town. They got this guy from somewhere in the southwest corner of the state. So keen to get rid of him they wrote a glowing letter of recommendation – and we wound up with him.' And there was I thinking we were hard done by in the U.K. with our speed cameras and video surveillance on the street.

On the way home I filled up the vehicle. $74.62. Youch! Later, when I was flipping through some of the notebooks from my trips west over the past twenty years – I've brought the entire collection with me - I found myself complaining about $1.64 gas in Dodge City, Kansas. That was 2001. Ten years earlier, in 1991, I'd filled up at $1.15 a gallon - and was wistfully remembering the days when I lived in Albuquerque and it was as low as 89 cents. So, a 40% rise in ten years to 2001, and from there to now – 250% and still rising.

Friday 22 April

A couple of days ago I suggested that the word for that murky, dank weather was 'dreich'. Today it is unequivocally bracing. 'Bracing' is when you take your kids to the beach (I'm talking about England here), the wind is whipping up the sand and scarifying your goose-pimpled skin, the temperature is about 61 degrees (wind-chill 44) and the little buggers want to go and play in the North Sea, which is approaching its summer peak of 52. 'Bracing', you say. It's a way of persuading yourself that this *will* be good for you, even though it's freezing your nuts off. I should add that after I was issued a towel and a bar of floating soap (correct: soap that floats) and forced to bathe in the Baltic some years ago (the Swedish apartment I was staying in had no running water) the North Sea suddenly seemed balmy by comparison.

Anyway, bracing: that's what it's like out on the range this morning – and it hasn't half given me an appetite. The sun is shining, there's a stiff breeze from the southwest, and the meadowlarks are singing. The predominant colors just now are still a kind of part-pink part-russet (I think that's the bunch-grass) and a silvery green. There are great swathes of bunch-grass which, when the clouds come down and the mist hangs in the air, seems to turn a much rustier, almost orange colour; in conditions like that it almost glows, reminding me of the dead bracken that's so familiar to us Brits. There's still precious little green out there, but with yet more rain in the night we can expect the grass, when it does get going, to be pretty healthy.

The major excitement today has been the arrival of a trailer or, as I would call it, caravan. This was Kitty's idea. It's only a few days now till I can expect the first wave of turkey hunters, who will be driving in from West Virginia, she says. They will take over the house and this shy, retiring writer will retreat to his mobile lair and consider how to ingratiate himself with them to the point where they have to offer him a turkey. The trailer has electricity, bottled gas and running water and is very cozy.

Saturday 23 April

The weather remains stubbornly unfriendly: 42 degrees, grey and blowy right now, which is nine o'clock in the morning. Yesterday it did manage to creep up towards 60 down here by the river, but the wind was gusting at around 45 mph up on the range. I ventured out for a couple of short walks and was all but blown off my feet.

Good old Mother Nature. I was up at the ranch house this morning and learned that the two ducks Kitty adopted last year have been visited by a raccoon. It got in through a weak spot in the wire that covers the coop. Ate up the hen bird and killed the drake. Matt managed to track the perpetrator and dispatch it with his rifle – without, as Kitty pointed out with a grin, causing himself any damage.

Kitty likes having a few birds about the place. There's a little flock of guinea-fowl, excellent, she assures me, for gobbling up grasshoppers and ticks. And, talking of ticks – nasty little disease-bearing s.o.bs – I found one climbing up my sweater last night as I sat reading. You can't squash them: I had to take a knife to it. So, a nightly inspection of my naked self is now on the agenda.

I was reading another collection of Mari Sandoz' correspondence at the time. After she died, in New York City in 1966, her sister Caroline shipped four and a half tons of books, papers, letters, manuscripts and research notes from her apartment at 422 Hudson. Some went to the University of Nebraska at Lincoln, plenty to Caroline's house in the Sandhills, where I was privileged to look through them that time in 1993. Caroline put a lot of time into reading and collating this mountain of papers. The book I've just been reading is a collection of letters that she later published in the *Gordon Journal*.

Reading *Old Jules*, it's easy to dismiss her father as dirty, cantankerous and violent, simply a brute. Plenty of people do. He beat Mari when she was a baby, for crying. He beat her mother until the old lady finally turned on him with a shotgun. He banged his fist on the table and insisted that women were to stay home and raise children to populate the new country. So if ever a daughter had cause to be bitter about her father, Mari did. He scorned her attempts to make a career for herself. 'Writers and artists,' he famously wrote her, 'are the maggots of society.' When she was eleven and published a tiny short story in the Omaha paper, he locked her in the snake-infested cellar. 'Fiction is for serving girls!' he stormed.

Much, much later – on his death-bed – he did ask her to write up his life. I've always contended – and I'm sure I'm not alone – that *Old Jules* is an act of reconciliation between father and daughter. Mari clearly sees him, in the end, as a visionary, a man of historical significance, a western hero. So it was beautiful to read this in one of her replies to the hundreds of letters she got from people who had read *Old Jules* and were shocked by what they found in it:

'Don't be too disturbed about old Jules… I would not have him any different at all – a man of less impatience and less violence could not have come out from his sheltered and safe environment and stood alone, cap to his brows, gun across his forearm, against the entire world. Such ego, such courage, is given to few of us. The world is full of ordinary women and children to be sacrificed. And by one of life's paradoxes, we were not sacrificed at all. Instead we were given a close look upon the lightning such as is granted to few. I, for one, have no complaint to make over my singed eyebrows. What does anything in this world matter except that here and there walks a man who is unique and gives all the rest of us a glimpse of the life that is denied us in person?'

Sunday 24 April - morning

It's still unseasonably cool, my thermometer registering a high around 54 the last couple of days; and it remains cloudy, windy too; but that's good walking weather, and I've been getting out on a few short hikes along the southern side of the meandering Niobrara. You get a great view of the grassland from high up there on the bluffs. At a casual glance you think you're seeing mile after mile of nothing but grass, a uniform thatch of it. In fact it's a mixture of many different grasses, herbs, flowers, soapweed and cedar, with plenty of bare spots in between. This whole dune system is pretty much held together by the hungry roots of these grasses, sedges, forbs (in Britain we call them herbaceous perennials) and a few shrubs, but once a bald patch appears, the wind will start to work on it, and soon you have what they call a blow-out.

Counteracting the destructive work of the wind are tenacious plants eager to fill the gap – or give it a try. Getting down on my knees I was able to get a close-up picture of one of several juniper seedlings I spotted today, as well as what looks rather like a member of the rose family with its seven leaves and red stem. Years ago,

41

when I was down in Texas, I met an ecologist who lectured me at some length on the deleterious effects of the cedar. (I think we call them junipers at home.) He pointed out that they are invasive, that each one can take as much as 12-15 gallons of water out of the ground per day. On natural range, he added, the regular, spontaneous blazes will burn them off, but now we suppress fire - and they're getting the upper hand.

Sunday 24 April - afternoon

While I was up at the ranch this morning Kitty handed me a slim folder containing some historical information about the family who constructed the red house. Holger Arent, a cabinet-maker born in Denmark in 1864, met and courted Hedvig Petersen on board the ship that was taking them both to America in 1890. She had two brothers homesteading south of here on the Snake river. Holger and Hedvig married, settling in Omaha, where Holger had relatives. For some years they ran a confectionery and cigar store.

Times were tough. According to these accounts, in 1904 Holger filed on a claim under the Homestead Act, taking the whole family to live in a dug-out, then a soddy, right down here beside the Niobrara. A dug-out is just what it sounds like – a sort of hollow as found, for example, in the bank of a river, to be extended inward or outward as time and the availability of materials permitted. Plenty of settlers started out that way, and plenty then graduated to the sod-house, built, quite literally, of sod which would be laid like a course of bricks. The sod would be cut with a special plough, in strips eighteen inches wide. With walls that thick, a 'soddy' could be very cosy in winter and cool in summer.

42

But fuel was a huge problem. There was very little timber around, and people collected buffalo chips in the early days, cow-chips later on. For 'chips' read 'turds'.

The Arents raised eight children down here beside the river. It was only after their father died, aged 59, and was buried in the cemetery three miles east of here along the dirt road, that they built the home I am privileged to be staying in. The story that's told is of an insurance policy on Holger's life which yielded $800, enough to invest in some materials. His sons bought cement in town, but otherwise used native sand and a home-made mould to fashion every one of the red-painted blocks that make up this sturdy old place. The blocks are rectangular, with five flat faces and one, the outer face, raised, which give the place a more rustic look. Most years the Arents gather from around the country and descend on the red house to picnic and celebrate their common ancestry. With a little luck, I might get to meet them this year.

There's more to tell about the Arents, but there's plenty of time for that. Right now I'm off to bed with Mari Sandoz – or rather, her book *The Tom-Walker*.

Tuesday 26 April - early

I guess this is how many a hired man lives, in a trailer. It's very cozy, if a little chaotic. I've assembled the little table, folded down the bed and connected up the power, drainage, water and bottled gas supply. I don't think I've mentioned the water I drink down here. It's from a spring, it comes in at high pressure, and it's cool, clean, tasty. I'll be living out here in the trailer for three or four days while the turkey hunters use the house. They arrived last night, Mom, Dad, their son J, on leave from Afghanistan, plus his girlfriend and her little boy. They were out pretty early this morning – revving up the ATV at 0430. And when I emerged, rather late for me at 0640, there was a large dead gobbler draped over the branch of a tree in the yard, its brindled tail-feathers spread out to catch the morning sun. G – that's Dad – was in the house drinking coffee, the upper part of his face covered in what looked like mascara, or soot. 'No, wasn't me,' he said, when I asked him who shot the bird. 'That was J. Nice clean head-shot. All I did was scare `em off.'

I left him to catch up on his sleep, made some porridge and then set off for a walk. I'd been looking at a pack of cards my partner gave me last Christmas. Each one shows a picture of some animal's footprint, and the idea is you study them and eventually get an idea of what you're looking at on the trail. I'm learning fast. Today I came across a faint imprint of a boot and was soon able to figure out that it was made about 24 hours earlier by a guy in size 11s, weighing about 170lbs. It is of course my own, made the previous afternoon. What interested me was that, even in this sand, and with a fair wind plus a little rain overnight, the print was relatively distinct. Reassuring too, when you're trying to find your way home.

I've talked briefly about the grasses that bind these sandhills together. What I may not have made clear is that they appear rather in bunches, that there is generally bare sand visible almost anywhere you look, in between the clumps. And what I'm enjoying about this sand is that, even on a wet day, you can kneel down to examine a plant, an animal track, a fragment of rock, a possible arrowhead, and not get dirty. The grit just brushes off.

Tuesday 26 April - later

I went to Valentine yesterday, the county town. It's 61 miles east of Merriman, so 77 from here. After doing some grocery shopping I called on proprietor Duane Gudgel at the Plains Trading Company, a super emporium selling mostly books, with an excellent collection of Great Plains material, but a bunch of other interesting items – and some very fancy coffee. Duane has always been supportive of my project and suggested some time ago that if I wanted to learn more about range management and associated matters I should call in at the Department of Agriculture, who have an office in town. I did, was very well received, and picked up some handy contacts – but I'll get to that in due course. As I left town I popped into Radio Shack to buy a lead for the computer. The young lad who served me, and his dad, were named Sandoz and are related, 'somehow', to Old Jules and Mari.

Back here the sun had come out after another pretty dismal start, so I set off along the south side of the river. I haven't yet got into the habit of taking my compass with me, but must do so. This landscape can be hard to read. So long as you have the sun, or if the river is visible, it's easy enough to get your bearings, but even the river can let you down with its extravagant loops and meanders, contriving to flow west at times and sow confusion among tenderfeet. In places you can easily confuse the draws, or canyons, that lead down to it for the actual river, such is the density of tree cover. I have one other excellent landmark in the shape of a dark horizontal line just below the skyline to the north. That's a shelter-belt on the far side of the river, not at all far from home.

I've mentioned the soapweeds more than once. They're yuccas, and they're everywhere with their clusters of narrow, dark green, sharply pointed leaves. The common name derives from the fact that native peoples would pound the fat fleshy root in water and create a passable lather, although a rancher I mentioned that to one time told me, 'Sure, it'll clean you. Strip your danged skin off too if you don't rinse it good.' I believe the natives also pounded the leaves, extracted the tough fibres, and wove them into some sort of fabric. My good friend Don Green, a retired prof from Chadron State College and the man largely responsible for establishing the Mari Sandoz Heritage Center, calls the yucca 'bear grass'. But why, I asked him. 'Oh, I guess because you wouldn't want it to grab you,' he said. He's from the Texas Panhandle. Grew up around some pretty churchy people and now calls himself 'a cowboy pantheist'. He's threatening to visit me some time in July.

Well, it was 36 overnight but with little wind (yet) and the sun shining from a clear blue sky, it could be a really gorgeous day. I'd better get my chores done so that I can be out enjoying it.

Wednesday 27 April

I'm a little concerned about Spring. Where is it? It's 42 degrees this morning, and they're forecasting a high of 50. Down at Scottsbluff, according to the radio, they have light snow. I console myself with the thought that every cold day is another day without bugs.

Talking of which, my veil has arrived from home. I saw it in a little store in the Scottish Highlands last summer when we were cycling north of Ullapool ('Midge Veil: only £5.95'). I assumed it was a joke, a wee tourist souvenir, like the mosquito trap I bought years ago in Missouri, complete with metal spring and bait-hook. But that same day I spotted a seriously tough-looking Scotsman wearing one as he cut his grass. Suddenly the idea didn't seem so crazy.

The hunters were out early again - 0430h or thereabouts, and I was almost persuaded to get up. But as I lay there thinking about it the clock somehow ticked its way around to six-thirty. After breakfast I went exploring again. Hiked about a mile upstream and then squirmed my way down a narrow ravine towards the river-bank, maybe a mile from here. It's an abrupt change from the breezy, sunlit, elemental landscape of grass and sky to a much more complex environment where trees, vines, ferns and tiny patches of soft green grass all complete for the light that filters through the broad-leaved trees and cedars. It's much more like the environment I grew up in, playing cowboys and Indians in the woods at the back of our house, having to crouch low to avoid having your eye taken out by an overhanging branch, constantly scratched by thorns and broken twigs.

When I think about the settlement of the West I often compare the experiences of the earlier settlers in the eastern woodlands with those of the pioneers who came west. I wonder to what extent their different encounters with the natural world engendered differing views of Nature. I feel I'm on uncertain ground here, but I have gained a sense from my reading in American literature that the earlier, eastern view of the natural world that surrounded those first settlements was that it harboured moral as well as physical dangers, that reversion to a state of savagery that some commentators

47

observed and feared, whereas the mythos of the later west - that is the open, sunlit one beyond the Mississippi - sees in the natural world something healthy and invigorating. Perhaps that's a fanciful, simplistic notion, but it happens to tie in with the way I see east and west in this country.

Partway down the ravine, I came across a seep from the limestone which marks the source of a slender little creek. Further on it's joined by a second stream, cascading down over the rocks, which I followed until it, and I, forced a way through the undergrowth to the edge of the river.

I stayed there some time, watching the water flow by, listening to the cawing of the rooks, the hum of insects, the wind soughing in the tree-tops. Then I made the steep climb towards the source of the second stream. Partway up I came across what would almost qualify as a meadow, perhaps twenty yards square. All around it were tracks of deer, cattle, and something that's either a lynx or a bob-cat. I figured that out on the basis that felines don't leave claw-prints, whereas canines do.

Back home, I'd just settled down to work when there was a gentle tapping at the trailer door. It was young J's girlfriend. They were off to hunt up a turkey. Did I want to go with them?

They rigged me up in a camouflage jacket, matching hat and a kind of face covering - not unlike the veil I mentioned, except that it has a narrow gap for you to peer through – and the area thus exposed, around the eyes, they now smothered in the black stuff G was wearing the other morning.

We drove off slowly, through the woods towards the river. 'They're not far from here,' J said in a half whisper.

He'd been out earlier and had seen two or three toms and a bunch of hen birds. I was worried that the truck would scare them away. 'No,' he said. 'They see the vehicle and they think we're out feeding the cattle – and they're always interested in cattle food. It's when we're on foot that they get wary.'

We followed the river a couple of hundred yards to where it veers sharply north, and got out, walking quietly, half crouched. They both had their rifles at the ready. We climbed up a little rise, under a large cottonwood whose branches came down to a clump of shrubs. Nobody spoke; they just pointed. We would get in there and wait, because the birds were just around the corner, pecking away in the dead grass, but showing no sign whatsoever of coming our way.

After a while J took out his caller, a crafty little device that imitates the sound a hen might make when she's feeling romantic. Trouble is, the toms already had all the hens they could handle. They just weren't up for any more.

He called again, and we waited. K had her rifle raised and was looking through the sights. If I read J's hand signals correctly – we were being as quiet as mice here – he was now considering a flanking movement, getting around the little flock and driving them towards her gun. Here was my chance to be a hero. In something between a stage whisper and sign language I managed to convey my suggestion, that I walk away from them, get around the back of that hill, and approach them from the far side. J graciously conceded that that might work.

Ha! And again, ha! Even as I moved stealthily south, silent as a panther, the birds scattered to the north. The circle I then had to describe was, in the end, the thick end of a mile. I did eventually get on the right side of them, but by this time they'd crested a rise, done a quick risk assessment and decided there was nothing to be ashamed of in being… chicken. They flew right across the river, and settled down for a good laugh.

According to J you only get one chance with these birds. Once they get it into their heads that you're after them they are really very canny. So we trudged home, where they invited me to eat supper with the family. Big tender beef steaks, from a farmer friend back home in the eastern part of the state. G was concerned that he had yet to bag a turkey, but J had an idea. He'd been out the previous night, just before sundown, and had found where they were roosting in the trees. So that's where his dad will set off for, about four thirty in the morning.

Thursday 28 April

Our man 'Lightning' is about to depart, he tells me. When I called on him in his little room in the cattle-shed he said that Matt has had the okay from the hospital to resume normal work. Still, I could be seeing him again before too long. Mid-May, he reckons, he has a date with an angry bull at the Gordon rodeo. I told him I'd try to get there. I have fond memories of the rodeo after my trip in 2007 when I spent a few weeks in Utah and Nevada with the Senior Pro Circuit. These were guys – and gals – aged forty plus, in some cases seventy plus, who perform for hundred-dollar purses, mainly for the love of it. I got some great stories from my time out there, but never managed to sell a single one of them, which I have to say grieved me.

I'm enjoying *The Tom-Walker*, so far at least, rather more than any of Mari's other novels. I've tried several and never been swept along. Indeed, I have only ever completed one of them. This book is really quite shocking, considering that it was published in 1947. We have a rape, scenes in a bordello, a girl of seven offering sexual favors to her chums, and a hero who fears, much like old Captain Ahab in *Moby-Dick*, that the loss of a leg (in the Civil War) may have unmanned him. Her writing is, to say the least, uncompromising, and the story, so far, compelling.

The mail, I have learned, is delivered along Highway 61 three times a week. The mailman – I beg her pardon, mailwoman – drops it off at the end of the dirt road, four and a half miles away. I'm awaiting a parcel containing my hiking poles – not that the country around here really requires them, but they're a big help in crossing the river, and they're handy for cutting a way through undergrowth. I'm also expecting my *Guardian Weekly*, a digest of the more sober material from one of our quality papers, and a great comfort.

Well, the sun has melted away the clouds. Time to climb that dusty trail, do the online stuff, and get on with the day.

Friday 29 April

I was sitting in the trailer reading when G's wife called by to say that they were popping over to Kitty's dad's ranch, for the branding. Branding? What branding? Nobody told me…

It was a flying visit in the end; rather too much talk about going, and not enough concerted action. However, I was grateful for a ride in their truck. We bumped our way to the paved road, crossed that and drove another four or five miles over dirt, looking for – well, nobody was quite sure, because nobody actually knew where the cowboys would be. So we zigzagged along in a general easterly direction until we saw a gathering of pick-ups, and the outline of men in stetsons on horseback, collars turned up against the wind, kerchiefs keeping the dust out of their noses while they twirled loops of rope above their heads.

It seemed we'd got there just as the show was almost over. There were maybe three dozen little black calves still in the pen, and a very slick, well orchestrated operation was running like clockwork. Everybody knew exactly what their job was and got on with it, quickly, neatly. They had four or five guys roping the calves. Each one in turn was dragged, squirming and protesting to where a pair of cowboys wrestled it to the ground and held it perfectly still – one at the head end, the other at the rear - while a third applied the red-hot brand and someone else gave an injection. For the girls, that was it; they could stand up, shake themselves and trot away to find mom. For the boys there was the man with the knife, and their sex life was over before it got started.

I was surprised how little noise there was. Somehow you expect there to be a lot of yee-hawing, like in the movies. There was some bawling from the heifers looking for their babies, and some from the calves, but the loudest sound beyond that was the roaring of the two propane burners where the branding-irons glowed red hot.

It was all over far too quickly, and we were on our way back home. Nobody had seen Kitty's dad, but the general opinion was he would be back at his place cooking steaks - and perhaps a few prairie oysters.

Saturday 30 April - morning

The turkey hunters will soon be gone. The two youngsters left around five this morning with their little boy; G and his wife won't be leaving until around noon. He's still out in the hills trying to nab his turkey. Before I met these people I was mildly irritated at having to move out to the trailer, gather up all my things from the three-seater settee, which I've been using as a bookcase, and remove most of my food from the fridge. Already I have got to know them well enough to know that I'll miss them.

They're leaving me a fabulous souvenir, an eighteen-pound tom, or cock bird. Young J shot it, gave it to me, and then was kind enough to take it out to the wood-pile and dress it for me. I've dressed chickens and pheasants, but never anything that big – and he managed it far more adeptly than I would've done. It's now in the freezer, till I have someone to share it with.

While he was dressing it he explained that, like Matt, he was in the National Guard – and that's why, like Matt five or six years ago, he wound up in Afghanistan. He's been out there liaising with the police in Kabul, training them. He says he's in the safer part, well away from the fighting. He flies back out next week, and returns home for good in July when he's looking to go to college and take courses in business studies, and then maybe open his own bar.

G is going home happy. I was outside around seven o'clock when I heard two shots from the direction of the white bluffs, and half an hour later there he was, trudging up the road with a 21-pound bird on his back. It's already dressed, packed away in a cooler and loaded on the truck, somewhere amongst the baggage, the trash and their ATV. The leftover food they're donating to a hungry writer. As soon as they drive off I'll move back into the red house and have a long soak in a very hot bath, then lunch. I am starving.

Saturday 30 April - later

In a moment I'm going to talk about the waterfalls, meadows, and babbling brooks – yet another surprise and delight when I went exploring today. But when I left off I was salivating over the prospect of lunch, and I can report that it was damned fine. So fine that I'm going to rhapsodize about it for a moment. You do this sort of thing when you're alone.

Take four slices of bread – my own, home baked. A few slices of cheddar cheese. A stack of jalapeno peppers. Make 'em into sandwiches, and smear each surface with a little bacon grease. (One of the most useful things my old man taught me, back in the 1950s, was to conserve every scrap of bacon grease, even if you had to scrape it off your plate.) Now stick the sandwiches in a dry frying-pan over a medium heat and toast each side until the cheese has melted and the bread is crisp. Wash down with coffee.

And while we're at it, let's talk about coffee. Drip machines, filters, percolators? Phooey! What do they give you? Washing up. What you want is a very, very large spoonful of fresh ground beans. Drop it in a heated china mug, and pour in your water. Leave it to stand. Read a newspaper. Take a walk around the room, then nudge the mug a few times. Attack the crossword. Maybe drag a spoon gently across the surface of said mug and then, when the grounds have sunk to the bottom, gently blow any remaining bits away from you, purse your lips and start sipping. Sure, you may get the odd bit of grit between your teeth, but I guarantee this: that brew will hit the spot. And all you'll have to clear up is one dirty mug.

Okay, waterfalls, meadows and babbling brooks. I'd spotted some pine trees away to the north of the dusty road that takes you to the highway, and that interested me. I have yet to find any around our part of the river. These were east of the ranch house, but until I'd had a word with Matt I wasn't sure they were on his land. They are, he said, and that's a neat walk down the draw.

It starts off as deep gash in the earth, a bare sandy declivity that plunges a hundred feet in a couple of hundred yards. Suddenly the vast open grasslands are gone from view, the wind is silenced. It's you, the sand - pitted with badger-holes and the like - the sky, and a few animal tracks.

And then the first seep of water comes in from the eastern side of what is almost a canyon, and with it the first splash of green. Another few minutes' hiking and you're in amongst tall deciduous trees, and pines – although most of those are on the upper slopes, silhouetted against a blue sky. Two or three more springs feed the main stream – which is never more than a couple of feet across and a few inches deep. There are little meadows, waterfalls, four five six of them, which have gouged great chunks out of the limestone. The trees are now clad in honeysuckle (just breaking into leaf) and wild grape (still in winter retreat). It's a very different world down there.

Mostly I walked in the stream, emerging from time to time to get around another cascade or a collapsed tree. Even so it took me no more than forty minutes to get down to the spot where this creek slid into the main stream of the cool, olive-green Niobrara. There was a level grassy area on one side, the sheer white limestone bluffs on the other, quite a little sun-trap.

I sat for some time, listening. A woodpecker was hammering away, a dove coo-ing, and something – an elk? – was making a distant dry barking sound. And there were the two watercourses, the one babbling, the other, wider, stronger, quieter, giving out the occasional 'glup' as it cleared a submerged rock.

When I find places like this – and there are plenty, if you care to look for them – I am reminded of the many, many Americans who've looked at me and frowned and asked, 'Nebraska? What you wanna go there for?' I'm starting to think like a native, and prefer not to tell them.

They brought laughter... glamour...
carrot cake

Sunday 1 May

Spring is holding back, doggedly, determinedly. Yesterday it was wind. And, briefly, snow. I was driving back from Gordon when the flakes started flying for a few moments before the cloud was whipped away to the south and the sun shone again. All day, indoors or out, I could taste the dust in my mouth, feel the grit between my teeth. But by way of antidote, I am looking at two or three pictures I took on a hike the other day – of trees coming into bloom. Spring can't be far off now. And I'm ready: I bought a few packets of vegetable seeds in town.

After visiting the grocery store I went to the library, where I picked up a fascinating book and, like a flighty teenager, abandoned Mari Sandoz for the moment in favor of her father's mortal enemy. Dedicated to peopling the Panhandle with farmer settlers - preferably from his native Switzerland - Old Jules was vehemently opposed to the cattleman. In particular, he found himself in opposition to Bartlett Richards, proprietor of the huge - and hugely successful - Spade

Ranch.

Originally, Jules had settled down by the river, south of Hay Springs, maybe fifty miles west of here, but he always had a hankering to be in the Sandhills proper. In 1909 he staked a claim to the east, thirty-odd miles south of Gordon, way out in the wilds – to the horror of his long-suffering wife, who had somehow forged a social life at Mirage Flats, as the old place was called, and seen her children get proper schooling, despite his assertion that he could teach them better than any damned American.

Under the Kinkaid Act (1904), which recognized the improbability of anyone making a living on 160 acres in these dry parts, land in thirty-odd western counties could now be claimed in lots of 640 acres, a full square mile. Someone like Jules, who already had a homestead, was entitled to claim an additional 480. But with the river place still to be sold, and with his wife carrying a sixth baby (Caroline) a move wasn't yet possible. In any case, Jules took against this first place, and in August of 1910 sent Mari (now aged 14) and her brother James (aged 10) to look after a new holding, a patch of empty grassland beside a small lake and surrounded by hills, with not a neighbor in sight. They'd be comfortable enough. Hadn't he built a shack out there? He had, all except for the door, windows and floor, that is.

The two children would remain there, alone, until a devastating range fire in September prompted Jules to set out and see how they were doing. They were loving it. This brief spell in the hills was a crucial turn in young Mari's life – for two reasons. For the first time since she could recall, she had no baby to carry round on her hip while her mother worked outside, no overbearing father bossing her around; and she became intimately acquainted with, and fell in love with, the sandhills environment. Heretofore she had been familiar with the hills but resident by the river. This was a radically different, an elemental environment: no trees, no river – and no people, so this was an idyllic time, which the two children spent wandering the hills, hunting grouse and rabbits to fry for their meals, learning about the plants and animals, the weather, the character and moods of the land. Small wonder that Mari chose to be buried right there, on a hill overlooking the place.

But back to Bartlett Richards and the Spade Ranch. Richards, like many cattlemen, had played fast and loose with the law. He had carefully acquired lands around his spread which made it nigh impossible for neighboring farmers to access water, or the hay meadows. When Jules first tried to run a small herd of his own on the new place he found that Spade cattle (there were several thousand head, scattered over a great sprawl of land that stretched from Ellsworth in the south to the Niobrara, some 30 miles north) were soon trampling his fences.

Reading the first few chapters of this book, *Bartlett Richards, Sandhills Cattleman*, I see that I am living on what was actually Spade Ranch land. And I am curious to know more about this man Richards. He seems to have been an extraordinary character. Not a well child, at the age of 17 he was sent to a Wyoming ranch for his health, and – just like Theodore Roosevelt, just like Owen Wister, another invalid, who wrote *The Virginian* on the back of his experiences out west – young Bartlett thrived. By the time he was 19 he was managing three Wyoming ranches covering an area as large as his native Vermont. For the next 30 years he was a big, big player in Wyoming and Nebraska ranching. In 1910 he went to jail for offences having to do with his land acquisition. He grew ill, and died in 1911, aged 49, still in Federal custody.

A pause. It's only 1030, but I have just taken six loaves out of the oven. I will rip one apart for my lunch, I dare say. Then back to the story of the man who once ran his cattle over this very land. It occurs to me that just now this feels like the life of the gentleman writer that I dreamed of when I was eighteen. Whenever I am overcome with such a sentiment I pause and allow myself a contented smile. Most of the time this writing game is about struggle and hardship, penury and rejection. When it comes right, for however brief a moment, I am inclined to go out, look at the stars and grin.

I ought to add a note about bread-baking. I still find it hard to mention it casually, because people seem unduly daunted by what is a very simple task, and are consequently impressed that one can manage it. It's been a part of my life since 1971, when I happened to complain that the bread in the shops where we lived, in south-west London, wasn't up to much. The challenge was, can you do any better? I started then and have never stopped, even when, as now, I'm living alone. It's quick, easy and generally produces better bread than any you can buy. It's also a hell of a lot cheaper. There, that's that dealt with.

Tuesday 3 May

It was quite a sight, I dare say, and I am almost regretful that nobody was there to witness it. There I was in my down jacket and hiking trousers, a baseball cap on my head, pushing a large, wood-framed wheelbarrow around the open range and pouncing gleefully on every decent sized cow turd I could find. Add a flat tyre to the barrow, scatter a few hail flurries about me, throw in the curious buzzard that swooped low over my head, not once but twice – no, I don't think he could quite believe what he was seeing either - and you have the kind of opening tableau that a film director such as Wim Wenders might have dreamed up.

It's the gardening. That's what it's about. It was the kind of morning – sunny, cool, breezy, the sky dotted with puffy white clouds, the landscape still with its dun-colored winter coat on - that makes a guy want to do… something. Well, I'd bought the seeds, and Matt said he had a couple of rolls of chicken-wire up at his workshop – so let's go.

I worked up quite a thirst marking out my little plot, digging the first few rows with a trenching spade, gathering six barrow-loads of cow-chips and digging that in. If I keep up this pace I'll have the plot pretty well prepared by the end of the week – just in time for the arrival of the next lot of hunters, and my buddy Chainsaw Phil, who's flying in from the UK next Tuesday.

As I said, I worked up a thirst – which I satisfied with a cool glass of Fat Tire, sitting in the afternoon sunlight as the greeny-yellow finches (I think that's what they are) darted about the trees pecking insects from under the bark. There are still no leaves to be seen, but quite a bit of blossom about to burst into life.

It may be, of course, that I fail at this gardening caper. It may be that the cattle, or the deer, or the squirrels, or some other crittur – the grasshoppers, perhaps – will get my crops before I do, but this is a chance to do what I've long wanted to do: grow a few vegetables in a hot climate. Rapid results. According to the packets – of beetroot, French beans, zucchini, lettuce and tomato – I should be harvesting within 45 to 55 days of sowing. We shall see.

I have continued with the Bartlett Richards story. Of course, it's been put together by his son, so it is partisan. Well, fair enough. Other people have written him up from a hostile perspective, and described him as what my grandmother would have called a double-dyed villain. The book contains a number of Richards' letters. Those to his family reveal a tender, loving and deeply serious man. Those relating to his business and his calling as a cattleman put a lot of things in perspective for me. What I had never considered, for example, is the extent to which the fencing of the open range – of what was still Government land – might have been less about appropriation of resources and more about good management. No settler, no homesteader, was remotely interested in the Sandhills when Bartlett established the Spade Ranch. The area simply wasn't considered cultivable, and 160 acres of sand would never feed a family. It still bore the taint of the label given it by Major Stephen Long after his expedition of 1820, The Great American Desert.

Until the mid-1880s cattlemen had got away with a rough-and-ready open range system. Hell, the cattle were mostly free anyway, driven up from Texas where they'd run wild since the Spanish incursions in the sixteenth century. Turn them loose on the open range, fatten `em and ship `em east. Easy money.

Then came the devastating winter of 1886-87 when a

huge percentage of stock was simply starved or frozen to death, suffocated in the snows. Now the cattleman looked to fence off areas of range and keep the cattle from it during the growing season so that they would have winter grazing. They would fence off hay meadows too, and plow up strips of land as firebreaks. For the first time, they tried to manage the land, improve their herds, conserve the grass. Fences, however, were against the law. This was public, Government, land. But the point was, out west the law turned a blind eye. Well-managed ranches such as Bartlett's brought prosperity, trade, business, jobs. Why would the law question what everyone saw as commonsense practice on land that was no good for any other purpose? Wasn't it all a lot of fuss stirred up by eastern politicians clinging to Jefferson's agrarian dream? Well, I have 70 more pages to read, and poor old Bartlett is going to go to jail and die.

More digging to be done this morning, and more cow chips to be gathered – but only after I've got some air in that tire.

Wednesday 4 May

Here I am banging on about cowshit and I've been neglecting to mention the cattle that produce it. That's because the vast majority of them are out of sight, grazing peacefully on level pasture a mile or two from here. Yesterday evening there were still three recalcitrant heifers lurking in the enclosure, munching through their pile of hay. One more calf has appeared over the past day or two.

Matt is trying to persuade one of the cows, who lost her calf, to adopt an orphan, but she's not taken with the idea, at all. So he tempted her with a bowl of goodies, cattle nuts sweetened with molasses, then trapped her head between two steel bars, nose into the food. She'll stay there while the calf suckles, and he's delegated to me the job of releasing her after about 45 minutes. Never one to trust my short-term memory, I have set my phone alarm.

To more pressing matters. The mice are back. I had a sneaky feeling that my triumph was suspiciously swift and easy - a little like Desert Storm, I suppose, or, less controversially, Operation Barbarossa in 1941. Anyway, I was minding my own business yesterday when I heard the sudden snap of a trap beside the sink. This was in broad daylight. So yesterday evening I set all three traps, and caught two more of the little pests overnight.

Yesterday, at last, was a proper spring day. Started out at 31 degrees and by mid-afternoon had reached 73 – and left me with a burned upper right arm. But it was glorious weather for working, and I got two or three more rows of digging done, several more barrow-loads of manure spread in the trenches. The next task is to find a way of germinating my tomato seeds indoors.

I am starting to worry about bugs. Yesterday, every time the wind dropped, a cloud of little flying things rose from the ground. I mean within thirty seconds. They're not unlike the Scottish midges in size, but they don't seem to be biting. And as soon as the wind picked up again they were gone – all except the ones that managed to settle on my clothes, in my hair, on my bare flesh. They just sat there and 'aggravated the tar outa me' as a Kansas lady once said to me. And this morning, I *am* kind of itchy.

I have to report that Mari Sandoz has let me down again. Push the right button and I will enthuse, interminably, about her writing on the Great Plains region, its history, its landscape, its heroes and villains. But I have yet to complete a single one of her novels – unless you count *Son of the Gamblin' Man,* her fictionalized biography of the painter Robert Henri, born in Cozad, Nebraska. I've more or less given up on *The Tom-Walker.* As with all of her fictions – at least, the several that I've tried - this one parades before the reader her vast wealth of research material, in this case post-Civil War politics and economics and the vernacular of the day, but simply never grabs you and makes you want to know what happened next. And there's this insistence on cramming one colourful simile after another into her prose, as well as into each character's speech. Three, four, five, six per page, unrelentingly. I feel disloyal saying it, but her fiction simply fails as far as I'm concerned. I think it was a matter of survival for her. My understanding is that her history books were so painstakingly researched, took so long to write, and sold so slowly – steadily, yes, but slowly – that she could make more money out of these novels, and could knock them out far more quickly. It's rather as if she were running up table-napkins out of material left over from a carefully made dress.

It's a lot cooler today, and the wind is up. Probably perfect for digging, except that my body is reluctant and I feel very comfortable sitting at the kitchen table here pecking away at the keyboard. But I think it's time to go and release that cow.

Thursday 5 May

Twenty minutes before six in the morning, and across the river a lone coyote was having one last howl before turning in after a night on the prowl. Down in the woods the turkeys were awake and gobbling. A pair of geese were honking their way north across a pale blue sky, and on the fence-post a meadowlark trilled as the first tongue of sunlight licked at the underbelly of a solitary cloud, smearing it pink.

I'd gone out early to try and capture a few images of the dawn. There was ice on the car and enough of a breeze to have me reaching for my thick hat and gloves. I must have snapped twenty or thirty times, but when I got home, turned the heat up under my porridge and sat down at the computer screen I found two or three halfway acceptable shots. That was all. My mate Greg, a writer and photographer back in England, would say that's a decent return. In the old days, he says, you'd shoot a whole roll of film, and then another, and if you got one picture that captured what you were after you'd call it a success.

I had another strenuous day yesterday, and slept better for it – despite being startled when a grey mouse shot across the bedroom floor and disappeared into a corner closet just as I was folding up my *Guardian Weekly* and turning out the light. One more day – three or four more rows of digging - and I ought to have my vegetable plot ready. I'm having to venture a little further afield for the cow-pats, of course. Yesterday I found myself under the cedars, maybe five or six hundred yards downstream from here. After I'd piled up my barrow I took a walk around and was surprised to see several trees that had clearly been gnawed at, and in some cases felled, by what I could only imagine to be beaver.

'Sure, there's beaver down there,' Matt told me when he came down later to check on the three remaining mothers-to-be, and the orphan calf. 'Cause a lot of damage. There's a big old cottonwood they've chewed around. I mean, it's old and it'll die sure enough, but it don't need any help.'

I asked him whether they ever attempted to build a dam – no, the river's too swift and shallow – or whether he'd ever tried to get rid of them. 'Yeah, I have a guy comes out to trap them, time to time. Hasn't been around for a few years though.'

Matt says there are muskrat too – and I did see a number of neat round holes in the bank, maybe three or four inches in diameter. Old Jules Sandoz used to trap them for the furs – and would leave the entrails on the kitchen table for his wife to clear up. Mari and her brother kept one as a pet, the summer she and Jim spent alone on the new claim in the hills. She later wrote it up as the short story 'Musky'.

Well, they're forecasting 65 degrees today, so I'll be smearing sunblock on and paying particular attention to the tops of my ears, which got scorched on Tuesday. Later today I'm off to town – I'm down to my last bottle of beer - and I'll be calling in at the garage in Merriman to have one of Mercy's tyres checked. It's looking pretty unsafe to me. And there is no spare wheel – unless it's hidden somewhere I haven't looked.

Friday 6 May

I wonder whether things are about to change. It's not eight o'clock yet and it's 56 degrees. 71 yesterday afternoon, and they're forecasting 75 tomorrow. And as I look out on the hills it seems there is just a shading of green here and there where previously it was all dun-colored. But there's a stiff breeze, which will keep those midges at bay.

I tackled the tomato seeds yesterday – on the cheap. Used an old Cool Whip carton the hunters left, cut four little holes in the bottom and filled it - first with small rocks, then a handful of pulverized straw; finally I piled some sand with a little pulverized manure on top, and sowed half the seeds. We shall see...

There are only a couple of expectant cows left in the enclosure, and Matt has announced that he's about ready for branding. It'll be a little different from what I saw over at Kitty's dad's place: fewer cowboys, no lariats, and the use of chutes to direct the calves to a branding table. I'll be there, hoping I can help.

I took Mercy to town yesterday. The guy at the garage, Don, knew right away who the vehicle belonged to, and volunteered that he was pretty darned sure where the missing spare wheel might be. 'Why, he'll have needed to get something in the back and' – he gesticulated with his arms – 'he'll have thrown everything out. That's how he is. You go down to his yard; you'll soon find it, lying around.'

Don looked at all four of my tyres and pronounced them legal and safe in any case, but agreed that I didn't want to be beetling up and down Highway 20 without a spare. After that I had a choice: carry on to Gordon and get the few groceries I needed – plus the beer – or eat a cooked breakfast at the Sand Café, next door to the garage. No contest. And after a three-egg western omelet plus toast and hash browns I was ready for home.

I got to the end of the Bartlett Richards book last night. I wound up feeling very sorry for the guy, and his family. Sentenced to a year in jail (at Hastings), all his appeals squashed, and as soon as he gets there his health fails and within a year he's dead, not yet fifty. The bare facts are that he illegally fenced Government land. In mitigation, the law locally ignored what he and others were doing; and everyone agreed that ploughing up the sod – which is what the homesteaders would do - would destroy a fragile ecosystem. People even lined up to speak of his kindness and hospitality towards such people as did settle nearby – loaning them milk cows, supplying them on credit from his store. You could question all of that; but then you are left with the letters he wrote to his wife and children, and I'll quote from two. Firstly, one written when he was in New York on business, to Inez when their children were small, an example of the way he would sign off:

'Dear Longley [the baby] – I know he is a comfort to you. Tell him Daddy is glad to hear that he goes to sleep so well when he takes his nap. Kiss my namesake [Bartlett, Jr.] and promise him with your eyes his Daddy's tenderest love now and always. My heart almost bursts when I think of you and the children – but I will hold you all in my arms, as I now do in my breast, shortly. Your lover, Bartlett.'

And then there's this to young Bartlett, from jail, just six months before his end:

'I am greatly pleased to get your fine letter of March 10th and hear what you did with your Valentine present [he'd sent the boy $2, to be spent on 'something you want for yourself or others']. You have improved very much in your writing. Make a little longer tails to your Y's and G's below the line – and it will appear better yet. I am enclosing you a most interesting account of the migration of birds. Think of the Arctic tern which flies

22,000 miles each year to go from the Arctic to the Antarctic snows. Get your mother to read this… to you and Longley – for I want you to remember the interesting habits of birds.' It's hard to think badly of such a man.

Saturday 7 May

The last calf has been delivered. It was a huge one, and Matt had to pull it. But for all its size it was weak, barely able to stand, and there was never much chance it would survive. Sometime today Matt will take it out into the hills and leave it for the coyotes and buzzards. The mother is now suckling an orphan calf – and I'll be off to release her in half an hour or so.

I took a walk last night, just as the sun was going down. I realized that with all this gardening and manure-gathering I'd been neglecting to watch the plant life, and things are moving along fast. A splash of white caught my eye, two or three small trees part-way down the bluff above the river, maybe a third of a mile east of here. Steep as that hillside is – and with a 100-foot drop below to concentrate your mind – it's easy enough to walk on. The sand is very yielding, and there's always some kind of cattle-trail to follow along the contour. Mostly I can grab at a clump of grass; the roots are long and tough enough to hold me. Even as I approached the trees I could smell a heavy, sweet scent, not unlike the may blossom back home. I'm pretty sure it's a wild plum.

It was a surprisingly colourless sunset, despite the streaks of grey and white cloud. There was a very thin new moon high above me. For the first time in three or four nights up there I didn't see the heron flying home, or the geese, but the turkeys were gobbling away down by the river, blissfully unaware that another lot of hunters are coming next week. I stood for some time after the sun had gone, hoping that the western sky would light up, then started for home. That's when a kind of honey-colored something caught my eye, way up in a cedar tree. It was a porcupine, very still, spines flared. To me it was exotic; to Matt they're nothing but a damned nuisance, chewing bark, killing trees. 'I shoot `em on sight,' was his only comment this morning when I told him what I'd seen.

There was a moment last night when I half wished I had a gun down here. Something was scrabbling and shifting around under the cooker. Definitely bigger than a mouse; probably a rat, to judge by the gnawing sounds I was now hearing and the occasional clatter of something striking metal. I was reluctant to open the drawer under the oven in case it leapt out and escaped. After listening for some time I came to the conclusion that it was not in but *under* the bottom drawer beside the stove, and took the coward's way out. I made a tube of paper, half filled it with mouse poison, slowly opened the drawer and poured the poison in behind it. This morning, removing the drawer, I found that it had mostly been taken. So I brace myself for the smell of dead rodent in a few days.

My trip to Gordon yesterday bore mixed results. I ticked off a few items on my grocery list, but found the library – the main point of my going there – shut. Fridays and Sundays. And I kicked myself, because I have the schedule right here on the kitchen table. Just never bothered to look.

Well, the guy at the garage in Merriman was right. The spare wheel was at Kitty's dad's place all along. Matt went across yesterday and fetched it back, along with the licence-plate tags.

Today promises to be another fine one. It got down to 42 overnight but here we are, 0820 and it's 52 already – and they're forecasting 75 today, 80-plus tomorrow. Chainsaw Phil, who flies in Tuesday, will not be happy. He hates the heat.

Sunday 8 May

Henry David Thoreau. I've been here a month now, so I think it's fair enough to bring his name up. And if you want to skip the philosophizing and get on to the sex and violence – well, I apologize: there ain't any.

I first read *Walden* way back in my freight train days, sitting in a rickety caboose with a can of tea simmering on the cast-iron stove, paraffin lamps flickering, a string of 40 loose-coupled wagons rattling through the dark. Many a night I would sit and dream of a life in the woods as we left Sheffield, still a thriving steel city at that time, sped past the blazing walls of fire that were the coke ovens at Wath on Dearne, and out into the country heading for the cathedral city of York.

I read him again when I did a degree in American history and literature in my late thirties. I was mightily impressed both times. But it's not his thoughts on Economy I'm thinking about now – as pertinent in today's climate as they were 150 years ago, if you ask me. It's his essay on walking, which was on my mind as I wandered the hills and explored wooded valleys this afternoon.

Thoreau remarked that a seventy-year lifespan was just about enough time to allow a man (and a woman, I guess, but he didn't say that) to get to know the landscape within a day's walk of home. Within a ten-mile radius, that is. Ten miles out and ten back: home before dark.

So I found myself wondering, as I scrambled – at times crouched, occasionally progressing on my hands and knees – through the dense undergrowth that feeds on the waters that flow into the Niobrara. Wondering. How well can I get to know these 6,000 acres in one growing season?

I honestly think I will get a good overall impression, and that's about it. There is so much to see, so many micro-environments, so many different trees that seem to be holding their breath, ready to burst into leaf all at once; so many mysterious animal tracks, so many flowers. And then the grasses. There are no less than 71 pages of the damned things in my *Grassland Plants of South Dakota and the Northern Great Plains*. Okay, only a couple per page, but I am daunted.

My best hope, I conclude, is that I will be able to grasp what the great landscape architect Lancelot 'Capability' Brown called the *genius loci*, the spirit of the place. That'll do me.

Okay, enough philosophizing. My walk took me westward to the north-south fence that divides this place from the next one upstream. I headed north down a broad, gently sloping pasture which led me to a thicket of cedar trees marking the river's course. When I'd ploughed my way through them I found a narrow band of lush green grass by the water's edge, just a few feet wide - in places only inches. Opposite me, the tall white bluffs that form the northern bank. Here and there the fallen timber, the tangled grapevines, the over-hanging branches, were so dense that I was forced to scramble up

73

the bank and fight my way onward – hence the scratch-marks on my face this morning.

It was a struggle, but it was well worth it, if only for the bank of violets I found basking in the sun, and the discovery of a spring-fed stream entering the river. I took off my boots to paddle in the stream, which was cold, and ventured carefully into the river. It may be shallow but it flows very swiftly over a rocky bed, so you really have to watch your step. I was pleasantly surprised at how warm it was by comparison – and I'm now encouraged to think about crossing the river here and exploring the hills to the north.

Heading for home, I found that I wasn't able to stay on the bank for long: the bluffs now came right to the water's edge. So I climbed up the canyon, following the stream towards its source – and found to my delight a couple of strawberries in flower.

Monday 9 May

Today didn't get off to the best of starts. I'd driven up to the ranch HQ and was on my way back to the red house. As I approached the spot where the trail dips sharply between eroded banks of sand, I was distracted by the sight of Oscar, the white horse, silhouetted against a clear blue sky. I had the camera on the seat beside me. I am making a point of always having it to hand; you never know what you'll see next. I stopped, and snapped a couple of times. Then I set off down the incline. And there was Chief, the old paint, standing right in front of me. I slowed; he remained rooted to the spot. I was down to a crawl, but still he wouldn't move; so I stopped. Big mistake.

After an exchange of pleasantries, Chief ambled off in

search of better grazing and I put my foot on the gas pedal. Somehow Mercy had slipped into two-wheel drive, and before I realized it I'd dug myself in – deep. Both horses were watching, from barely fifteen feet away, as I got down on all fours and scrabbled away at the damp sand with my bare hands, then got back in, gave it another try, and dug myself even deeper.

By now, not only were the rear wheels embedded axle-deep, but the exhaust was buried too. I trudged back to the house – about two-thirds of a mile – put on my boots, shouldered the spade and the trenching tool, and set off up the hill. As I plodded along I could see the car, in outline, at a crazy angle to the trail, and there were the two culprits, standing guard, looking as guilty as sin. What a picture. And what a shame my camera was on the front seat. By the time I got up there and pulled it out they'd 'lit out for the Territory', as Mark Twain would have it.

All's well that ends well, I suppose. I excavated about a cubic yard of sand, got the car moving, then went back and made the road good again. I now have a spade in the back seat, and it's staying there. By this time it was eleven o'clock and the day had heated up. 86 degrees when I checked the thermometer. So after lunch I slung my boots around my neck, put on my sandals and waded across the river. I described a sort of circle to the north and east, re-crossed the river and made my way towards home, pausing only to take note of a few clumps of wild plums for future reference.

I'd forgotten, of course, that my sandals were still on the far bank of the river, but that gave me an excuse to cool off one more time before going home. Later, I sat in the living-room and read a superb short piece by Mari

Sandoz, published five years before she found fame and literary freedom with *Old Jules*.

In 'The Kinkaider Comes and Goes' she visits old haunts in the sandhills and comes across a faded wooden sign, 'Pleasant Home', attached to a fence-post by a single nail. There's precious little to indicate that a home had ever stood on the spot, just an old cookstove abandoned in a clump of ragged sunflowers. And that triggers her recollection of a woman who had lived there when she was a child, a spinster music teacher from Chicago who loaned Mari poetry books, and the novels of Joseph Conrad, until the dreadful winter of 1910-11 made her so ill that she decided to quit.

As so often with Mari's early work, the setting is no more than a device to allow her to reminisce about her own childhood, and the weeks she and her brother spent alone on the Kinkaid claim, which was to become the orchard place. It's a beautiful piece, elegiac in tone. Reading it now, after being here a full month, I found that it touched me in ways that it hadn't before, and her superb evocations of landscape already mean that much more to me. I won't go on about it, but I strongly recommend it. And I must add that it's made me think that now is a good time – and this is a good place - for me to re-read *Old Jules*. It's probably my favourite book, not just of hers, not just of the West, but in all of literature. But now I must head for bed. Early start tomorrow: I am required at the ranch for 0730, for branding.

Wednesday 11 May

I was awake at 0430h this morning, and up by five. It was the humming noise in my left ear. Took a while to figure it out, but I'm pretty sure it was the last echo of those bawling calves yesterday, all 175 of them – and their mothers, matching them note for note for nine long hours.

We were lucky. Very lucky indeed. After Sunday's 87 degrees, branding day dawned grey, cool and foggy. Well, they said it was foggy. They should try North Yorkshire in November, when you struggle to see across the road. By my reckoning the visibility was several miles, but, yes, I had to admit there was a slight haze.

Good old Matt. The way he handed me that clipboard and gave me my instructions made me feel that I really had to be on top of my game; otherwise the entire operation would fail. Oh yes, these cowboys recognise talent when it washes up in their front yard. Writer, huh? Here, grab yourself a pen and keep count.

There was a system, and once it got started it was going to be pure poetry. I just knew it was. But first, we needed an overview of the situation to hand. Matt had drafted in his buddy Rob, Kitty's cousin from up-river, and a little feller about six years old, Rob's son. They all took turns to offer an opinion as to the best way to separate the mother cows from their young, and herd the calves into the chute for processing. The cattle soon got wind that something was up and milled around in the pens, bawling, raising dust and shitting all over each other. Confused young ones trotted about, their faces obliterated by green crap. Matt was on the rail, looking over the sea of dark bodies and trying to make himself heard above the racket and through the dust.

It all came down to swinging the right gate at the right time, guiding the mothers one way, the youngsters the other. With one hand working a rawhide switch, the other rested on the gate, they were mostly succeeding – sometimes with the aid of an out-stretched leg. Gradually, the first lot of forty or fifty calves were gathered up in the little pen where cousin Jake, aided by the boy, manhandled them one by one towards the jaws of the table. There they were trapped by the steel bars across their bodies, rotated so that they lay side-on, and delivered to Matt the Knife.

Meanwhile three of us tried to get the propane burner fired up. The cigarette-lighter had seen better days, but with the help of some scrunched-up paper – and at the cost of a few singed hairs around the wrist – we had us a flame, and the branding-irons were soon glowing red. There were several of them: the big round O and the back-to-front E for Matt's herd, the X for Kitty's mum's, the Spanish 5 – partway between a J and a 5 to look at - that is her dad's brand.

Then it was down to business. And with the three different herds involved, the guy with the pencil was soon working his fingers to the bone. Not only was I keeping a tally of bull-calves and heifers under the names of three separate owners but I was working the gate that sent Matt's out onto the range, the other lot into a pen

'Bull! Matt!' Clang.

'Heifer! Dick!' Clang.

'Bull! Charlene!' Clang.

'No – heifer!' Good job I had an eraser. And then it turns out somebody – we could safely blame Lightning, now that he was back across the border - had put the tag on the wrong ear, and this heifer belonged over there, in the other pen.

So the cowboys dropped smoothly into their respective routines. There was cousin Eric wrestling the calves into the trap, twisting their tails to encourage them forward, stepping briskly aside to avoid getting crapped on, and following each one through with the fresh plastic ear-tags and an array of syringes, plus some large yellow pills to shove down the throat of any beast whose rear-end output was beyond the call of duty. They call that scouring. Matt dealt with the bull-calves, and Rob worked the branding-irons, holding them firm against the wriggling, bawling calf. Funny how, no matter where you stood, the wind blew the stink of singed hair right in your face. As for the calves, cute little six-week-olds some of them, with spindly legs and narrow hips - their eyes bulged with fear, their tongues lolled. Some bawled when the hot iron seared their flesh, some were silent.

Castration – even after I'd watched it a hundred times I found myself wincing – is a deft operation. Matt used a short, slender blade, maybe two and a half inches, to slit the sac. And then, rather than dig around for the testicles and risk infection, he probed with his fingers in the calf's belly, squeezed, popped them out, pulled hard until he'd got several inches of the string stretched out, and – cut. Into the bucket. It seemed to bother the beasts a lot less than the branding and medication, and they trotted off to find their mothers looking a little dazed but otherwise unconcerned. Never knew what they'd missed.

The whole deal could put you off meat for a while, I suppose. But Kitty's lunch, served in the house at noon, was irresistible. Big juicy beef steaks, fried onion and potato, pasta salad and biscuit, followed by a dessert cake with ice cream. Damned shame we had to stumble back out to work afterwards.

We were done by about four, hot, dusty and thirsty.

Suddenly the place was almost quiet, just the roar of the propane burner, the calling of calves for mothers and vice versa as they spread out south of us. Rocky Mountain oysters, anyone? Par-broiled on the propane burner? Our scribe and tally-man said he was a brave feller – so brave indeed that he could admit to quaking in his boots at the very thought, and decline the offer. I've eaten proper oysters; I even ate snails once, out of bravado. But I was young and foolish then.

Wednesday 11 May - evening

It's some time since I mentioned the Arents, the people who first settled down here where the red house stands, and built it, by hand. As I mentioned earlier, when Holger Arent and his wife Hedvig (formerly Petersen) came out to this part of Nebraska she already had two brothers on a homestead to the south, somewhere along the Snake river. Peter had come first, and by 1893 was ready to send for his brother Julius and their mother. Hedvig was supposed to have come three years earlier, and did indeed set sail from Denmark in 1890; but she met young Holger on the voyage across the Atlantic, stayed with him in Omaha and got married. I'm repeating myself, but only because I want to think again about the way they had to live in their early years down here.

It's years since I first read about dug-outs – probably in Willa Cather's frontier novels – but I've never really sat and thought about them. Living in a hole in the ground: it's what a lot of our ancestors did, nothing more, nothing less. Except that we call them cavemen. Of course, when you reach out and touch the river-banks here you can see that it made a degree of sense in a land that lacked trees, clay, or any of the customary building materials. If you go down to the bluffs, where they're made of firm, but easily crumbled limestone – yes, it's easy to see that you could fashion a decent living space out of that; and it would have the virtue of being cool. Clean too. But crumbly. A lot of it you can break apart with your fingers

Clearly they were cramped in their dug-out, this family of ten, so they added a room to the front of the cave, built, the record says, of stone – which they apparently gathered from the river-bed and cemented together.

Holger, you may recall, was a cabinet-maker. So he broke up packing-cases, gathered willow from along the river, and built the family's furniture. Reading between the lines, I would guess they had left their business in Omaha with very little in the way of assets. Think about it. You have a family of ten, you live in a thriving city, you run a cigar and confectionery store, and one day you pack up, hop on the train, and go to live in a hole in the ground in cattle country. It's surely not a decision you would take lightly. Things must have been pretty desperate.

We are told - I have been given access to a few precious accounts based on interviews with the children in their later years - that the dug-out extension had a roof of chicken-wire, covered with canvas and straw, and that there were lots of rattlesnakes.

The Arents had at least some cattle, and the children were kept busy seeing that their stock didn't mingle with the herds belonging to the neighbouring rancher – who at this time must have been Bartlett Richards, although in the scant reminiscences that I have seen he isn't mentioned by name.

Before long the family put up a single-storey sod-house, comprising two rooms. The walls were eighteen inches thick, providing insulation against the summer heat and the winter cold. The roof was made of willow poles covered with more sod. With the nearest wood for fuel being seven miles away along the Snake, the children were sent out to gather cow-chips for the stove. They had no proper shoes, just 'moccasins' fashioned out of old overalls. I have to say I feel for them: the other day I knelt down a little too close to a prickly pear and was forced to utter a number of profanities.

The Arent children had plenty of contact with the Natives who every year would come down from the reservation, just to the north, set up their tipis and pick wild berries. These they would form into cakes and dry in the sun and wind for winter food. They'd strip the bark off the red willow and smoke it. And then they'd come and try to trade for the Arents' dogs. They had quite a liking for dog-meat.

It's interesting to note that in those early days the family drank river water. They took precautions, of course: left it for the sand to settle before they drank it.

Of the pictures which are on the wall here, there are a couple taken from across the river of what appears to be a wooden house with a pitched roof, right here where the red house now stands. That's odd, because nowhere in this history is there any mention of such a dwelling. There's a picture of a narrow footbridge that was constructed across the river, probably not far from the point where Matt now crosses on his ATV, or All Terrain Vehicle – what we would call a quad-bike in England.

Thursday 12 May

It feels like old times again. The house is full of turkey hunters – plus Chainsaw Phil - and I'm back in the trailer. It's 42 degrees out there, and has been most of the day; and windy, and wet.

The trip to Rapid City and back seemed longer than it ought to have been. But there were compensations – like finding a supermarket with a decent range of fresh produce. We stopped in Chadron on the way home and I introduced Phil to my Olde Main Street Madam, Jeannie, who served us coffee and brought me up to speed on her struggle with the police chief. The latest is that he interviewed her at some length and covertly recorded the conversation. Jeannie is a lovely, kind-hearted person but you wouldn't want to get in a fight with her. Behind the bar is a photo, taken a few years ago: there she is sitting astride a big chunky bike with a bandanna round her forehead looking – well, like someone you don't mess with.

We got back here as it was getting dark and just had time to meet the hunters before they crashed out. They'll be revving up their ATV around four-thirty – and I dare say I'll be up shortly after that, planning an induction day for my tenderfoot friend.

I mentioned the other day that I thought it might be good to re-read *Old Jules* while I'm here and getting more accustomed to the Sandhills. I managed Chapter 1 today, during a lull in proceedings, and wasn't disappointed. I've said it before, and I'll say it again: I do not believe that there is a better piece of scene-setting in all of what we call the literature of the West than the opening page of this book. Every time I read those first few paragraphs my heart beats faster.

Friday 13 May

As my old rat-catching mate Walter would have said, 'By heck, if it gets much colder I shall `ave to put on another pair of braces.' [*NB: When we Brits say braces we mean suspenders.*]

I thought I'd seen the back of this weather, but here I am sitting at my table in the trailer, the heating full on, wearing five layers: T-shirt, shirt, thick fleece, goose-down jacket, waterproof coat. Then there are my trusty moleskin trousers and the hat with the ear-flaps that kept me warm in Lapland earlier this year. Minus 20, it was. Outside, under the apple tree, whose blossoms lie bruised and battered, my thermometer has hovered between 42 and 43 degrees since yesterday morning. The wheelbarrow, which last week was full of cow chips, is now full of water. I'd say we've had close to an inch and a half over the past twenty-four hours. The rain has more or less stopped, but the wind, whistling down from Canada, persists.

So, yesterday, as the weather swept in over t h e bluffs, Chainsaw Phil and I had a point to prove. Two of the hunters, fresh from the 90-degree heat of Georgia, took a look out the window, stowed their guns and drove to Mount Rushmore; the other two stayed home and watched action movies. We Brits, determined to show our vigour and fortitude, decided we would go hiking – after we'd paid a visit to town.

I'm getting to like Merriman. And I'm starting to find more to do down there. For a town of 118 souls it's a regular little beehive of activity. First call was the post office - where a parcel awaited me. After we'd signed for that we went to the garage to put another $60-worth of gas into Mercy's tank and hunt up Don. I needed to tell him how right he'd been about the spare tyre the other day – that it did indeed show up in Rick's yard. He nodded. 'Yeah, I told ya. I've known him a long time.'

From there we leaned into the screaming wind and staggered around the corner to ranch supplies. I'd not met the lady in there before, but as soon as I mentioned mouse poison she looked me in the eye and said, 'Guess you're up at the red house.'

Now how would she know that? 'Why,' she said, 'ya drove up in Rick's old Chevy, that's how. 'Sides, everyone who stays up there complains about the mouse problem. That's $2.89... plus your tax.'

Exhausted by this social whirl, we repaired to the café and ordered the lunchtime special. Ribs in barbecue sauce – with hash browns, green beans, biscuit, and a trip to the salad bar. Ribs? I'd call it a generous portion of a pig that happened to have a couple of bones in it. That was at noon, and I didn't even think about food again till eight at night.

Back at the red house we were ready to face the elements. We gritted our teeth, leaned forward at 45 degrees, and trudged toward the tops, before descending to the riverside about a mile from home as the crow flies. Down amongst the cedars we found much calmer, more temperate air and I was moved to unzip a few inches of my raincoat.

We followed the river-bank around three or four sharp curves, squeezing through the overhanging branches, inches from the fast-flowing stream. Along the way I spotted two or three encouraging signs that there may be good times just around the corner: a Plains wallflower, some sort of sweet pea, and a couple of sprigs of peppermint.

Saturday 14 May

The fun started in earnest when we got to Chadron. We'd taken one look at the weather this morning – windy, overcast and 42 degrees – and hit the road. Drove to Gordon and checked out the airport. Nice blacktop runway, beautiful lounge with a sofa, reclining chair and coffee machine; they even have a refrigerator loaded up with soda-pop. But no aircraft; and no people either, just a phone number or two pinned up on the notice-board beside the deserted office.

I'd better explain. About a couple of years ago the Chainsaw decided he wanted to learn to fly. And knock me down with a feather if he didn't take off for New Zealand, shack up with a long-lost uncle and come home several months later brandishing a pilot's licence. So now, everywhere he goes his eyes dart to left and right and it's 'Right, where's the airport, mate?'

'Airport?' I said, when he got off the plane at Rapid the other day and threw me the question. 'Take your pick. They're dotted along Highway 20 like pearls on a string.'

So next stop it was Rushville. Grass runway, nice red wind-sock but not much in the way of sofas; or soda-pop for that matter. As for Hay Springs, that was way across the fields and didn't look as though it had a terminal building at all.

'Tell you what,' I said, 'we've come this far. Let's try Chadron. College town; 5800 inhabitants. We're bound to find something there.'

Inside the airport terminal we met a duty supervisor who had a think and said, 'Maybe you oughta talk to our manager, fellow by the name of Doug Budd.'

Now this is where you have to stop a moment, shake

your head and admit that – yep, it really is a small, small world. 'Doug Budd of Crawford, Nebraska?' I said. 'Used to ride broncs?'

'Why, matter of fact he did.'

I knew very well that he did. When I was with the veteran pro circuit I interviewed him. One thing he said always stuck in my mind. I was watching him strap on some body armour and a kind of sheath around his leg. 'It's for my knee,' he said. 'Keeps popping out.' And then he climbed up the fence, eased himself across it and lowered his stiff body into the saddle. Clang! went the gate and he was away around the arena, clinging to that bronc while I winced at every jolt and jar.

Once we'd got the reminiscences out of the way, Doug suggested we would be better to try Alliance, 56 miles to the south. And then he started talking technical jargon with The Chainsaw, who wanted to know about radio procedure.

'Well,' said Doug, 'some guys get out on the runway and call in with 'downwind' 'on the base leg' and ' on final', but I don't say anything. You don' have to talk to anyone if ya don' wanna. A lot of these places don't have control towers. You just need to keep your eyes open.'

'Because?'

'Because there's a lotta guys flying around without radio. Some planes don't have `em.'

While I digested this, Phil thanked our man and went outside, rubbing his head. 'Hats,' he said, when I caught up with him. 'I promised myself a cowboy hat and I reckon it's time I went and got me one.' We spent some time in the ranch supplies shop. The fact that I came out with a cultivator for my vegetable garden is neither here nor there. The Chainsaw was overcome by the sight of so many stetsons, and emerged with a black one and a straw one, plus a mean-looking leather belt.

As a one-time geologist, Phil now wanted to get out to Toadstool Park to look at strange rock formations, but of course, as I explained en route, you can't go to Toadstool without taking the dirt road to High Plains (pop. 2) and the old Cook Shack. Last time I was there they still had 5 cent coffee. Phil was impressed by the population figure, but I pointed out that this was a bit of fiction promulgated by the owners of the café. When I first came across Nenzel, on the other hand, one of the towns along Hwy 20, it really did have '2' on the sign as you zipped through. Come to think of it, so did Buford, Wyoming, when I was there in 1999. Nenzel boasted a city park, a pump, a picnic bench and a barbecue grille. I know. I had a lunch there in 1996, brewed coffee and freshened up afterwards in the toilet. Since then I have met at least three people in my travels who claim to come from there, and the official count has rocketed to 13.

The Cook Shack was between meals when we arrived, and we were the only visitors, but the guy rustled up a solid sort of lunch of shredded beef, beans and beer, after which we took a stroll around the little town they've rigged up there, complete with general store, boardwalk and an iron calaboose, made by Barnum of New York and shipped west in segments to be erected on site – an early example of the flat-pack idea.

From there it was a short drive to the park, a place of strange grey hills formed by various rivers having crossed a level stretch of land and deposited all sorts of sands, gravels and half-formed rocks, some no more than a sort of very firm clay, which yields if you push it with your thumb. The Chainsaw was in geology heaven, reminding me that he did get a degree in the subject several decades ago.

By the time we got back to Merriman it was around nine, and we were both thinking the same thought. Beer. Unfortunately, we caught the Sand Bar on an off night. They had an impressive range of spirituous liquors, but very few beers, all of them in cans. They had a pool table and a television. The proprietor was behind the bar, her partner on the other side, propping it up and chain-smoking. As Phil remarked, 'If you own the place I guess you do as you please.' I'd like to say we livened the place up, but apart from inviting the usual question – 'Where ya from?' – we didn't manage to distract either of the incumbents from a very bad western, staring James Stewart in a wig. We sank a couple of Pabst Blue Ribbons and drove home along a dark and deserted Highway 61. The house was empty. The hunters had moved on. They were about to be replaced by trail riders.

Monday 16 May

They arrived in convoy before I'd managed to shower. They'd driven all night. The van, the truck and the trailer all crept cautiously down the dusty trail. Suddenly the yard was full of horses, nine of them, and hay-bales, saddle-blankets, tack – plus eight women: four or five college kids with a handful of adults; plus the one with the beard, Joe, who seemed to be responsible for it all. He comes from over the border. Iowa, which he pronounces Ioway.

The Chainsaw and I stood well back as tack was sorted and horses were saddled up. These gals might have been up since three in the morning and driven six hours, but they wanted to be out in the hills right away. As we shifted our supplies into the spare fridge in the garage, one or two of the women loaded up the kitchen with enough grub to feed a small army. Then they took off across the river.

Phil and I went outside and assessed the day. It had been another cold start, but the cloud was higher and thinner now and looked as though it might break. Perfect for a hike. As we walked the mile and a half up to the ranch-house the sky started to clear from the east. I wanted to show Phil the draw I'd walked down a week or two ago, the one that leads through the pines to the river.

It's always interesting going with someone new and seeing a familiar place through their eyes. Phil was immediately attracted to the steep sandy slopes to right and left of the gully, down on his knees picking up pieces of rock that had been washed out of what he referred to as horizons. He clearly wanted to linger.

We found fossilised bone fragments in various shapes and sizes, one or two flinty pieces that looked as though they may have been worked, and agreed that it might be fun to spend a morning on the slopes looking for arrowheads. I know that Kitty found a couple of buffalo skulls along that same watercourse a few years ago.

With all the rain we've had the little creek was running well, seeping out from the sides of the ravine, snaking its way through fallen trees, dropping clean sand here, gravel there, and cascading over jutting rocks. More and more of the trees down there are coming into leaf now, and I was noticing what I'd failed to see last time I came this way, that a lot of them are silver birches.

We followed the creek down to where it comes out into the river, and worked our way upstream, once more surprised by the amount of damage wrought by the beaver – which we have yet to see in the flesh, although we could clearly see where they had their runs from the water up the grassy bank. In places they'd simply nipped off young junipers, stripped the bark, and laid the leafy branches neatly on the ground The beaver have also attacked – and felled – some much bigger trees, trees with twelve- to fifteen-inch diameter trunks; and they've girdled eighty-year-old cottonwoods and killed them off.

We arrived back home hot, thirsty and picking ticks off our clothes. Matt, who'd called by to see whether the trail riders wanted to move some cattle for him next day, agreed that beaver were really quite a nuisance down there. Phil artfully shifted the conversation from gnawing trees to felling them and pointed out that there's a tall specimen growing right alongside the back of the house that's probably damaging the foundations. In no time flat we'd agreed that he would borrow Matt's chainsaw, live up to his publicity and have it down.

After we'd eaten, and as the light faded, we lit a fire down by the river crossing, maybe a hundred yards from the back of the house. There's a lot of fallen cedar down there: very old, very dry, and it burns very hot. Within half an hour we were sitting round a huge blaze, scalding our faces while the chill worked its way into our backs and the river ran silver under the light of an almost full moon.

Then came a certain familiar sound – both Phil and I have raised daughters and know it well – as the gals stumbled, shrieking, down the track clutching blankets, drinks, folding chairs and goodies. We graciously

91

declined their offer of 'smores', the graham cracker, chocolate and marshmallow concoction beloved of girl scouts – and, I'd guess, dentists – but I accepted an invitation to help myself to carrot cake when I went back to the house and made myself a bedtime cup of tea.

Today the gals will ride again – those who aren't too sore after seven hours in the saddle. Phil and I will take that tree down, and around four this afternoon they'll be off back east.

Tuesday 17 May

Today is cool. 48 degrees, windy and threatening rain. I suppose I could move back out of the trailer and reclaim my quarters in the house, but (a) the very thought of re-arranging my stuff yet again fills me with weariness, and (b) Matt tells me we are expecting one last turkey hunter some time this week. I'll cook some porridge and consider the novel sensation of feeling like a real man.

I think I must have just turned three when my sister (who is eleven years older than I am) took me blackberrying down between the railway lines near our home, twenty miles south of London. What you had there was the fast electrified line that by-passed the towns of Merstham, Redhill, etc., and the slow line which ran parallel to it but through the stations. The two were probably separated by a hundred yards of rough grazing dotted with hawthorn trees and brambles.

I was in my push-chair (stroller). My sister – and perhaps a brother or two – busied themselves picking berries. As soon as the first basket was filled she placed it on my chubby little knees and told me to look after it. The next thing I remember, a huge brown head with bulging eyes, and a massive face full of off-white teeth leaned over my right shoulder, snorted excitedly, and dug into the berries. I screamed blue murder – and from that day forth was terrified of horses. I well remember my steely resolve to be a good father and take my daughters – we're talking thirty years later now - to pull up handfuls of grass and 'feed the pretty horses'. They were all a-tremble with excitement; I was quaking with fear.

So-o-o, a roll on the drums and three hearty cheers. Yesterday I mounted one – and managed not to fall off. Of course, one of the lady trail-riders had to remark, 'Let's see if you can do it again without pulling the saddle off.' But then, we all know what these western gals are like. Not your shrinking violets. They wanted me to trot around the yard. I was more than satisfied to be on its back, and quite keen to get off. One day, maybe.

We were sorry to see the trail-riders head back to eastern Nebraska and Ioway, as I now call it. They brought us laughter, glamour, carrot cake… and lots of fresh horse manure for the garden. And before he left, Joe the wrangler guided me through fixing the toilet, whose cistern mysteriously cracked and flooded the basement yesterday morning. I'm glad I didn't have to tackle that one alone. I suppose I could've called on The Chainsaw, but he was fast asleep – despite all the shrieking as the younger element speculated on what lay beneath my vegetable bed. They'd spotted the rude wooden cross that Matt put there, with the inscription 'R.I.P.' They were planning a movie: me as the crazed Professor, Phil as the Buzz-saw Killer, the bodies in amongst the potato crop, and all sorts of dark doings in the basement. On NPR just now they announced that more and more school-kids are being taught competency in financial management. Maybe they ought to be teaching boys how to fathom the female psyche.

Anyway, Phil came to life with a mighty roar in the p.m. He got the chainsaw cranked up and was ready to attack the elm whose roots are surely rocking the foundations of the red house. There are a couple of nasty cracks between the blocks, rear and side. After careful preparation and a lot of frowning, he rigged up a rope for me to pull on, lest the tree decide to crash back into the house. The felling took but a few minutes, the dismembering a little longer. What was a thirty-foot elm is now a neat little pile of foot-thick logs and a stack of branches, three to four feet long.

Wednesday 18 May

It's been a quiet day down here, reflecting the mood set by dull skies and a stiff breeze, with just an occasional glimpse of sun visible through a veil of grey. Pity about the clouds, because tonight there's a fat full moon hidden away there somewhere and we shan't see it.

Mostly I've busied myself with domestic stuff, going down into the basement to crank up the washing machine, cooking a leek and potato soup, and further preparing my vegetable garden. I salvaged various bits of newly felled timber, a few abandoned poles, and threw up some crude defences against any critturs that want to try their luck with a former destroyer of vermin. Sowing however, is on hold. Spring is dragging its feet. It's getting quite green along the river, underfoot, and indeed on the hills in places. But then you look at the broad-leaved trees that surround the red house and see such a lot of grey, bare branches. Those big old cottonwoods are particularly reluctant to come into leaf.

The only time I ventured up onto the range today was

to hunch behind a sheltering cedar tree and send a couple of texts home before taking a short walk along the top of the hills. There I came across what I take to be a turkey's nest in a blow-out, a patch of bare sand enlarged by the action of the wind. The eggs were stone cold, and there was no way of knowing what kind of condition they were in, other than breaking them.

Despite the cold, new flowers are starting to emerge. I'm seeing little white phloxes, close to the ground, and a lot more of the western wallflowers. Down by the river, I found what I took to be an exotic species of fungus. It is roughly the shape of an old-fashioned thimble, but framed in a sort of lattice-work of rubbery, yellow-brown flesh. It looks dangerous, but Phil thinks it's a highly prized Morel mushroom, quite rare, quite delicious and retailing at a very high price.

This weather is threatening our plans for the week. So long as it stays cool neither of us fancies a river trip. You always spend longer than expected in the water and it just isn't warm enough to be pulling canoes off sand-bars, negotiating the occasional barbed-wire fence or portage. As for flying, which is very much on the agenda, we need the wind to drop. It was a steady 25 mph today, gusting towards 40 and whipping up the dirt. That would not be comfortable. So we await developments, acutely aware that we have to get to town sometime soon: we're down to our last four beers.

Thursday 19 May

The girl in ALCO was quite sure. We are on flood alert. All of us. Until Tuesday.

I didn't argue. I thought the threat of inundation was concentrated on the Platte and Missouri rivers, hundreds of miles from here, but what do I know? Only what NPR tells me – and that it's unseasonably cold and cloudy in Cherry County. So maybe she's right. And this evening as I write this, we're still twenty minutes from sundown but it's almost dusk already. Outside, as I watered the lawn just now (yep, that's a euphemism), the apple tree was still blooming, the grass had grown ever lusher, and the sky was a dark, menacing shade of grey. Rain fell steadily and inside the house Phil scampered up and down the stairs trying to head off the leak, which just now was plip-plipping into a bucket underneath the stuffed elk's head.

I feel sorry for Phil. He comes all this way from England, lured by my talk of camping trips, canoeing, and steaks barbecued over a roaring fire, and what does he end up doing? Chores. Still, as he points out, at least we haven't got bugs. He was dreading bugs, and even now is chasing a moth around the kitchen – or is it another of those hornets that are emerging, dopy, from their winter slumbers?

Today, after I'd shifted all my effects from the trailer back to the red house, we decided we needed some action. Now, if your need for action is so great that you drive to Gordon on a Wednesday afternoon, boy, you're in trouble. But, improbable as it may seem, we managed to while away some hours there – mostly between the library, the café and the hardware store - and come home reasonably well satisfied that it was time well spent.

Phil and I both have a history of serial house re-modeling. So we both like hardware stores. Once we were in there we found all kinds of things to interest us – and in my case, an ambitious project was soon taking shape. We were ogling the knives and guns. Brits do this in the U.S. of A., simply because we rarely see firearms at home, and almost never handle them. There aren't many animals, or people, worth shooting. As for knives, we are no longer allowed to possess – or rather to carry in a public place – a fixed blade longer than three inches. I recently had a dainty little knife with a four-inch blade confiscated by nasty, officious little security people as I boarded a train to France en route to a three-week hiking trip in the High Pyrenees.

On the matter of firearms – and before I swing back to our home maintenance theme – Phil remarked, 'Isn't it odd that in a country with so many guns there aren't fewer lawyers?'

So anyway, there we are in the hardware place and suddenly it occurs to me that the main entrance here at the red house has no screen door, just the hinges where one used to hang. 'Got it,' I said. 'I'll buy a screen door and we'll rig it up.' As it happened, they were out of stock, but the guy has ordered me one to arrive next week, meaning I shall have to hang it myself.

No sooner had we got home than Phil decided to tackle the toilet. The repair that Joe the wrangler and I had sorted out hasn't been effective, the result of a faulty gasket between cistern and bowl. So this evening the Chainsaw fitted a new gasket ($2.95 from the hardware store) only to find that the cistern had a crack in it. Fortunately, down in the basement, we found a purple tube of adhesive, 'Amazing GOOP', with its sound advice 'keep out of reach of children'.

Our trail-riders, when they took off, left us some excellent grub, including a cubic yard or so of ground moose meat, which we got stuck into this evening, served up with pinto beans and tortillas. Tomorrow, weather permitting, we plan a fossil hunt, providing we aren't flooded out.

Friday 20 May

I have a good friend called Don who grew up in west Texas, in cattle country. Whenever he's making plans he always adds the rider, 'If the good Lord wills it and the creeks don't rise.' Well, no creeks as such here, but when you get puddles the size of the one that's threatening to inundate the big barn you're inclined to re-think. It's roughly the size of a nice little pond we played in when I was a kid.

So… no fossil-hunting today. In fact, it was a minor miracle that we coaxed Mercy up the trail to the ranch-house to do our online things. As the day wore on the rain got heavier, and we had an entertaining spell mid-morning re-deploying the buckets – with some success, I should add. After an early lunch we took one look outside and agreed it would be a reading day. I'm going through *Old Jules* again, and the Chainsaw is reading it for the first time. He keeps putting his copy down, frowning, and saying things like, 'He really was a deeply unpleasant man.'

I have to say I've never really formed a fixed opinion of the guy. Yes, he beat and abandoned his first wife. Yes, he drove the second mad. Yes, he so disgusted number three with his personal habits that she fled after two weeks. And he treated number four like a skivvy. Then he beat their three-month-old daughter for crying. It's some rap sheet.

And yet, and yet… he was the one who went out in a raging blizzard to deliver a neighbour's baby, the one who stood up to the hired guns when they tried to frighten the settlers off land the cattlemen wanted, who brought to justice the crazed pyromaniac across the river after he'd set off a series of prairie fires and loosed off the shot that almost killed wife number four.

And then I remember that this portrait is written by the very same daughter who was beaten by him, and bullied, but who finally came to see beyond the old man's temper, his egotism, his bombast – and chose to dwell on his heroic qualities. A partisan reader may not like it, but there is genuine tenderness, an affection for the old man in some passages.

I am left looking at Jules Sandoz and saying to myself that, rather like Popeye, 'He was what he was.' We need to remember that while some people wrote of Mari's book that she had besmirched the good name of the American pioneer, she received infinitely more letters confirming that her father was not particularly unusual, that you had to be tough, occasionally brutal, to survive those times, that domestic violence was routine back then and that her portrayal of pioneer life was spot-on. Let us not forget, either, that the old man did mellow in time. Some years ago when I interviewed the youngest of the Sandoz children, Caroline, she remarked that Jules never frightened her. 'We laughed at him,' she said, 'and ran away; and with his crippled leg he couldn't catch us.'

No, I find myself far more interested in his daughter. Before completing *Old Jules* she wrote several drafts of an autobiographical novel based on her upbringing – and worked out a considerable amount of rage and bitterness, mostly about her father. And then, after his death, she started researching the history of her region in the newspaper archives at Rushville, Hay Springs, Chadron and Gordon, and interviewing oldtimers, both white and Native. She found that his name cropped up over and over as a major player in the early settlement of the Panhandle, an energetic advocate for the small farmer, a tireless opponent of big money interests, a man of culture and learning who made good on his promise that he would grow fruit in the apparently barren S andhills. So I find myself fascinated by the way her view of him shifted, in her apparent forgiveness of his earlier transgressions, her ultimate gratitude, I suspect, for the gift of intelligence, the habit of research, the priceless experience that his pioneering impulse passed on to her

– not to mention her own dogged determination to plough her own furrow.

The rain eased in mid-afternoon, and I scooted up onto the range to make a phone call. I was walking back down when a large truck appeared in the yard. 'Aha,' I said to Phil, 'here's our turkey hunter.' I was both right and wrong. It was indeed a turkey hunter, but he'd brought five more with him. The party consisted of two fathers and four sons, aged about fourteen to nineteen. They're with us till Sunday. They use bows and arrows – or at least, that's what they're carrying. We did the formalities and left them to it while we talked flight plans.

Saturday 21 May

Renting a plane is no simple matter. Phil has already had to jump through several hoops, both in the U.K. and here, in order to demonstrate his competence as a pilot to the FAA (Federal Aviation Authority); now he had to convince the guy at Valentine that he could indeed handle a 1965 Cessna 150 - and that would require him to perform a check flight, with the owner sitting alongside at $135 an hour.

We'd got off to a later start than we intended. It began with us getting most of the way to Merriman before realising that the Chainsaw had forgotten a couple of papers. Like his pilot's licence, for example. Then we remembered that Valentine is on Central Time, meaning that it was almost noon, local, when we got there – and found that the rental man couldn't figure out how to get the computer-operated fuel pumps to deliver – so how about we came back in an hour or two?

No problem: the delay gave us time to browse in Duane Gudgel's bookstore. Phil finally got his check flight around three, while I called in at the Natural Resource Conservation Service. I had an appointment with a guy who does range surveys all over northern Cherry County. I wanted to ask him if he would be willing to take me out with him some time so that I can fire off endless questions about soil, wildlife, plants, water supply and management techniques. The people I spoke with were courteous and friendly, and almost apologetic as they explained that there are security and confidentiality considerations, as well as the usual personal liability issues. These all require security clearance, and I have been given a 35-page procedural manual with a series of questions attached, which I must answer and mail in.

I returned to the airfield just in time to see the Chainsaw land, taxi, and help shove the plane back in its hangar. By this time it was gone four o'clock and any chance of flying today had gone. But we're happy to go back Monday morning when the weather promises to be better. We had one more call to make before heading home, to collect a brand new toilet for the red house. In fact, not just one but two. When we phoned Kitty she was so impressed with the price she figured we might as well replace the upstairs one as well.

Sunday 22 May

I suppose it counts as a walk, even if I did spend much of the time on all fours burrowing under fallen trees and squirming my way down narrow ravines, tangled up with underbrush and clinging to the thinnest of roots to prevent myself dropping ten or twenty feet at a time. At one stage, after slithering down a muddy slope into a slow trickle of water I found myself teetering on the edge of a rocky eight-foot high waterfall. Nothing for it but to grab an overhanging branch, swing out and jump into the spongy green mess at the bottom.

And you know what? It was fun. It was a little like being an eight-year-old boy again. I was even tempted to roll up my shirt-sleeves when I got back to show off my scars and scratches. It was beautiful down there, with the broad-leaved trees all clad in their spring colours. As ever, I'd been trying to follow the river-bank – this time in pursuit of more Morel mushrooms, which the archers are keen to help us cook. I found a solitary one, which I later added to the three or four the archers had found. By the way… archers? They've nabbed two turkeys, both with guns. I have to say I'm a little disappointed. I had visions of them dragging home a couple of toms every day, pierced by arrows and looking like porcupines. But they're great company, so we can't complain. And the bonus is that George and Jack, the two dads, are an absolute mine of information on the Sandhills flora and fauna. They both work for environmental agencies within the state and are intimately connected with this landscape, always willing to share their knowledge – especially when it involves horror stories about poison ivy, ticks, deer flies, etc.

My walk, scramble, call it what you will, took me into a flat, swampy area under a grove of old cottonwoods. I'm very fond of cottonwoods, although I've cursed them many a time when trying to make a camp-fire: they just don't like to burn. The bark intrigues me, being thick, deeply fissured and grey – and nutritious. Oldtime mountain men and explorers often kept their horses fed on it through the winter.

As I splashed my way across the standing water I disturbed a heron from way up the top of one of the trees. No sooner had that one flapped its way noisily over the river than another one got up, then a third and a fourth. Looking up I saw perhaps eight or ten nests, and over the next few minutes about a dozen birds took off for the hills.

I ate a picnic lunch down by the side of the river, then, with the weather deteriorating, decided to head for home, which meant a steep climb up another creek-bed towards the pines. Here I came across the first choke-cherry blossom I've seen so far. It has a sweet, heavy scent, not unlike the may blossom we have in England around this time. And there, growing right beside it, was the yellow flower of the golden currant whose berries, my book tells me, ripen in late June and make excellent jam, wine or pemmican. By the time I got to the top, out onto the grassland, a rain-shower was sweeping in from the west. I whipped out my raincoat and headed for home. It was time to get ready for a party.

Monday 23 May

The party wasn't what I expected – but then neither was the host. I'd seen Ken Jackson last year at the Cowboy Poetry event in Valentine, but I didn't get to talk to him. A lot of these people who perform in public carry their 'larger than life' personality with them 24/7, and can be quite hard work. I wasn't sure what we were in for. His place sits above the Niobrara just east and a little north of here. Ken is a tall man with a large white droopy moustache and a real friendly manner. Unlike most 'personalities' I've met, he is interested in other people; he asks you questions and listens to your answers. But the first thing that struck me when he shook my hand was the strong smell of beer. Blimey, I thought, not even six o'clock. Then, just as I spotted it, so did he: the bottom of his coat was dripping all over his boots. 'Guess it ain't the brightest idea to keep your beer in your pocket,' he said, squeezing it dry and extracting a half empty can of Busch.

He took us into a sort of open garage. It looked more like an antique store, with various artefacts in bone, horn and metal on display, including a large cast-iron stove which, he informed us, used to live in the basement of the red house, but had originally come from Fort Robinson. Fort Rob is an old cavalry outpost - now a museum - about a hundred miles west of here. It's where Crazy Horse was killed, and where Old Jules was hospitalized after his friends dropped him down the well and crushed his ankle.

We didn't linger in the garage. The wind, like the stove, was cold, so Ken took us through into a proper old-fashioned den. I can begin to list the contents, but that's about all I can do. He had a collection of old books about the West, another stove, more ornate than the first; he had posters, photographs, paintings, an entire collection of those Time-Life books about the American West, whiskey bottles, beer labels, guns, antlers, knives, a brass bedstead – or was it iron? – and a human skull, believed to be 200 years old.

This was the beginning of a tour that took us next to the bunkhouse, where there were yet more books and paintings, photographs from the old ranch days, a display of arrow-heads, from ancient rounded ones, ten and twelve thousand years old, to the more recent, delicately crafted variety. From the bunkhouse we took in the various accommodations – it's a kind of guest ranch he runs out there – after which we piled into our vehicles and drove down towards the river. With the archers, Phil, myself, Ken, his wife and their daughter, we made up a party of a dozen or more. We were going to look for Morel mushrooms. Sounded to me as though it was going to be a lot of looking around for not much return.

Local knowledge: you can't beat it. Our path wound its way between densely packed trees close by the river, the trail ever narrower. And then, rather like a wagon train that had found the ideal spot to camp, we fanned out in a clearing, stopped and piled out. I guess we were down there an hour. And I'd say we picked eight or ten pounds of the things, perhaps more. They were everywhere, singly and in clusters, poking up from amongst the dead leaves, around the fallen, rotten timber, the new ones a pale honey colour, the larger ones dark brown, almost black.

Back at the ranch, the ladies sliced them in half, washed and dried them, then dipped them in beaten egg and flour before plunging them into a deep fryer. I have never tasted a fungus - anywhere, in my entire life – that tasted less like a fungus. If I'd walked into a restaurant and been handed a plate of these I would've sworn they were a species of fish; and a very tasty one at that.

Tuesday 24 May

The archers left yesterday afternoon while we were out in the hills. We had decided it was time to go and hunt arrow-heads, fossils and such things. We set off down the draw that runs north towards the river, and made a beeline for the sandy bank we'd looked at last week. We soon started to find more of the fossilised bone fragments. Some seemed relatively soft and chalky; others were much harder and had been suffused with minerals at some stage of their formation. Quite a few were shot through with crystalline substances. This was all very well, but what we really wanted were arrow-heads, like the ones we'd seen in Ken Jackson's display cabinet. Ah well, I thought, I guess you have to be patient, thorough, persistent, and just a little bit cleverer than we are.

You also need to be lucky. While Phil ploughed his way steadily towards the top of the slope, bending to inspect the different strata, I tried sifting the heavier material that was scattered more or less in bands on the surface. We were both finding different types of bone, tossing them across to each other to admire or comment upon.

Suddenly Phil let out a yell, and loped northwards, feet sinking several inches into the loose sand on a forty-five degree slope as he pointed towards a dark shape that protruded from the east side of the canyon, towards the fringe of pine-trees. What I saw looked like nothing more than a fat, twisted soapweed root, and I was about to tell him so. I'm glad I didn't.

As I have mentioned before, the Chainsaw has a degree in geology (City of London Polytechnic, 1984). He reckoned that what he'd found was most likely the hip joint of a hippo, rhino or elephant, possibly a mammoth. Something very large, at any rate. We did a fair bit of digging with our bare hands, hoping to find the entire skeleton of whatever giant beast this came from, but, being weak-willed, hot and thirsty, we gave it fifteen minutes before deciding that a bottle of Fat Tire might be more rewarding. Later, armed with plastic bags, we returned to the scene and lugged our entire collection back to the red house.

Wednesday 25 May

I've found the wildlife around here fascinating, and am getting to know a number of creatures I've never had much to do with before. I'm particularly enjoying the presence of the turkey-buzzards. Most days when I'm out, particularly on the tops, they'll swoop a little lower and check me out, their dark shadows flitting across the grass. I often stand and watch their flight, the elegant way they climb without appearing to expend any energy, the lazy circles they describe, high in the sky.

Having said that, I do worry about two particular types of crittur. One is bugs, especially those that bite or sting, although later this week I'll be collecting that screen door and should feel more protected in the house. The other is snakes. Up till now I've not been too worried about them. This past weekend, however, I've had a couple of unpleasant surprises. The first was that time down by the herons' nests, where I all but tripped over a brown and white thing as it slithered across my boot. Then on Sunday, when we were driving home with the giant fossil, we parked up and decided to look at one or two blow-outs on the top of the bluffs, just upstream of here. That's where people have been telling me you find arrow-heads. We put in half an hour or so, failed to find anything, and set off towards the house, which was when something slithered across our path. Olive-green along its back, canary-yellow underneath, it was about two or three feet long.

It made me jump about three feet, sideways. The snake stopped, probably frozen in terror, and stared at me while I pulled out my camera. Then it moved on a couple of feet, and I'm sure it was that movement, sinuous, silent, effected without benefit of any limbs, that troubled me. As I took the photo, I was feeling quite disturbed inside, yet at the same time I couldn't help thinking that this had the look of a child's toy snake, made of rubber and spray-painted in a factory somewhere in Asia.

I took a couple of snaps and we headed home. We were almost there when Phil remembered the car, which we'd left at the top of the trail. Just as he disappeared from sight I spotted a large, fat snake coiled up beside the track. I repeated my sideways manoeuvre, and heard myself gasp. My first thought was, 'rattler'; but it was making no sound and seemed either very calm or very frightened. I wasn't even sure that its eyes were open.

I was – pardon the expression – rattled. No question about it. But I did fire off one shot with the camera before I saw Phil trundling down the hill in the car. I made a careful note of the snake's precise position in relation to a large soapweed and ran towards him, flagging him down. By the time we'd walked the thirty yards back to where I'd left him, the snake had vanished. The green and yellow specimen, I have since discovered, was a racer, the big fat thing a bull snake, known for occasionally imitating, and being mistaken for, a rattler. Both are pretty harmless.

Thursday 26 May

Yesterday's adventure nearly didn't happen, and I have to hold up my hands and say it was entirely our own fault. I used to do a lot of tinkering with cars, not because I was interested but because I could never afford a decent one. I never got much further than replacing brake-shoes, adjusting carburetors and fitting a replacement door or window from junkyard purchases – and I gave all that up some time ago. Living in town, I haven't owned a car in eight years. The Chainsaw claims more recent experience, but the fact is, neither of us is used to vehicles with automatic transmission. They simply aren't very common in Europe. I did have one in about 1985, when I lived in a noted crime hot-spot. It was a BMC 1300 in British racing green. Cost me 100 pounds or about $160. It had a walnut dashboard, leather seats, drop-down drinks tables in the back, and when you put it in drive and turned the key it went backwards. Think you're smart? So try stealing this, you lowlife scum. But apart from that, I've only ever driven automatics in the U.S. of A. And I may as well say it: I grew up around grizzled old motorists who liked to wear leather gloves at the wheel, and regarded a two-pedal car as… yes, effeminate.

So there we were, outside Merriman post office, crawling around on our knees looking under Mercy's wheel arches. It took two of us – combined education three degrees, a pilot's licence and a merchant seaman's certificate – to work out that we had no transmission fluid. I'm getting too old to be embarrassed by my own ignorance these days, and the guy at the garage – already open at 0630h, thank goodness – resisted the temptation to pour scorn on two Tenderfeet as he explained the problem. With transmission fluid, he said, you take a level with the engine running, and with that he poured in a couple of quarts.

After that it was plain sailing. We arrived at Miller Field just a few minutes late, I sat and Googled while Phil did his pre-flight checks, and half an hour later I was squeezing myself into the little cockpit, camera in hand.

'Right, you need to keep your feet off those pedals.' I did as Phil instructed, shuffling back until my knees were under my chin. 'And your knees off that.' More shuffling and wriggling.

Take-off was surprisingly quick and easy. We were soon skimming the Valentine roof-tops and heading for open country at 80 knots, climbing to around 1500 feet above ground. One thing I never realized was that the altimeter gives you a reading from sea level, so it pays to know how high those hills are below you – and to be aware of the radio masts en route.

We were heading west towards Merriman, keeping Highway 20 to our right, the river away to the left. The ground below us seemed featureless and flat, just the spider's web of thin trails leading across the dun grass to every water-hole, the long straight north-south roads that marked the section lines. I fumbled with my camera but couldn't switch it on: my hand was shaking. I was reminded of a flight I took a couple of years ago when a friend in Albuquerque persuaded me to go up in a microlight – arms and legs dangling in space, nothing between me and posthumous fame but a huge creaky wing and a small puttering engine; the only photo I took that's worth a damn is of the runway as we came back in. In the Cessna, I found myself hunched up every time we banked to starboard, fearing that I would be forced against the flimsy door. Might it fly open? 'Course not,' said my pilot.

We were circling above Merriman. Right beneath me was the café, the bar, the gas station, with a tanker pulled up at the pumps and someone walking towards the office. Across the road the monolithic concrete grain elevator gleamed white as the sun finally broke through the clouds. Banking hard left we headed south, following Highway 61. Up ahead were the dark meanders of the Niobrara and away to the west the bright green circle formed by Matt's center pivot.

Now, with Phil throttling back, I started to feel a little bit more relaxed, allowing myself to lean against the rickety door and study the ground, picking out the ranch house, the workshops, the dusty trail that leads to the red house, the black dot cattle, the gleaming of sun on water as a bend in the river appeared between the cottonwoods. We were losing altitude, barely a thousand feet above the pasture, and I was clicking away like crazy. My fear had vanished and I wanted this to go on – if not forever, then at least until I'd had my fill.

We circled low and slow, once, twice and a third time. I spotted my vegetable patch, the guinea-fowl on the ranch-house, and, as we straightened out and headed east, the Jacksons' place down towards the highway. We followed the river back to town, and touched down just two hours after taking off. We parted with $120 apiece and agreed that it was money well spent.

Saturday 28 May

Chainsaw Phil is back in England. We left the house at 0545h, drove to Rapid City, and I left him at the airport where he awaited a noon flight to Minneapolis. He looked decidedly glum, if slightly dotty, as he made his way towards the security control wearing his black stetson with the straw version on top of it. He liked it here.

I was surprised at how lonely I felt when I got back to the red house. I've had two solid weeks of hunters, trail riders, hunters with bows and arrows, and the man himself. I've got thoroughly used to having company and will have to adjust all over again, although it won't be long before I'm back in Rapid collecting my partner. She's coming out for her vacation.

The consolation right now is that spring, surely, is here to stay, despite a further three-quarters of an inch of rain last night. It's getting up into the 60s most days – 69 today – and only dipping into the 40s at night. And the soil is nice and damp. We've accumulated roughly a third of an average year's rainfall in the last two weeks. So today I put in an hour or so on my vegetable plot. Even as I raked the soil and sowed my lettuce, beetroot and green beans I could hear George the archer, who listened to my grandiose plans a few days ago and said, 'You're very ambitious.' Was that the assessment of a man who was overwhelmed by my energy and vision, or does he know that come July all my work will be destroyed by deer, raccoons, grasshoppers? We shall see. I have also put out half a dozen tomato plants and sown a few of what the Americans call zucchini squash but we call courgettes.

After that, well, for the first time in a fortnight I had time to wander at my own pace, checking up on what's happening out on the range. So I put on my boots, stuffed some fruit and a water-bottle into my small back-pack and set off for a hike.

Sunday 29 May

I still haven't quite shaken off the blues. Stepping outside this morning and seeing the space where the trailer used to be – Matt hauled it away yesterday morning – didn't help. There's just a patch of lush green grass marking its outline – or was, until a posse of cattle swooped down from the hills and had a good munch.

Today I stayed in bed until 0730h – quite the latest I have slept since I arrived. After breakfast I washed – myself, my clothes, the dishes – and fixed up a sprinkler for the vegetable plot; then I thought about a hike, and decided against it. Why? Partly because I had some reading to do, but partly, I may as well admit it, because of the damned snakes.

Yesterday I had a close encounter with a rattler. Close enough to be startled – and to get a decent photograph. At first I thought it might be a bull-snake, but then I saw, and heard, the rattle. I was barely half a mile from home, and found it lying, stretched out in the grass, As soon as it saw me it re-arranged itself into the strike position, coiled up like a – well, to me it resembled a cow-pat as much as anything.

'Looks about a five-year-old,' Kitty said, counting the segments when I showed her the photo. Once again, I felt I'd coped okay when I actually came across it; it was afterwards, back at the house, that I felt myself shaking. And again when writing this.

I did go out briefly this evening, and I found myself treading carefully. Instead of studying the sky for the turkey-buzzards, or casting my eyes over the sweep of grass looking for newly-emerged flowers, I kept a close watch on the ground immediately in front of me as I tip-toed up the hill, startled by every exposed soapweed root, hopping away from every cow-turd, even at one stage jumping as the strap of my camera snaked its way around my bare arm. To think that yesterday I crouched down not ten feet from what I thought was another bull-snake, leaned towards it and took two photos…. I'll recover my nerve, I guess, but it may take a few days, and I will be far more cautious than I have been.

But on a brighter note, I spotted a tiny white flower yesterday that reminded me of the wild garlic we see at home. I tasted a slender leaf and detected a distinct onion flavour. Back here I looked it up in one of the books and confirmed that I'd found one of the wild onions that the Natives used to collect – and the homesteaders too. I shall watch out for more, and maybe dig up a root.

Monday 30 May

Matt was looking exceptionally pleased with life today. He was off to his buddy's place in South Dakota to cut up the wild hog they shot some months ago in Georgia. The head, I hardly need reminding, is in a freezer in the garage down here. As soon as they get the taxidermist on the case I will have another stuffed companion to look over me when I sit reading at night. At least, I assume it'll end up here: last I heard Kitty was saying there was no way it was going to decorate their living-room.

The first cricket of the season sneaked in yesterday. I actually saw it nip in under the door, and it's chirruping away from somewhere in the lounge. And last night I was awoken by the same sort of scurrying noises that kept me awake my first few nights here.

Despite that harbinger of warmer weather it's been another dismal sort of day, the temperature struggling up to about 59, the air damp, the ground wet, the sky overcast, and the wind blowing at about 25 mph all day. Back in England we would say, typical public holiday weather. So although I was up at 0530 I didn't venture out until late morning, and even then it was with a weary sort of 'I can't sit here all day' resignation. My daily drive up to the house to hitch a ride on the Internet signal involved several four-wheel skids and re-arranged the trail comprehensively. It's odd to see ground that is so sandy when it's dry produce so much gumbo as soon as a bit of rain lands on it. I've got enough of it stuck to Mercy's wheel arches and body-work to start up a business: hand-crafted adobe bricks. I bet they'd snap them up in Lincoln, or that fancy part of Omaha where the warehouses used to be.

Later I went for a wander around on foot. I can hardly call it a hike: I was out and back in a little over an hour. I was glad I made the effort – if only to see the shaggy-coated coyote who loped away from me at the top of the hill and melted into a fold between the hills. They seem to have a way of moving fast without really putting much effort in. There's a very funny description of a domesticated dog giving chase to one in Mark Twain's *Roughing It*.

My walk took me down into yet another of these

draws that lead, eventually, to the river. Not for the first time I was defeated by a tangle of fallen trees and had to climb a near-vertical slope to extricate myself. I might have continued, but I had on my very expensive, very cosy, very precious down jacket. I never expected to be wearing that at the end of May. The sides of the draw were scarred by run-off, and I found myself inspecting the many bare patches, part of my ongoing search for an arrow-head. I found the usual fossilised bones, several fragments of rock that may or may not have been worked by hand, but nothing that really leaped out at me.

I'm about ready to pay another visit to town for the library and post office, but tomorrow is Memorial Day, and everything will be shut.

Tuesday 31 May

I've been worrying about my mood, which has been down-beat. I think I've been fretting about whether I'll manage to translate all this experience into something readable, but today I had an email from my sweetheart, who wrote, 'Trust the place; I am sure it will bring you new things to do and think about.' What a wonderful thing to have a wise woman in one's life – especially when you do crazy stuff like deciding to live alone in the Sandhills for six months.

The morning was, yet again, grey, damp and cold. 51 degrees when I got out of bed, pretty much the same two hours later when I slipped and slithered up the hill and along the trail to the ranch-house: 15 mph on the good stretches, less than that on the gumbo. I'd been emailing for maybe ten minutes when the dogs stopped barking at me and turned their attention to a vehicle heading in from the direction of the highway. Moments later I was looking at five smiling faces and a frisky young pup, the first wave of the annual Arent family reunion.

It felt odd to be telling these descendants of pioneers to come on down and make themselves at home in the house their ancestors built, by hand. Among this first party was the octogenarian Frances, whose mother Margaret was one of the eight children raised here before the First World War. They insisted on eating outside in 57 degrees with a stiff wind and no sun. I told them I would expect no less of people with Viking blood in their veins, and I salute them. These are a people who sailed to North America a thousand years ago in open boats, a people who colonised Greenland; even more impressive, they elected to settle in the north-east of England because it was so mild. Now that's what I call tough. It took me thirty years to acclimatize myself to the weather up there. I made my visitors hot, brown, sweet English tea, which they pronounced good. They didn't stay long. They took a look around the place, ate their food and departed, leaving me a plate of fried chicken and potato salad, as well as some delicious home-made brownies.

After they had left I just had time to clear my plate, go back to the ranch-house and complete my online business before a convoy of three more vehicles arrived. This lot had been busy at the cemetery, decorating the family graves. It's a Memorial Day tradition. (I only found out later that Memorial Day was intended to allow people time to garland the graves of their old soldiers.)

These visitors too were planning a picnic, and they got lucky. The sun came out, the temperature shot up to 70, and the wind dropped. I had to come clean and admit that I'd already had one free lunch, but they still gave me a large bag of fried chicken which I've since stripped of its batter coating and boiled up with carrots, onions and potatoes to make a hearty stew that'll feed me for several days.

After they'd left, a dark cloud rolled in from the west, the temperature plunged back to 53, the wind got up to about 40 mph and whipped up the dust; then it rained, heavily, and the radio gave out a tornado warning for half the state. Normal service had been resumed.

Not that I cared much by now. I was having a treat. I'd discovered earlier that it is possible to download podcasts of some of my favourite BBC radio programmes. I do this all the time at home, but somehow I'd got it into my head that it was impossible from over here. Copyright or something. But I was wrong, and I have never been so glad to be wrong. I could've danced.

Picture me, my belly full of chicken, a glass of single malt whisky in my hand, sitting in the recliner, listening to one of my favourites, *Desert Island Discs*. That show has been running since I was knee-high to a grasshopper – in fact, it dates back no less than seventy years. Each week a well-known person is interviewed and asked to select eight records to take with them to a desert island where they have been shipwrecked - with the records, a gramophone, and a power supply. Yes, I know… but it makes great radio.

So… creature comforts. I think that a part of me had felt that so long as I was living here I needed to engage with the landscape, the people, the experience of solitude, twenty-four hours a day; that to distract myself with DVDs, iPods (I brought neither), would be to cheat. Then I started thinking about those pioneers, and the violins they brought with them, the pianos, the books, the social events they organised, the dances and spelling-bees; and I remembered that beautiful story of Mari Sandoz', "The Christmas of the Phonograph Records". Old Jules fritters away a legacy on box after box of wax cylinders, and wakes up the whole household at gone midnight to listen to the new-fangled device; all the neighbours crowd in, and Mary feeds the five thousand as the novelty of recorded music, the joy at diversion, the magic of song, the memories of a dozen old countries, enchants the whole community.

There was a strong strain of self-denial in my upbringing. It's not a thing you rid yourself of easily. But I'm working on it.

'You'll be the talk of the town in that car'

Wednesday 1 June

I learned a few things from the visitors yesterday, bits and pieces that help construct a history of the red house. Number one, they pointed out the site of the wind-pump, whose stone well-casing is behind the garage, along with a couple of galvanised jags of metal which must have been part of the frame. They took down some of the old black-and-white photos and showed me what they say is the old dug-out, twenty or thirty yards or so from the pump – although by the time the picture was taken it was probably used as a root-cellar. In two of the pictures is a house with a pitched roof, presumably an earlier one that was knocked down to make way for this. Nobody seemed to be able to identify that.

The red house is built on quite a slope, and the Arents put up a solid retaining wall to either side of the front elevation, presumably to hold back the upper part of the garden. That's still there, although it's slightly misshapen now, and there are gaps in it. I'm tempted to conclude that it was built of the same stones that formed the front of the dug-out, which, we are told, were taken from the river. In fact, I'd be willing to bet it was. One of my visitors, poking around out there, reported that he'd seen a bull-snake slithering into the wall. He was perfectly calm about it. 'They eat rattlers,' he said. 'Hunt them down and eat them. As soon as the rattlers smell them, they keep away.'

Did I feel reassured? Well, yes I did, until someone added – quite unnecessarily – that these critturs also like to hang out in cellars. Did my informant know that that's where the washing-machine is? I'm still trying to figure that one out.

When the visitors showed up I'd been worried that I might be intruding on a family affair, but they made me feel very welcome, and seemed to enjoy talking about their connections with the place. Frances, the daughter of Margaret, told me that she lived here for a year or two in the early 1940s, when she was in high school. I didn't quite understand why she had been sent here, but it had to do with the fact that Hedvig had died (in 1941) and the house was about to be sold. The sale would mark the end of the Arents' association with the house. Frances also told me about how the Indians used to come down from Pine Ridge every autumn to camp along the river and pick berries, and how fascinated they were by the little blonde-haired tribe that the Arents were raising. So taken were they with one child – I forget which – that they wanted to make a trade and take the kid home with them. 'What?' I asked. 'You mean, swap one of their children for one of the Arents?' 'Oh no, not a child – they were offering a pony!' It made Hedvig jumpy every time they came back over the next few years.

After everyone had left I went up to look at the graveyard that sits on Matt & Kitty's land, over towards the highway. Just a handful of Arents are buried there:

Holger, Hedvig, and their son Martin, who died shortly after his mother. The cemetery was looking very neat after its clean-up job. I know that Kitty mowed the grass the other day, and it looks as though some of the flowers have been replaced. Plastic, mostly – but they have a long year ahead of them. Sitting there, I wondered how I might find out more about these people.

As night fell I helped myself to another glass of single malt. There is a bottle of Glenlivet sitting on the work-counter here. It's been here since I arrived. I've sat many a chilly evening, occasionally wrapping my sleeping bag around me as the snow flew outside, and all the time knowing that a certain warm glow was available. I wasn't particularly cold last night. I simply cracked. As Matt remarked when I confessed to what I'd done, 'Hell, ain't there a statute of limitations on things like that?'

Thursday 2 June

I slept close to ten hours last night. Perhaps it was the warmth: the temperature only got down to 64, making it by far the mildest night since I got here. I suspect, however, that it was not wanting to wake up and face today's task.

I used to be inflicted with a passion for what we Brits call DIY, or Do It Yourself – and for some reason I just can't think what the American phrase is. But I'm talking about home repairs. When I was young, energetic and foolish I would tear down brick walls, rip up floorboards, build closets with my bare hands, re-lay drains, attack simple wiring and plumbing jobs and climb triple-extension ladders to dab paint on the furthest extremity of the gable. I've scraped, painted, wall-papered, drilled and plugged, built up huge collections of tools, knocked lumps out of hundred-year-old houses - and myself - with the best of them. And I did all of these things several times over as we moved from one house to the next, each one larger and more challenging than the one before. And then one day I decided I'd had enough. I should add that I got divorced. Not once but twice. I no longer own a house and I feel no sense no regret whatsoever. One way or another those passions have dissipated. And it ain't as bad as it sounds. It leaves you feeling kind of peaceful inside.

But the fact is that today I am confronted by what ought to be a simple DIY task. I am hanging the screen-door I bought last week. Correction: I plan to hang the screen-door. Because I know, deep inside myself, that a job like that is fraught with hidden complications. The way I saw it, it would be a case of two hinges, six screws and – as we like to say back home – 'Bob's your uncle.' Job done. Then I opened the cardboard packaging and saw the various parts, and the instructions.

But even as I balked and started muttering about needless add-ons I stopped, and said to myself, 'Come on, are you a man or a mouse?' And immediately I recalled Groucho Marx's answer to that one. 'Put a piece of cheese on the floor and you'll soon find out.'

I shall pause here, eat my oatmeal, and come out fighting.

Thursday 2 June - afternoon

I don't think I've mentioned the fact that some years ago – 1999, I think it was – I wrote for a TV soap. We were Britain's second most popular, with 12 million viewers four times a week. That's one fifth of the populus. I hated it: the ludicrous plots, the shallow characters, the unseemly wrangles in the story conferences, the tears shed around that table, the petty jealousies amongst the writers (there were 14 of us). There was just one thing I loved. The money. I dug myself out of a huge black hole in eight months flat, paid off $25,000 of debt, then got the hell out. But I learned a few things about cliff-hangers. (This is a really, really cheap shot….) Yep, I'm going to leave my screen door right there, and reveal the outcome tomorrow.

Yesterday was a bitty day. First of all, Mercy. The front offside tyre (yes okay, tire) had been leaking air, very slowly, for some time. When I went out yesterday it was, like yours truly as he opened that screen-door packaging, visibly deflated. I drove up to Matt's workshop, where he has a compressor and air-line. But he was out, and I couldn't figure how to work things. Didn't want to screw up. So I did my Internet stuff, slung my laptop over my shoulder and legged it back here.

A few hours later I walked back up. It takes about 25 minutes. I enjoy it more than anybody would realize. At home I regularly walk to town from where we live (just outside the cathedral city of Durham) and, depending on which route I choose, take 30 to 40 minutes. I relax, think deep thoughts, improve my cardio-vascular health. Over here I seem to have stopped relaxing as I walk. Instead of watching the sky and conjuring up deep thoughts, I watch the ground, and wonder whether it's true that the Native peoples used to prescribe a brief nap as the best resort if you're out alone and get bitten by a rattle-snake.

I was barely halfway when I spotted it, lying like a discarded length of rope across the trail in front of me.

As I stood there, deciding that it definitely was a rattler, it coiled itself up in the 'prepared to strike' position' and shook its tail feathers, so to speak.

I edged slowly around it and hurried home, where I added snake-proof boots to my shopping list. Later, when I went back to the workshop and went online again, I found that most fatalities from rattlesnake bites in the U.S. befall young males who try to attack or kill said snakes. Those youthful passions. Land you in trouble every time.

We got some air into Mercy's tyre, but in the time it took to drive down to Merriman half of it was gone. She now sports a brand new one, and I shall try to make sure that every time I park I do so in a way that displays it to full advantage.

Friday 3 June

NOTICE: As of today all visitors to the red house must pass through the Crazy Limey Memorial Screen Door. Yes, it's up, it's swinging, and it's been keeping insects at bay for a little over twelve hours.

I feel a bad pun coming on, and here it is. There is a fly in the ointment. I still have to install the 'door closer'. As it stands – and it stands rather handsomely – the shiny new door requires to be pushed open and pulled shut. Later today I shall attempt to rig up the little gizmo that automatically closes it. Only then will it be the thing it says it is on the accompanying literature: a *Swinging* Screen Door (or, for the benefit of any Hispanic readers, *Puerta Oscilatoria Mosquetera* – which to my ear conveys a hint of romance.)

I simply ran out of steam yesterday. The job had drained me. First there was reading the instructions, which were trimmed down to so few words that I had to sit and ponder them, and juggle all the various bits of hardware, until lunchtime. Okay, I take lunch any time from eleven onwards, but trust me, it took some pondering. Then I had to find a hacksaw to work on the Hinge Adjustment Channels. I was so exhausted by figuring out what the hell they were that I had to pause for a cup of tea.

Having trimmed the aluminum Channels to the required length I was left with a couple of nasty jagged edges, but this is where a little of that frontier ingenuity came in: I filed them smooth using a small chunk of native rock.

I now faced the most daunting challenge: working out how and where to fit the strike plate. The instructions weren't exactly helpful and clear: 'install on wood jamb or aluminum Z bar to firmly engage latch bolt.' The latch bolt, yes, I could identify that; but, leaving aside my utter ignorance of what a Z-bar might be, how was I to tell where it would hit the door-jamb before I'd installed it? This is where quite a chunk of the afternoon went, not so much in deciding where to put it, but agonising about what to do should I have it in the wrong place.

I made my decision, drilled guide holes for the screws with that sharp slender attachment on my Swiss Army knife for which I've never really found a use, and screwed it in place. I won't go through it blow by blow, but will say that attaching the door handle and associated parts was a long and tedious business of frustration and puzzlement which necessitated the use of some strong language. When I'm required to drill three holes through a brand new aluminum door, in very precise locations, I tend to knot up inside. Once I'd got those items fitted I

126

found that my striker plate did indeed need adjusting. Here I could have done with a nice sharp wood chisel, but made do instead with my trusty Swiss Army knife to take out 1/8 of an inch of timber and re-seat it.

After a celebratory beer I went outside. I could see something odd on the path, just a hundred yards from the house. Hm, I thought, as I approached a wriggling writhing knot of reptilian confusion, that snake's got two tails. First things first: it was not a rattler. It was not even *a* snake. It was a pair of them, and they were - how shall I put this? – *at it*, in broad daylight, in a public place.

Friday 3 June - bedtime

Question: where do all the bugs go when they realize they can't just waltz in through the front door? Answer: they hammer at the kitchen window. It got up to 91 degrees yesterday and was still around 70 some time after dark. So I guess this is a taste of things to come.

Saturday 4 June

Matt took one look at the car and gave a wry, cowboy type of grin. 'Why, you'll be the talk of the town in that car,' he said.

Very possibly. It was, I have to admit it, the first time I'd washed Mercy since I got here. But this week has also been the first time the ground has been clear of snow or rain for more than a day or two. So I took out the hose-pipe, grabbed a sponge from the kitchen and started on the dirt that had accumulated over the past two months.

Later I took a stout, sharpened stick and chipped away under the wheel arches and around the fenders, shifting several pounds - many pounds - of hardened sand, silt and cow-muck that had set like brick.

There's no question that a car runs better when it's clean. Nobody has ever explained why, but it just does. With one new tyre and a bit of a glint on the chrome, Mercy seems to be leaping up the dusty trail, straining at the leash. But I resisted the temptation to go for a spin, as our parents used to say. Instead I decided that, snakes or no snakes, I needed to get out for a walk.

I set off with my hiking pole, my British walking boots, and my new straw hat. It's the model that the Chainsaw wore when he was here, but there was no way I was going out to be seen out and about in matching head-gear. That would really set the tongues wagging. It's only a year ago that the lady at Chadron State College library asked me, in a hushed, confidential sort of tone, if I were gay. 'Whatever gave you that idea?' I asked, squaring my shoulders and deepening my voice. 'Well,' she said, 'you keep talking about your partner, and…' What do they say about the Americans and the British? Two nations separated by a common language.

I ended up taking two short hikes. First I walked one of the steep draws that drops down to the river, just east of the ranch house. At the back of my mind was the huge fossilised bone Phil and I had dug up. Maybe the subsequent rain had washed out a mammoth skeleton. But then again, maybe not.

Things have come on down there. What I earlier thought were grapevines are showing more evidence that they are indeed. Several of them were smothered in buds, so here's hoping. Down by the river the lush grasses reminded me of home – and of the fact that in England most of a grass's work is done by midsummer. I am aware that out here they have spring and summer grasses, that while quite a few now bear seed heads, there

128

are many others that have hardly started their growth. I'm still mystified by a number of the flowering plants I come across on these walks. Neither of the two books shows everything I'm finding.

I wasn't too concerned about snakes down in the draw, but later in the afternoon when I walked along the top of the bluffs upstream of here, I took great care. I am learning to study the ground in front of me all the time, and only to look around at the sky, the horizon and so on, when I'm stationary. It makes for slower, but safer progress.

The landscape still has a wash of winter colours. The greenness is coming on patchily, as though in no great hurry.

Sunday 5 June

I have been here two months now. I have started to get to know the place, settled into a few routines and feel pretty much at home. And now summer has come. I suspect that this is the way it's going to be for the next three or four months: hot days, pleasant nights, and a constant war against insects. I have finally put away my thick moleskin trousers.

I busied myself around the place yesterday morning. It felt like a typical Saturday at home. Started off by making a final adjustment to the screen-door project: it now swings shut with a satisfying slam. Then I gathered a barrow-load of rocks and assembled them in a neat circle to make an outside fireplace. If I want to sit outside on an evening – and I do - I need protection from nasty flying things. My arms are bitten in several places already. It'll help when I get the long grass cut around the house. For that I need to borrow a mower, but just for fun I got out the old wooden-handled scythe that I'd spotted down in the cellar, rubbed some of the rust off it with a stone, and spent a few minutes swinging away. It works, after a fashion.

Later I spent some time arranging my papers. The fact is, I had them all in order before the first wave of visitors arrived, 'filed' in date order along the settee, and had never put them back. That's done now. I have no excuse for not being scholarly.

Monday 6 June

I was up early on Sunday morning and was up at the ranch house for eight o'clock. Matt was planning to brand a couple of dozen strays that escaped the earlier round-up, but his buddy was running late and wouldn't be here till ten. Time then to take the mower down to the red house and get the grass trimmed. It now looks a little like a garden down here.

Wednesday 8 June

I think I'm at a turning-point. In fact, I'm sure I am. I've been here two full months, and have four to go. And there's a job to be done. The funds that have enabled me to put my paying work to one side and come out here come from a body called the Harold Hyam Wingate Foundation. I believe their wealth originated in a chain of London cinemas. I applied for a scholarship in order that I might make sense of my twenty-year interest in the work of Mari Sandoz and attempt to write something about her life, the environment that shaped her. I also made the bold, the reckless claim, that I would attempt to introduce her to a British readership. Already I'm beginning to wish I'd never said that.

I feel as if, so far, I've been doing all the easy stuff: getting to know a bit about these Sandhills, settling into a ranching community, familiarizing myself with the plants, wildlife and weather, establishing routines. Then, the other day, I looked at my new screen-door, my tidy garden, and realized that I'd more or less run out of what writers call displacement activity. So I am about to start on something.

Meanwhile, let's tiptoe back onto safer ground and talk about plants. A couple of days ago Matt looked out at the hills and said that the oldtimers always reckoned if they turned green like that you knew things were good. Many years they don't fully lose their winter colours. Everywhere I look as I walk around I see new, vigorous growth.

Some of the grasses have flowered, and I'm concerned about their names. Will I learn them? Will I even find them in these picture books? But I keep reminding myself of something I decided years ago. It's more useful to know what a plant or animal looks like, or smells like, how it behaves, when it appears – to experience and enjoy it - than to fret over what it's called. Either you get to know that or you don't. You can even give a plant your own name, as the ancients did. No mistaking the prickly pear cacti, however, which are putting out new leaves. I'll be interested to see whether they bear fruit. Last year I was down in New Mexico in September and the red *tunas*, as they call them, were abundant. Sweet, fleshy, and full of seeds.

Despite the rain, Matt is irrigating. Has to, he tells me, because the water disappears through the sand so quickly. I'm seeing the same on my little garden plot, and am watering regularly. I stopped to watch the CPI yesterday. I was curious as to how it could take three or four days to complete its cycle. Now I have an idea. There are eight segments to the arm, and at the base of each joint is an electric motor. Every minute or so they kick into life, the rubber-tyred wheels turn, advance a few feet, and stop. It's a marvelous system, but expensive. To install one now, I have been told, could cost around $70,000.

Thursday 9 June

Ask any writer: getting started is the hard part. Especially when you find reasons not to do so until eight o'clock at night. I ended the day having gone on a three-hour hike, during which I considered eleven different openings to the thing I plan to write. I returned home and baked six loaves, then finally sat down and wrote 246 words, few of which will survive the first edit. But… I have started, on something. And I will proceed, however rough it is. It's far easier to edit a piece of bad writing than to conjure up the words with which to fill a blank screen. The fact is, I have spent way too long on the opening. That old dictum about grabbing your reader in the first paragraph imbues them with such enormous significance. You feel that they have to be just perfect. As ever, I should have stuck to the thing I tell anyone who ever asks: don't worry about the beginning; you can come back to that when you've finished. Just… get started, and forge ahead. But who ever takes their own advice?

I might have done more had it not been for the weather. The temperature had dropped a full thirty degrees since Monday, and with a stiff breeze to keep the insects at bay it was perfect for hiking. I set off up the hill and headed roughly south and west. No particular aim in view, until, after two or three miles, I hit the north-south fence-line and decided to follow it, away from the river.

I soon found myself fascinated by the many and varied fence-posts, their ages, their state of decay. That's what I love about hiking, especially when you're on your own, the way it frees your mind up to absorb things you'd normally overlook. I don't think Americans realize how free we are in most of Europe, and certainly in the U.K., to wander around the countryside. Our 'green and pleasant land' is cross-crossed by a series of ancient rights of way, dating back to Medieval times or even earlier, and most are still sign-posted – even though some farmers take an almost malicious delight in plowing them up. One of my several walks into Durham takes me across a field which is ploughed and planted every year. And every year people like me, plus various fellows legging it home after a night out, have to trample a new path, diagonally, across a field of winter wheat, or barley, or oil-seed rape. I make a point of it, even though I hate to tread on a young plant. These are rights granted to our ancestors, centuries ago, and I do not wish to see them eroded.

However... fence-posts. There's an attractive mixture here, of stout old juniper posts, knotted, grey and crooked, and of heavier timbers cut from pine. Here and there a run of neat, round, machine-cut posts treated with some kind of preservative. There are also quite a few that look way too slender to do the job required of them. Matt calls them twigs, and makes dismissive references to neighbors who 'won't spend a cent' and prefer to rustle for make-do posts down in the woods.

And now I'm going to have a quick gripe of my own. Neither my Wildflowers, Grasses and Other Plants of the Northern Plains and Black Hills, nor my Grassland Plants of South Dakota and the Northern Great Plains is proving as helpful as I'd hoped. I found what I thought might be flax, but can't find it in the books. Anyway, it's bursting out all over the place, and is a very attractive shade of blue. One that I have identified is a segolily, a delicate, pale yellow thing. The book tells me they are edible, particularly the bulbs, which are credited with saving the lives of many a starving Mormon after their early crops were destroyed by crickets. I also found the first rose of summer, crouching low to the ground but blooming happily and smelling divine.

I'd been following the north-south fence for about a mile when I hit the one that runs east-west, followed that for another mile or so, and then turned north, cutting across a jumble of hills and worrying, every time I dropped into a hollow, that I might get lost. Along the way I disturbed any number of lizards, several curlew, and what I took to be grouse. Back on higher ground, of course, the river came into view, its banks looking more green and lush than I have yet seen them.

Friday 10 June

I have had another quiet day, and because the weather is still grey and cool – I correct myself, it was flat out cold in the morning - I stayed around the house. 53 degrees at eleven o'clock? I even put the kitchen heater on for a few hours, and when I went to sit in the lounge to think about a few things I had on my trusty down jacket.

First of all I thought about my writing. It had been on my mind all night, keeping me awake. Had me up at

0520h. I pulled out my travel journals, looking for an account of my first visit to the Sandhills in 1993. I soon had notebooks, files and loose leaves scattered around me, but had found nothing to add to my memories of that trip. Then I dug into two fat envelopes full of research notes on Mari Sandoz, most of them gathered around that time. Perhaps I'd find something in there. I started reading... and when I awoke it was lunchtime. Well, ten-thirty, which is good enough for me.

My day seemed then to go from bad to worse. I frittered away the afternoon doing a cryptic crossword and reading an old *Omaha World-Herald* that the hunters left here. I read it from cover to cover. I even scanned the want ads, the way I used to twenty and thirty years ago when I was searching for clues as to what made America tick, trying to decode their strange language.

It was early evening before I managed to put a few more words down. They didn't come easily, and I was soon tired again, and hungry. While I ate my re-heated, leftover shepherd's pie I went to my collection of downloaded podcasts and listened to another old edition of *Desert Island Discs*, the BBC radio program I mentioned a week or two ago. This one dated from about 1999. The guest was Ian McEwan, a seriously successful author back home and one in whom I have always had an interest. He was the first graduate of the M.A. course in Creative Writing at the University of East Anglia in 1971. That's where I did my Master's in 1989. We had the same mentor, the late Malcolm Bradbury, who had taught at Iowa in the 1960s and become infected with the idea of teaching writing – something at that point unheard of in the U.K., and viewed with deep suspicion.

McEwan, as he stated on air, was lucky. He was the only applicant to, and only student on, a course that was not so much up and running as rumoured. I remember Bradbury telling me when I interviewed him for the *Guardian* in 1990 that he and Angus Wilson had received this application, told the young graduate to come along, and played it by ear from that point on. British amateurism at its best.

As it happens, I've never got on with McEwan's work. I remember reading his first collection of short stories, and the first novel, *The Cement Garden*, and finding the subject matter too dark – no, too nasty – for my taste. Incestual rape? No, not for me. Patricide? Not really. Other people didn't have that problem, and the guy rose to literary stardom. He later won the Booker Prize.

But… what I was going to say is this. On *Desert Island Discs* Ian McEwan, at the time of the recording busy writing *Atonement*, which has since been made into a hugely successful movie, revealed that 'for me at the moment a good day is 200 to 300 words.'

Can you imagine the sigh of relief with which I polished off my shepherd's pie and sank back into my chair with a glass of Glenlivet? I'd spent all this time chastising myself for not being productive enough. I'd convinced myself that my dismal total of 561 words marked me as a total failure, and an idler… and here was a Booker Prize-winner telling the world that it added up to not one, but two good days' work. I should add that when I was writing corporate histories, working from researched material, interview notes and the like, I frequently put out 2,500-3,000 words a day. And while we're on the subject I must mention Mark Twain. When his publisher told him that the manuscript he'd sent in was 12,000 words short, he supplied the missing verbiage within twenty-four hours. But, as he admitted in his autobiography, he only wrote 3,000; the other 9,000 he stole.

Well, it's still cool out there, but the sky is clearing – just a few grey clouds being ripped to shreds by a stiff wind, and tender young leaves being strewn across my vegetable plot. I must get out today, and then crack on with my 2-300 words (an idea that still makes me laugh).

Saturday 11 June

I set off for a walk yesterday with no particular direction in mind. Even as I left the red house I wasn't sure whether to turn right and go up the hill, or follow the trail around towards the ranch house and take it from there. I did neither, choosing instead to take the path that heads north through the tall cottonwoods, close to the river.

I say close to the river. In fact, it's even harder to follow the river here than it is in the opposite direction. The curves are so tight, the loops so exaggerated, the draws so steep, that you have two choices: either try to stick to the river's edge and spend half a day scrabbling up and down the bluffs while you make two or three miles' progress as the crow flies; or look for a straighter course by skirting the top of the many draws that cut deep into the hills, which takes you well away from the water. I chose the latter option, but even so I ended up dropping and climbing, then dropping and climbing again as I tried to shave a few hundred yards off the distance. And before long, as always happens, I got into a steep narrow draw that took me down to the river's edge.

The delight of such a walk is the huge variety of micro-environments you encounter, from dry, sunny slopes where parched grasses crackle underfoot, to lush green spots beside the dense shade of a cedar thicket; from easy going along well marked cattle trails to steep descents down jagged scars in the soft rock. And all the time, on a day when the temperature never got above 68 and a stiff wind kept the puffy white clouds moving swiftly across the sky, there was this constant alternation between being hot and feeling deliciously cool.

I heard the snake before I caught sight of it, maybe three or four yards ahead and to my right, lying coiled in the sunshine, mouth agape, tongue flickering. It was making a noise that was somewhere between a hiss and a rattle. I stood still for a moment and looked along its length. No, no rattle at the tail end. This was a bull-snake, doing what people tell me bull-snakes do, impersonating a rattler. And very convincingly. I snapped a portrait and hurried on.

When I'm hiking anywhere near the river I am constantly aware of the birds – or absence of them - mostly because the crows start up a panicky caw-ing as soon as I get near the trees, and relay the message to their neighbors upstream. Yesterday a hawk of some kind flew up and down the river, way over my head above the tallest trees, making a sort of *kai kai kai* sound. And I saw a pair of herons unfold themselves from the undergrowth and take off up-river. There's something primeval about those birds, always a thrill to see.

Back on higher ground there are usually far more birds. Yesterday, for example, I scared a pair of grouse, the previous day a couple of curlews. And that got me thinking about ground-nesting birds. I have no idea what they were, but everywhere I went there seemed to be things the size and colour of sparrows, but with long tails, certainly faster in flight, and with flashes of white, either under their wings or on their bellies. By chance one got up from a patch of rough grass barely twenty feet ahead of me, and there, barely visible, was its nest, or rather a neat, round hollow a couple of inches across in a thatch of dead grass, more or less hidden from view by the leaves of taller grasses. When I got right up to it I could see the two tiny eggs. Less than a quarter of a mile away I found a second nest – once more revealed when a startled bird got up and tried to distract me. Otherwise there's no way I would've spotted it.

Sunday 12 June – early morning

The washing-machine is rumbling away in the basement, and any time now I'll be rumbling through the red house with the vacuum cleaner. It's only a day or two till I drive to Rapid City to collect my sweetheart. Some time between now and then I'd better shave too. It has surprised me to find just how slothful and slovenly a guy can get when there's nobody around to impress.

But never mind domestic hygiene; what about personal safety? That's a question that reared its head yesterday. It was mid-afternoon, there was a warning out about severe thunderstorms in the area, and I could see clouds building up to the north-west. So I decided to take a nice simple walk: up onto the top, and head due south till I hit the fence-line, then turn around and come back. I would just see what I could see, and at the same time get a good view of any thunderheads that might start building up.

139

The first thing that caught my attention was a cluster of delicious-looking fruit, hugging the ground. They looked just like plums, and very tempting. Very perplexing too, because this is barely the middle of June. Turns out they're the fruit of the Groundplum Milkvetch – although I didn't know that until I got home and looked them up. I couldn't believe they would be poisonous, so I cut one in half and dabbed a tentative finger onto their flesh, but I couldn't really taste much. The book tells me they're supposed to be juicy (which they certainly are), sweet (hmm...) and taste like raw string-beans. They're popular with livestock and deer, and rodents, who will cache them. And they're also known as buffalo beans, which I think I prefer as a name.

What I'm obviously not so aware of, now that I'm looking out for reptiles all the time, is the direction I'm taking. I was hardly concerned yesterday. The sun was out, the wind was settled in a northerly direction, and the fence-line I was aiming for was about half a mile, perhaps a little more, beyond the horizon. I plodded on, probing the ground with my stick. It was only when I realized that the wind, which had been behind me, was in my face, that it occurred to me to get my bearings. I was in a dip, and by this time the sun was obscured by clouds. As I climbed out of the hollow I saw ahead of me, across a broad level area of range, cattle dotted around a windmill, and beyond that, two or three miles away, a familiar ranch-house - Matt and Kitty's place.

I wouldn't have thought it possible, but within twenty minutes or so – less than a mile - I'd deviated from my course by 180 degrees. I hurried back towards home. The wind was gathering strength, a veil of grey was sweeping across the north-western horizon, and I could smell rain.

For the rest of the afternoon, and well into the evening, I was in and out of the house as the wind rose and fell, as white and grey and yellow-bellied clouds appeared, swelled up and disappeared. There were a few drops of rain, a flicker of lightning, and that was it. This morning the sky is clear and blue. Great drying weather. I must go and fetch that laundry and hang it out.

Sunday 12 June - evening

I'm writing this on Sunday evening as a cricket chirrups insistently – irritatingly - from somewhere in the kitchen, which is where I do my writing. An electrical storm illuminates the sky to the north, not that I can see much of that: I'm using blankets as blinds in the kitchen windows, to keep the insects at bay. They have an uncanny knack of locating the gaps between inner and outer frames and squeezing through. Various other bugs keep pinging against the lamp-shade, while others are massing at the front door. I am itching, and I don't know what to blame. I suspect the culprit is some tiny, barely visible species of flying creature that's hitching a ride on my clothes and in my hair every time I go outside.

This morning was pretty much given over to domestic matters. First, as mentioned, the laundry, which dried in about twenty minutes; then the garden. I brought the mower down from Matt's workshop, re-set it to cut the grass quite a bit shorter than last time and got to work. As well as trimming the lawned area under the trees and around my new fire-ring, I cut a swathe through the rapidly growing weeds that surround the place, opening up a path to the river. Then I took the barrow and collected a few loads of fallen branches, fuel for the barbecues I'm planning over the next two or three weeks. I made sure I gave every piece of timber a good kick before I bent to pick it up.

I walked up to the ranch this morning, just for the exercise. Matt was busy doing a few repairs. Some time this week he's going to be harvesting the triticale that's growing under the Centre Pivot. As soon as it's dry he'll bale it and sow a new crop: millet. The machine which cuts the hay and lays it in windrows needed a few adjustments. One of the bars that rakes up the cut hay and feeds it into a channel from where it emerges in rows - I'd guess it's twelve or fourteen feet in length - had got bent, so while I held it in position across a makeshift bench he straightened it with a few hefty blows of his hammer. Nice to see an artist at work.

After I'd done my online work, perched on the tailgate of an old pick-up, Matt offered me a ride down to the red house. Sure, I said, and hopped into the cab. The idea was to cross the river and drop off some salt for the cattle in the plastic tubs he has scattered around the pasture. The problem is that when they're empty the wind takes them... and drops them off where it will. And so we started on a search for the lick-tubs, which took us westwards, through a gate into pastures I didn't even realize belonged to the ranch, and to some spectacular views over the river, snaking between the white bluffs and bordered by lush green areas of long grass and shrubs.

It was slow going. We inspected every draw, many on foot, in search of the missing tubs. We startled a bull-snake, which glided swiftly down a gopher hole. And we paused to look across the river, through Matt's field glasses, at the site of a historical incident, the burning of a number of wagons by the U.S. cavalry during the period of the Black Hills Gold Rush. I was intrigued to see the site, albeit from a couple of miles away. One or two people had already mentioned it to me, and just last week I found a copy of a map made by Mari Sandoz which pinpoints the same incident. I look forward to exploring it on foot some time.

We only found one lick-tub, down under some trees, sheltered from the worst of the winds. We filled it with a mixture of salt and minerals. I never knew that cattle needed so many additives. Reading the label off the sack I see that they include calcium, magnesium, potassium, copper, zinc and selenium.

I finally got home two and a half hours after Matt had offered me a ride – to save me time. But… live and learn, that's always been my motto. Something new every day.

Monday morning it really has to be housework. That is, all the chores I couldn't be bothered to do today; and then around five thirty I borrow Kitty's truck and set off for Rapid.

Tuesday 14 June

I am very careful at home, very 'green'. Or at least, I try to be. I manage most of the year without a car. I buy no processed food and bake my own bread. I can think of very few poisons that I use regularly. I avoid cosmetics, spray deodorants, air fresheners, insecticides by and large. I use soft soap in solution against aphids. When I find caterpillars on the brassicas I'll often just squish them with my fingers. I generally get away with the non-chemical approach. Yes, England's is a very benign environment. Nature's out to get you, I suppose – or more specifically a slice of your crops - but it's a very... gentlemanly war she wages.

Over here, clearly, it's different. In the few days since I got this screen-door up, the weather has turned much more summery. The bugs are out in force and I'm in danger of becoming a prisoner in my own home. So this morning I nuked them. That is, I took a two-gallon sprayer from Matt's workshop, deciphered the faded instructions on an ancient bottle of malathion and sprayed the front walls of the red house and the grass. To coin a phrase beloved of soccer fans back home, 'it's all gone quiet over there.' I wonder how long for.

One disadvantage of living down here by the river – apart from it being bug heaven, I suppose – is that I don't see so much of the sky as I'd like to. Just now, for instance, as I went up the hill to make a couple of phone calls, I was surprised to see thunder-heads building to the east. Down here it seemed a perfect, sunny afternoon.

Well, I've done the housework. The place is presentable, and so am I: showered, shaved, and wearing a clean shirt – or rather, one that was recently clean. I expect Old Jules felt a bit this way when he went off to meet the latest candidate for matrimony. In fact I managed to get myself ready for the trip to Rapid way too early, so I killed a bit of time outside, enjoying a relatively insect-free half-hour pottering about the garden, inspecting the lettuces and French beans.

To tell the truth, progress has been slower than I had hoped, but now that the warmer nights are here I think I'll see things take off at last. The one thing I'm worried about is that all that cow manure I put in the trenches may be an awfully long way down. Still, my observation of the grasses in the blow-outs is that they seem to send their roots down to an extraordinary depth in search of moisture. We shall see....

Wednesday 15 June

The drive from here to Rapid never sounds as though it's much, but every time I do it it exhausts me. At about three and a half hours' driving time it's just long enough for you to need a proper break en route. I left here about five-forty Monday afternoon, stopped for a dinner at Chadron, got lost in Rapid looking for our hotel and didn't make it there till about ten thirty, which just left me time to check in and zoom off to the airport. A's plane was on time and, despite a nightmare trip - seven hours in Minneapolis with no U.S. cash - she was awake enough to agree that a beer was a good idea.

It was simply delightful being re-united after two months apart. I don't think I'd allowed myself to realize how much I missed her, and have already caught myself imagining how desolate I'll feel when she goes home.

Tuesday we had a late breakfast in Perkins, right next door to the hotel. I generally avoid chain restaurants and will happily cruise around looking for an FRD, or family-run diner, but there are times, and this was one of them, when you need to eat substantial amounts of grub *right now*. And the good thing about this outfit is that they do a very reasonable imitation of porridge.

So, we were well fortified as we ventured into Safeway to stock up for three weeks – and my goodness I needed to be. When we emerged an hour or two later we'd racked up close to $300 in purchases.

Next stop was Cabelas, the outdoor specialists from Sidney, Nebraska, who have recently opened up in

Rapid. The mission? Protective wear. The damage? $120. But I am now the proud possessor of a pair of full-length snake-proof boots. There can be no question: I am a fellow to be reckoned with. A. went for gaiters, reinforced with that stuff they put in bullet-proof vests. Kevlar, I believe.

We finally got away at around three, made Chadron about five, and called in at the Olde Main Street Inn. As ever we had a warm welcome, and sat down to enjoy a cool beer. And, because it was such a nice afternoon, Jeannie suggested we take our drinks around the back and sit in her garden, with its flowers, shade trees and fountain.

I never realized that there was a law in the U.S.A. that prohibits the possession of an open container of alcohol in a public place, but there is. And when you have a cantankerous chief of police right next door you'd better be aware of it. Thus it was that we had to decant our drinks into china mugs in order to cross thirty-some feet of public space.

Relations between the good citizens of Chadron and their elected officials have reached the point where the recall option has been invoked. I only have a foggy idea of what that entails, but I gather it requires a sizeable number of signatures from among the electorate – and in Chadron they have had no trouble reaching their target. Sounds to me like someone's going to be run out of town on a rail before long.

We finally made it back here just as darkness fell, and stuffed all the groceries into fridges, freezers and cupboards. If war breaks out, we're good for a few weeks at least.

There is no plan for today. Who needs one of those?

A. is still catching up on her sleep and I need to tidy up my books and papers so that we have room to sit down. Later I guess we'll air our new protective wear, and see what these snakes are really made of.

Thursday 16 June

There's always that bit of vanity, isn't there? Even as I tried on the snake-proof boots in Cabelas I was thinking, 'But what will I look like in them?' No, it was more like, 'What *will* I look like in these things, all laced up to my knees like some posh Victorian motorist off for a spin?' Well, having put on my cowboy hat, and said boots, and studied myself in the mirror, we have the answer: Indiana Jones.

But before we talk about our hike up-river I need to mention Matt and Kitty's dogs. They have one each. Kitty's is an elderly sort of fellow. His name is Hoka. It's a Native word meaning badger. He has a badger's coloring: black and white. Hoka is an attentive guard dog who knows that it is his duty to bark at anyone who shows up at the house, particularly when nobody's around. There's no discretionary element in this: you show up, you get barked at. Period. So every day without fail, when I go up to sit and do my emailing, I have to withstand this verbal, canine barrage of threats and abuse. Matt's dog, Cinch, is younger. He's mostly black with tan highlights. He used to do a pretty convincing impression of a ruthless killer whenever I appeared. One time I got out of the car, walked over to the workshop to chat to Matt, and he went and barked at the car all over again. But then he's not much more than a pup, and he has learned that I pose no threat whatsoever. The other day when we were out hunting lick-tubs and I sat in the

147

passenger seat of the old pick-up, why, Cinch wanted to sit on my knee and lick my face. So the situation is that instead of having two manic dogs going at it every time I approach the house I now just have the one, waddling over, tail wagging, barking insistently, and repeating every few minutes until I drive away. That was until today, when the guinea-fowl decided to join in. Not barking, you understand, but making an unholy racket while I tried to compose emails to my several correspondents. I wonder whether they realize that I have eaten guinea-fowl. I think I had them wrapped in bacon.

I've finally heard back from the NRCS at Valentine, the Department of Ag guys who do range surveys. The Feds have rejected my response to the security examination, not because they think I might be a terrorist, rather because the exam I sat was the 2010 version and would I please now do the 2011 one. I have put it on the list.

We were blessed with superb weather yesterday: bright sun, temperature in the upper seventies, and a delicious cool breeze. We walked along the top of the bluffs overlooking the river, swung around the head of successive draws and then descended one I'd tackled before, which brought us to a creek and a waterfall. The one trouble we had as we dropped into the dense woodland was bugs, in particular a nasty little deltoid thing which I think may be a deer-fly. I don't think they bit us a great deal, just circled our faces and necks with evil intent.

By the time we got to the river we couldn't wait to peel off and get in. It was around six when we got back home, thirsty and hungry. We lit a fire and prepared a barbecue. My idea of a barbecue – and A. shares it, I'm glad to say - doesn't generally involve charcoal. It involves sticks. Keep piling them on, crack a beer, and wait until there's a nice bed of hot coals. And then, while you're eating your T-bone steak, throw on more wood to make a smoke-screen against the bugs.

Today we're taking it easy until the afternoon. Then we're planning to pack up our tent, hike across the hills and camp out under a moon which is a little past full but still fat and bright.

Friday 17 June

Everyone knows that the essence of good comedy is timing. And we got it dead right. To the second. We'd had a leisurely morning, scouting around the grounds and down by the river armed with our snake-proof gear, hiking sticks and a framed photograph of this little settlement taken before the red house was built.

The wind-pump is clearly shown in the picture, and its remnant foundations are right there behind the barn, so A – who is a much more thorough person than I am – has decided to try and figure out, once and for all, where the dug-out and the post-and-wire footbridge used to be.

Just as we were coming to the conclusion that the dug-out might have been in a hillside opposite the house we had a visit from Don, the guy whose trailer I slept in when we had all the hunters, and Kitty's mother. They had some sort of business down in the cellar. Having known us all of ten minutes Charlene invited us to pop over to her place south of Cody and use an empty house she has down by the river. 'Give yourself a break,' she said. 'It's comfortable there. It even has a TV.' I told her we might just do that.

By the time they'd left and we'd had lunch it was time to get our camping gear together for the hiking trip. Matt, when I mentioned our plan, had frowned and said, 'They're talking about rain later on.' I was tempted to tell him that the online forecast spoke of a 10% chance of a shower, but I kept my mouth shut. You don't go around telling your host that he's talking out of his rear end. By the time we were ready there was a bit of a grey cloud to the northwest, but otherwise mostly blue and white skies.

Did I mention timing? As we stepped out of the door, packs on our backs, boots tied around our necks in preparation for the river crossing, there was a clear, sustained rumble of thunder. We looked at each other and laughed. Across the river, as we hit the rising ground, it was clear that there was indeed a patch of dark, purplish cloud to the east; but as far as we could tell the weather was coming from the south. There was a smudge of greyness to the west too, but overhead it was still fairly clear. We were following a two-track, on a line that would take us between the two showers. Perfect.

Half a mile later, I have to admit it, the view ahead was a little more ominous. But even so, there was this long swathe of blue sky to the south that looked as though it ought to be heading our way. We'd be fine. Even when a few fat drops of rain started to fall, that brightness was still there. The only thing was, it seemed to keep shrinking.

'Okay,' I said, 'let's sit under this cedar tree and wait for it to pass.' Half an hour later we were still sitting there, clasping our knees, watching puddles form in the wheel-tracks. The brightness had vanished, and the only variegation in the sky was between the purple-grey clouds to the east, shot through with occasional lightning bolts, and the milky grey stuff to the west, which seemed to be the source of the large odd-shaped hailstones, which were whacking against our shoulders, pinging about our ears and bouncing across the grass like so many homeopathic pills. On the basis that this was supposed to be a vacation, we decided to retreat. We trudged back the way we'd come, getting wet in places that our waterproof clothes should have protected. Worse, my feet were squelching inside the snake-proof boots, which Cabelas claim to be 100% waterproof. But as I remarked, in between hailstones, at least it was warm.

This morning it's bright and breezy and we are planning another adventure that requires half-way decent weather. We'll be re-tracing the Old Jules Trail, taking photographs and notes, and submitting all to Chainsaw Phil, who has decided that a website is required. Our aim is to enable ordinary college-educated mortals like us to negotiate the trail linking the significant sites in the Mari Sandoz story.

Saturday 18 June

We drove to town, headed west along Hwy 20, past Gordon and Rushville, and turned south past Walgren Lake towards the area where Old Jules first settled, Mirage Flats. There really isn't much to see there now. The croplands are all the evidence you need that he knew about land. It was his cussedness that got the better of him, driving him way out into the hills. We soon found the main point of interest for the literary pilgrim, the stone marker at the site of the well where Jules broke his ankle.

I have always been troubled by that incident, or rather

151

by the way Mari deals with it. Jules has just finished digging a well, having been lowered in a bucket to a depth of 65 feet. His Swiss friends who are operating the windlass, Nicolet and Tissot, play a joke on him, jerking the rope as they pull him to the surface. It breaks, Jules falls, crushing his ankle. They haul him up, horrified by what they have done. Despite his injuries, Jules insists that they get to Valentine and file claims on their property. So, desperate as his situation is – he's in no condition to travel sixty miles to Fort Robinson for medical help and will treat himself with morphine - he sends the two men off with the registry fees. Two weeks later, they still haven't returned, and he is at death's door when he's picked up by a passing convoy of soldiers and taken to the fort. There he is treated by the legendary Dr Walter Reed, the man who would later become famous for developing a cure for yellow fever. When he announces that he must amputate the gangrenous leg, Jules tells him, 'You cut my foot off, doctor, and I shoot you so dead you stink before you hit the ground.'

The thing with Mari Sandoz is, she always has a massive amount of research material to hand; and she likes to weave it all in. But there are occasions in this particular book when she chooses to skip over certain events, to mention them in passing. Of course, if she lingered and told us everything she knew we'd end up with a 900-page monster; and let's remember here that Little, Brown & Co., publishers of the *Atlantic Monthly*, who awarded her the non-fiction prize for her manuscript in 1935 and published the book, insisted she cut a considerable amount of material to bring it down to a manageable 135,000 words. Perhaps some of the cuts came here, because as far as I'm concerned we don't quite get enough on Old Jules' feelings towards his partners, or the effect on her father of this stay in hospital, which lasted several months over a winter. It's there – but slipped into the narrative in passing. First he writes to Rosalie, the sweetheart he had hoped to bring over from Switzerland to marry him. I'm a cripple, he says, no use to you now. Then, to quote from the text, 'he wrote no more, saw no one except the breeds and the enlisted men who taught him American card games, profanity and smut.' And then she moves on.

There's no question that Jules is portrayed throughout the book as bad-tempered, foul-mouthed and dirty-minded, but we also see his high-minded side: politically engaged, proud of his European cultural roots, dedicated to the cause of the landless, anxious to bring culture to his family. Is it the case that the young pioneer, still not long away from Switzerland, still very much the former medical student, was finally brutalized and corrupted by this entire episode? Somewhere in the correspondence from which she quotes, we are reminded that back home Jules was remembered as a fastidious dresser, a man whose daily shave was of great importance. I think Mari may be trying to tell us so, but I don't think she pays it enough attention. It is actually very hard to admire the old man as much as – I suspect – his daughter would like us to, and I feel that's because she didn't pave the way as carefully as she might have done. But that's very much her style, to weave in the little details, the clues, in fragments and demand that you concentrate. Blink and you miss it.

From the site of the well incident we moved on to the river place, the homestead where Mari spent her earliest years. Her father had settled along the north bank of the

Niobrara with his second wife, Henriette, on the place she'd claimed in April 1887. He soon fell out with his neighbor to the south, one Freese. A long and bitter feud ended after Freese was found guilty of certain acts of arson, and, subsequently, shipped off to the insane asylum. Soon afterwards, Jules and Henriette settled on what had been Freese's land, registering a claim there in March 1892. You can see why he would make the move. On the south bank there's a broader, flatter stretch of ground, ideal for his orchards and field-crops.

We pulled up at the cattle-grid that guards the entrance. There we found the faded sign-post – 'Old Jules River Place'. A short walk took us into a fenced corral. Through there and over the barbed wire we found the faint track that took us up the bare, flat-topped promontory that is Indian Hill. This is where Mari used to sit when she needed, and had the opportunity, to be alone. You can just imagine it, a young girl sitting there, perhaps even lying down to render herself invisible as she watched the clouds go by and seethed at the circumstances of her life as she saw them: cowed by her tyrannical father, unloved, constantly burdened with the care of the latest arrival so that her mother could work in the fields while her father smoked, or attended to his stamps, or fired off another letter to the government, or disappeared on a hunting trip. In that unpublished manuscript I read down in Caroline's basement years ago there are a number of references to her hearing through the flimsy walls of her room the 'ugly' sounds of her parents making another baby, and to her rage and disgust with the brute realities of life. She would have had plenty to think about on Indian Hill.

From the river place the trail seemed far from

obvious. Do you follow the track that wanders down to the Niobrara, or climb the one to the south, more of a gully at first sight? We tried both and ended up taking the second alternative, grateful that the weather was dry, because it was one rough old trail that stretched ten miles or so across open pasture to a tiny Swiss cemetery where we found the graves of the *Grossmutter* - Mari's maternal grandmother – and Emile Sandoz, Jules' brother, shot dead on his own front porch by a hired gun in one of the disputes with cattlemen.

Sunday 19 June

It's a gorgeous morning: bright, cool enough to keep the bugs at bay, with the water rippled by a stiff breeze and sparkling in the occasional moments of sunlight. Pelicans circle lazily, convincing us they're about to land but always shearing off in another direction. Yesterday afternoon, after we left the Swiss cemetery, we drove here to Smith Lake, put up the tent and dined on chile beans. Then, with a couple of bottles of Moose Drool to quench the thirst, we watched a spectacular sunset.

We have already had a visitor. Jeff is a biologist who teaches at Boulder University and writes a column for the town's *Daily Camera*. He's photographing turtles. He showed up as I sat drinking my coffee and watching a stick bob up and down on the lake. He explained to me that the stick was in fact a painted turtle – and that the log a little further out was a snapping turtle. He'd had reports of painted turtles trying to lay eggs in the road around the other side of the lake, and was off to investigate.

Half an hour later he was back, offering us a close-up view of the little fellow he'd picked up: plain on the back but vividly patterned on the underside, red, brown and yellow. These are harmless little things, he told us, whereas a snapper will bite through a broom-stick – should there be one to hand, that is. People like to try to grab its tail, he said, and have no idea how agile it is. It'll extend its neck, turn around and have a finger off at the drop of a hat.

Monday 20 June

We were in no hurry. We walked around the lake for a while before resuming our journey, heading south on Highway 27 till we came to the trail that leads to the orchard place and Mari's grave. The orchard place was the valley home, deep in the empty Sandhills, that Jules took up in 1910. It's the place that a 14-year-old Mari was sent, with brother Jim, aged 10, to watch over, just the two of them, quite alone. It's the place that so branded itself on her young mind that she wrote a clause in her will saying she should be buried there.

We didn't go straight to the grave-site. We wanted to leave that until last. Instead we drove down to the old place at the far end of the broad, flat valley, past the remains of the orchards that Mari's sister, Flora, had nurtured after the old man died. The low, white-painted, single-storey house looks well maintained, waterproof, solid, not unlike the kind of cottage you'd find in Scotland. But it's deserted. I found myself wondering why nobody has ever considered setting up a sort of retreat down there. It would surely appeal to writers, artists, scholars or photographers, perhaps even musicians. It would be ironic, wouldn't it, to start such a scheme in the home of a man who famously denounced writers and artists as 'the maggots of society'?

To the south of the old home place is what was once Flora's home, now rented out to hunters in season. To the north is what's left of Jules' experimental station, where he tried out new varieties of fruit. Beyond that the summer grasses, ripe and tall, wave in the breeze.

We should have gone from there to the grave-site, but we still had plenty of time so we decided to go the extra yard. When Mari was seventeen she went, against her father's wishes, to sit the exam which would earn her a teacher's certificate. At first, he was enraged, but when his thunder had died down it typically gave way to boasting about how well he'd educated his kids. Mari had a number of teaching jobs over the next few years, and during the time of her brief marriage. It was after her separation from Wray Macumber that she taught at the Hunzicker school, and lodged with a family in a sod-house, not many miles from the old orchard place. The house features on some of these old guides, which I suspect were compiled by her sister Caroline.

The question today was, does it still exist? Could we find it? I was dubious, A much more optimistic. We agreed that we'd give it a few miles, and drove on south along Highway 27. Nothing. Not even a sign of a sign. Okay, we said, we'll turn around the first chance we get – like in this ranch entrance here.

And then I remembered all the many times I have knocked at doors in remote places out here, all the many strangers I've approached – and the sometimes remarkable results of these chance contacts. 'Tell you what,' I said, 'let's drive down to the house. You never know.'

We passed a ruined house on the way in. It had a pitched roof and seemed to be rendered in cement. Of course: that's how they kept those old sod houses going so long. This was in fact what we were looking for – not the squat, flat-roofed soddy of the history books, but a large, square, two storied place, once home to our heroine.

According to the Hamiltons, who now ranch this land and came out to meet us, the place has been empty for fifty years, probably more. They told us that some time ago they'd had a visit from a couple of elderly gentlemen, probably in their eighties, who said they'd grown up in the house. We spent a little time poking around outside. It really was falling apart, the windows broken, the walls crumbling, the roof caved in, and inside were piles of earth and litter where animals had set up home and burrowed through the floors. It was a rather depressing prospect, more so when we learned that the ranchers told us they were thinking of demolishing it for safety reasons.

We drove back up the highway and turned in towards the old orchard place, swinging north this time to the last of our pilgrimage sites. Mari Sandoz' grave sits in a small fenced-off enclosure, a modest granite block bearing the legend ' Mari Sandoz, 1896-1966.' In a mail-box is a pencil and a ring-bound visitor book, full of thoughtful entries written by all manner of readers from Nebraska and around the world. I think this was my fifth visit, and every one has had new meaning for me as I've struggled to piece together two remarkable lives: Mari's and her father's. I'm not sure why I've struggled. Perhaps it's that every time I read the books that outline their courses I am distracted by the incidental detail, the asides, the colour, the sounds and scents with which she decorates her portraits of people and places. I still struggle to piece together the narrative of actual events, but I'm happy to be sent back time and again, by that very confusion, to what I consider a great, great book.

[Since I first wrote this entry I have learned, from *Backstage*, the autobiography of my friend Ron Hull, the reason why the grave was sited where it is. Mari's will stated that she should be buried at the top of this particular eminence. On the day of her funeral, which was in mid-March, the weather wintry, her sister Caroline stopped the party h a l f way up and declared that, in the conditions, this was far enough.]

The grave used to overlook the fruit trees which Old Jules planted along the sides of the hay meadow that forms the valley bottom. The first time I came here they lay in rows, felled, the bark stripped by successive years of weathering. I took home a single grey twig for a souvenir. They've all gone now.

We'd just got our tent up as the sun was disappearing. The ground below the grave wasn't the best for camping. Each possible site we inspected was either uneven, stony or infested with poison ivy. But the fact is that wherever you camp down there you are surrounded by this huge sweep of emptiness that was once the Sandoz home place and orchard.

We climbed the fence and walked up the hill through the patchy grasses and soapweed to watch the sun set through a few streaks of high cloud which lit up, orange and red. Behind us the purple of evening crept in from the east and suddenly we felt cool. We prepared a hasty supper, then realized that we'd forgotten to pack any eating irons. So we gathered a few dry stems of last year's sunflowers, and used them as makeshift chop-sticks.

In the morning, after we'd broken camp, we walked around the hay-meadow and ventured into the last remaining patch of the Old Jules orchards. The trees bore the remnants of their blossom but had succumbed to some kind of pest, their leaves mildewed and curled up.

Tuesday 21 June - early

Yesterday was a recovery day. We slept well when we got home, despite having to do the nightly bucket check. I mean the quick round of containers upstairs which catch most of the drips when it rains – which it is doing every day right now. If we look after the pails, and empty them regularly, we manage to prevent the water getting down to where we sleep.

We did contrive a short walk in the early evening and, as ever, I got distracted by the flora. The first sunflowers are appearing here and there, and that means that, despite the weather, summer must be on its way. How many more times will I say that, I wonder? All along the riverside the trails, which were, a few short weeks ago, easy to follow are now encumbered by thickets of shrubby leadplant. My *Grassland Plants* informs me that Native peoples used to smoke its leaves or, on occasion, boil them for a kind of tea. Reading this inspired the thought that American café proprietors start using *Amorpha canescens* instead of that dreadful stuff that comes in bags and masquerades as tea. It *cannot* be any worse.

Tuesday 21 June - noon

Mid-summer's day by my reckoning, and the rain has stopped falling. Instead, it's sweeping across my field of

160

vision horizontally, chased by a gale-force wind and heading for the Wyoming line. This weather seems extraordinary. Last night, I hear on the radio, they had tornadoes away to the south and east of here, along the Platte river, with hailstorms and 70 mph winds. More rain is forecast for today.

Yesterday, however, wasn't too bad. The temperature peaked at around 61 and there were occasions when the sky appeared to be lightening. It reminded us of a British summer Sunday, and naturally we resolved to make the best of it. But first, we were going to tackle the turkey, which has been in the freezer since the first hunters left, back in April.

We cut off the legs and put them to one side, which enabled us to cram what remained into a large oval tin with a raised lid. We packed a few onions and carrots around the bird, laid several slices of smoked bacon over the breast, poured in about half a pint of cheap red wine and popped it in the oven.

We now came to the hard part, namely the red house stove, which has two main temperature settings: red hot elements, and grey lifeless elements. I exaggerate slightly, but you see the problem. With the temperature set to 325 degrees, we presumed that we could afford to leave things a while. Big mistake. Within an hour there was a smell of scorching meat around the place. The wine had boiled dry and the top of the bird was starting to look like overdone roast beef.

I won't turn this into an epic tale, much as I am tempted. What we did was pay close attention for the next four hours or so, basting the bird regularly, adding several more glugs of the red stuff, and then turning the oven off. Scorched or not, the thing was cooked; of that we were sure. And it would still be warm when we came to devour it.

By this time the weather had eased and we turned our attention to the vegetable garden. You see, food is never far from my mind – and why should it be? It's essential to our well-being. Out there the little tomato plants were starting to bend to the will of the easterly blast and the zucchini squash were in danger of losing their first precious leaves. This is where it pays to have a partner of Scottish descent, someone blessed with the twin virtues of resourcefulness and thrift. My kind of gal. 'What we can do,' she said, 'is rummage through the garbage, pull out those used milk cartons and fruit juice containers and make some sort of protective sleeves.'

No sooner said than done, whereupon A. adopted a pose worthy of the Chainsaw at his most pensive and said, 'What about that upturned sink you have over the barbecue pit?' That's now protecting the infant zucchini.

I should add here that, although we are enduring miserable weather, I've never been happier. This is the true nature of your average Brit: rarely more cheerful than when facing adversity. Roll back the clouds, send in the sunshine, whack the temperature up to 90, and he (or she) will sag visibly and start complaining.

Now that A has caught up on her sleep – the best word to describe her work schedule at home is punishing – she's full of ideas. She'd been looking at the photographs of the place taken in the 1920s, possibly earlier, and wondered whether the remains of the suspension bridge might still be visible. We set off along the river-bank, heading upstream and picking our way carefully between the many swathes of poison ivy. We soon came across what was left of one of the piers on the north bank, almost encased in a wild grapevine. On the south bank we found another - still wrapped with heavy gauge steel wire and anchored into the bluff. Its partner lay on the ground.

As to the original dug-out, we are stumped. People say, airily, 'Oh, it's there all right,' but the bluffs are so scarred by rock-falls and wash-outs that it could be any one of a dozen sites.

If our archaeological researches did nothing else, they stimulated our appetites. The finished turkey didn't look all that appealing, but it tasted just fine. There is no other standard by which to judge it.

This morning, after A had got up, I suggested that we might go for a picnic. Then I paused for the laughter to echo around the rain-swept bluffs. But who knows? As my grandmother used to say, peering through the gloom towards the west, and desperate to get five of us children out of the house, 'It's definitely brightening up over there.' She was half-Scottish.

Wednesday 22 June

Just once in a while you plan something and it all comes out the way you hoped it would. It's a good feeling. Yesterday looked as though it was going to be a complete non-starter. Wind, rain and a temperature hovering around the mid-50s: it wasn't very encouraging. But then we got into the afternoon, and there was this hint of an improvement, an odd patch of brightness over the bluffs to the west. By three thirty we'd made up our minds to go out, and I had just the ideal walk in mind – east of the ranch house, and down the steep draw that leads to the waterfalls. It's the place where Phil and I found that massive fossilised bone a few weeks ago.

There were no relics this time, but there was an extraordinary little plant – several, in fact. Tiny flowers, but enormous seed-pods, bladders the size of a small plum splashed with pink patches – and once more I have failed to locate it in either of the reference books.

We followed the little creek and descended into the trees. We hadn't gone very far at all when we stopped to look at something or other. It may have been a plant, or a rock, perhaps just the light coming through the birch leaves. The point is that we were standing quite still when we spotted a doe, thirty or forty yards away, browsing on a clump of currant bushes. Beside it was a very young fawn, its coat a bright orange colour, dappled brown. Out came our cameras, and to our surprise the two animals obligingly moved a little closer.

I don't know how long we'd been there, standing in the running water, motionless, when there was a movement in the underbrush just in front of us. There, less than fifteen yards away, was the buck. Where it had come from we weren't sure, but it was settling down under the pine trees, apparently for a rest. There was no question that it had spotted us, but it seemed quite untroubled and just sat there chewing, occasionally casting an eye over towards the mother and fawn who were still browsing, working their way slowly towards us.

We were expecting all three to take off at any moment. They didn't, although after a few minutes the buck got to his feet in a resigned, languid sort of way and came to have a closer look at us. Finally, some fifteen or twenty minutes after we'd first spotted them, they decided we weren't to be trusted, and took off, swiftly and silently.

We splashed our way downstream until we came to

the first of the cascades. You can't get down that from the top. You have to go around it and maybe a hundred yards downstream, then walk back up, which is what we did. As we approached it, A peered into the hollowed-out rock face behind the falling water and said, 'What's that black thing?'

Bingo. As I said earlier, sometimes your plans work out just right. I'd missed her birthday last month, and the flowers I sent via the Net simply failed to arrive, so I'd stashed a bottle of champagne at the bottom of the falls for future reference. How lucky can you get? As we climbed up the bank clutching the bottle, the sun came out and we were able to sit on the grass above the creek and savor the chilled contents.

We completed our walk to the river-bank, and came back up the easy way, via a steep trail that gets you through the woods and out onto the open grass within minutes. There was still quite a bit of cloud about, but there were enough breaks to allow the sunshine through. We were now at that time of day when the low light starts to emphasize the slopes and dips of the hills, and illuminate the flowering grasses, a much paler, more milky green here than at home, and contrasting sharply with the purple clouds on the horizon.

Today we're off adventuring – after I've had my hair cut down in Merriman at 0815h. I booked that slot last week, forgetting that I need a good thirty minutes to get down there, so I'd better get my skates on.

Friday 24 June

I realize that we haven't had much news from the ranch recently. It's haying time. Matt started cutting a week or two ago, got halfway and had to suspend operations while all that rain was falling, but has now got the first lot baled up and is busy cutting the second.

Saturday 25 June

The calm after the storm. It's a beautifully still morning, 61 degrees. There's blue sky to the west, the clouds are swiftly clearing to the east, and we are hoping to take a long hike. But do we trust it? Well, we certainly don't trust the online forecast for Merriman that I've been looking at these past few weeks. To be kind to it, let's say the website looks pretty and always manages an upbeat tone. As for forecasting the weather, well, as we say in Yorkshire, it's about as much use as a chocolate fire-guard. Yesterday we were promised sunshine, a few clouds and a 10% chance of a shower.

We'd been invited to call in on the Jacksons and said that we'd be at their place around seven. The steep part of the track that leads up onto the pasture from here has been cut up and re-shaped several times this week by the rain and is becoming more and more of a challenge. As we looked out, half an hour before we left, it seemed to be getting dark towards the west. I put on the radio, to be greeted with the news that there was a severe weather watch for the Panhandle.

The trouble with living down here by the river is that you only see so much of the sky. You don't get the big picture. But even when we drove up to the top it was hard to read the clouds. Looking to the north, we could see that rain was coming, but how much? We got out of the car, paused a few moments to watch the lightning bolts carving vivid lines through the grey wall, shrugged our shoulders and carried on.

The wind got up about half a mile later, just before

we turned into the yard. I'd wound my window down to see whether the rain had started and it hit me like something solid, rocking the car sideways. Matt and Kitty were out closing doors, generally battening down the hatches. 'Keep going!' Kitty yelled. 'You'll get blown to the highway at least.'

For the moment this seemed like fun: we were indeed propelled along the dirt road at a fair old lick. Then, just as we got to the cemetery, the rain hit us, a thick grey curtain of it coming in from the north, meaning it was striking my side of the vehicle – which was good news, since A had wound her window down and was snapping photographs.

Already there were puddles along the road, and had I had a sturdier car I would have driven on the grass, but with highway tyres (old ones) – forget it. By now it was almost dark, despite being an hour and a half from sundown.

When we got to the highway we took stock. Was it safe to go on? What would happen if we turned back? I called Ken, shouting to make myself heard above the wind, the rain and the crash of thunder. 'You got four-wheel drive?' he asked. 'Sure.' 'Well, you ought to get through, but don't drive on the gravel. Drive on the sod.'

We nosed out tentatively onto the highway, peering through sheets of rain, drove the few hundred yards to his entrance and stopped at the autogate. The puddles had engulfed both the drive and the surrounding grass, the rain was still lashing down, and the light had just about gone. We turned around.

We got home rather more easily than we'd feared. If the rain had done anything it seemed to have filled in a few cracks on the final slope down towards the red house. And I don't think we'd been back twenty minutes when we looked out and saw the rain had stopped and the hills to the south glowed in a strange orange light which suffused the whole sky. Sunset.

Sunday 26 June

The river was the colour of *latte*, the sky a mixture of dark purples and milky grays, and there were drifts of white under the eaves of the red house. We'd been awoken by hail banging against the window and a dull roaring sound from the hills. The front door had blown open, there was no electricity, and although the kitchen light did flicker into life a couple of times, it soon died again.

Outside – well, it's a painful business talking about outside. The tomatoes are more or less wiped out. I think one or two may struggle on but my hope of a late August harvest is looking like a fantasy. The French beans have also been knocked back, but I think they're sturdy enough to make it – some of them, at least. The beets I'm not sure about. Their leaves have been pounded flat, but they do have new shoots at their core. The zucchini squash I am fairly upbeat about. The larger leaves have holes shot through them, the others seem bruised, but there appear to be enough sound ones to suggest they might recover. We'll find out over the next day or two. And who knows, it may not be too late to re-sow all of the above.

As to the lettuces, crop one is mashed. They look like the cabbage we used to get served for school dinners. May recover, may not. The seedlings of crop two are more or less drowned in wet sand. But the good news is, we ate the first thinnings last night with our T-bone steaks. They were nice. Gritty, because I didn't wash them thoroughly enough, but nice. And, as an old lady said to me the day I moved to Yorkshire in 1973, 'You have to eat a peck of dirt before you die.'

It was soon clear that the trip Kitty and Matt had planned was off. They were going to take us out to the Snake river, and an ancient Native site, south and east of here. We've been keen to see the place, because we suspect it tallies with a site Mari Sandoz marked on one of her many maps as the spot where one Monsieur Laboue established a trading post in 1830 and conducted business with the Sioux and the Ponca. She suggests that he was the first white man to settle in the Sandhills.

I can't see us getting Mercy out of here, not today at least. The small lake which appeared to block our exit has shrunk a bit, but the track is gouged in several places and there are a few horribly soft spots.

Aha! Electricity. Out goes the scented candle A found in the lounge, and on goes the main light.

Monday 27 June

We had presumed that after Friday's storm, and Saturday night's, and Sunday morning's, the weather would settle down. You could argue that it did - into a pattern. Yesterday we had two more storms. It was the morning offering, which hit as we sat in the car outside the ranch house, that did the damage.

We had prepared to leg it up there, and so we had the laptop, camera and phone all wrapped up in a waterproof stuff-bag, inside a back-pack. But before we set off we thought we'd take a short walk on the tops above here to see what the weather was doing – or what it was likely to be doing, because, to be honest, it's far harder to 'read' a cloud pattern here than it is at home. In Britain most of our weather comes in from the Atlantic fully formed. You get a rain area off the coast of Ireland, say, and it sweeps across us, trailing sunny spells and showers in its wake, with the wind backing north-westerly. Here, on the Plains, they brew their own weather. You'll see a cloud forming, think little of it, and an hour later it may indeed have melted away; or have grown into something huge and violent. It is so hard to predict.

Anyway, as A and I came down from the tops we ran into Matt, out on his ATV with Cinch the dog. Soon as we mentioned that we were thinking of walking up he pulled his 'crazy Limey' face and said we should drive. We were looking at the gouges in the track, but Matt was looking at Mercy. 'Four-wheel drive?' he said. 'Short wheel-base? She'll go about anywhere. Just follow me.'

And so, as fresh storm-clouds moved in from the west, we set off, straight up the side of the hill, which I would estimate at somewhat steeper than 1:3. Mercy seemed to take it in her stride, but what you need to remember is that we were bouncing over great tussocks of bunch-grass, gopher holes and soapweed roots, and all with no shock absorbers. You might say it was a bumpy ride. But we stuck to Matt's rear end – and got there, as low, dark grey clouds gathered above us, forming a strange, menacing scalloped sort of pattern on their underside.

Up at the ranch we'd just managed to get a couple of emails off before the signal died, then sat and watched as this new storm unleashed its violent winds, torrential rain and hail. The noise as the roof was bombarded with stones approaching golf-ball size was almost physically painful. I kept expecting the windscreen to go, but it held, although the cracks have spread across it like tentacles and sort of joined hands in the middle. The yard was a sea of water, complete with white-capped waves, and behind us, when the rain eased enough to allow us to see, two large lakes were forming between us and the road home.

That was now the question, how would we get back to the red house, because we needed to, if only to check on the buckets in the attic. The rain and hail had moved east – at 35 mph according to the radio – and there was clear sky visible towards the western horizon. We told Matt we would walk.

'What are you, crazy?' he said. 'You can drive.'

'But what about those – those lakes?' I said.

'Jest plough through `em. Get a good speed up and go. Then drive on the sod.'

We did as we were told – and sailed through. As to driving on the sod, that required us to take ever wider diversions around huge puddles that stretched to thirty and fifty yards either side of the track. But we made it – at least as far as the top of the slope down to the red house. There we pulled up, preferring to check it on foot first. Mercy is still there this morning, parked on the grass. We won't be driving down here until some radical repair work has been done. The rain has gouged out craters four and five feet deep, up to thirty feet in length, and left sheer, unstable walls of sand on either side of the track.

Tuesday 28 June

The stormy weather seems to have gone, for now at least, and all around us we see the damage the rains caused. The most obvious and dramatic effect is on the draws, which seem to have crept further into the higher ground as fresh wedges of earth have slid into them. The flood of water that rushed down the hill in front of the house has dumped a large area of pale sand, perhaps twenty yards by twenty and a foot deep

Yesterday we drove down to the highway, headed towards town and parked where the road crosses Leander Creek. Matt had suggested that there would be a good hike down there. All I've seen of this creek up to now has been what's visible from the road, a broad sweep of sand patterned with several thin trickles of water. Normally, by this time of year, it would be dry – or so we've been told.

We followed its serpentine course for a mile or two before the pangs of hunger had us hunting out a place to eat lunch. But before we found one we came across another former settlement, marked by the concrete foundations of a small construction, possibly a storehouse. Lying in the grass amongst remnant half-bricks and shards of pottery and glass, was an iron pump, with its long curved handle lying in the grass a few feet away.

Back along the creek we found a sheltered spot, ate our bread and cheese, and brewed up coffee on the trusty meths stove. Even as we sat there we saw several large slices of the sandy bank, undermined by the torrent, collapse into the turbid, foaming waters.

On the way back to the highway we had another look at something we'd spotted on the way out, across the water on the far bank. It was white, sizeable, and buried two or three feet below the ragged line of grasses that fringed the freshly cut bank. Could it be a buffalo skull? Sure it could. At the very mention of the idea, A was off across the river with me in pursuit. 'Of course,' I said, 'I s'pose it might be a root of some sort.'

It was: a hard, woody root which, I have since discovered, is formed by the bush morning-glory, and was occasionally eaten by Natives - when sufficiently hungry.

Wednesday 29 June

Today we have been blessed with dazzling sun and a cooling breeze. The grass was gleaming, meadowlarks trilling, and we had a spring in our step as we set off to view the site of the wagon-burning that Matt showed me some weeks ago.

We crossed the river, climbed up onto the north range, and headed west. After a couple of miles we turned towards the river and were soon walking close to the bluffs that overlook it. Steep as the bluffs are, we managed to find a way down to the water's edge: there was plenty of loose soil to give us a foothold, plenty of branches and tufts of grass to hang onto. And of course we carry hiking poles, which give you that extra point or two of balance.

Down on the river-bank we found a perfect spot for a swim - and lunch. I think I am finally getting A attuned to the idea that the midday meal can take place any time after eleven, and that, if it gets towards twelve, I am not the best company. I believe we ate deer sausage and hard boiled eggs, but that's a minor detail. What was most memorable about the meal was our anticipation of a hot drink. We'd brought the Trangia stove, and our china mugs. I think I'd got as far as lighting up, and had the kettle almost boiling, when we found that neither of us had actually packed the coffee.

So we draw a veil over lunch, and move on. We'd managed to hit the river much closer to our objective than we'd realized. Once we'd crossed we had barely 400 yards to walk and there it was, right in front of us, a metal sign on a post, which read, 'Location of John Gordon's train of wagons burned by U.S. soldiers May 25 1875.' At this stage the Army were still enforcing orders to keep white settlers and gold-seekers out of the Black Hills. I am sketchy on my history here, but I should imagine that that all changed after the 7th Cavalry were wiped out at the Little Big Horn a little over a year after this incident.

[I have since found a written account of the Gordon incident. In February 1875 John Gordon got up an expedition to the Black Hills to look for gold. He left Sioux City, back on the Missouri river, on 13 April, shortly after another outfit, the Sioux City and Black Hills Mining Company, had departed under Ben Andrews. Both groups headed out along the Niobrara. Infantry and mounted troops were sent out from Fort Randall with orders to send back any parties attempting to enter Dakota Territory. On 6 May, near a ford on the White river, the Andrews party was stopped and the entire company sent back east under military guard. Gordon's party, meanwhile, followed the terraced road on the southern margins of the Niobrara. On 12 May, near Reunion creek, his caravan of twenty wagons was intercepted by Captain Fergus Walker's troops. Gordon claimed that he was heading west of the Sandhills to set up a new town, and refused to go back. To make his point he declared that this place where he'd stopped would be ideal, and had his men set up camp. Capt. Walker, outnumbered five to one, also made camp and waited. Two days later he sent a courier to Camp Sheridan to request military assistance. Capt. Anson Mills, with a cavalry unit, reached Gordon a few miles east of the Antelope Creek/Niobrara confluence, loaded up six of Gordon's wagons with enough food and supplies to get them back to Sioux City and turned them back, with Gordon under arrest. The rest of the wagons, fourteen in all, with mining supplies and equipment, he burned.]

So, not the most visually thrilling of sites, but an interesting history - and of course it's the history of the man after whom Gordon the town was named. There was a metal box at the bottom of the marker post, and inside, wrapped in an old sack which bore the legend Victory Race Horse Oats, was a visitors' book, which we signed.

Down below us on the river-bank we now found what they call the Thayer place, yet another abandoned homestead gradually collapsing back into the earth, just the shell of a substantial wooden building, still standing, with another nearby that lay on the ground in sections.

We had a choice now – to re-cross the river and head straight home, or to circle the heads of the several draws on this southern side. And guess what? We backed the wrong horse. What the map told us when we got home was that we'd walked out in more or less a straight line, covering barely three miles, whereas our return journey now described a massive U – probably seven to eight miles of rough going. We got home seven hours after leaving. We were hot, tired, dirty… and very grateful for that stash of chilled Fat Tire in the fridge.

Thursday 30 June

I had intended, when I set out on this six-month adventure, to camp out as much as possible. So far, the weather has been against it, but on Monday A and I finally managed to get out into the hills and get the tent up. We didn't go far; that was never the idea. We just wanted to be somewhere where we would be surrounded by grass and sky. We found it where I'd hoped we might, at the top of a draw barely a mile from home. We put the tent up on a patch of level ground, scratched a hole in a sandy spot, and gathered firewood from under the cedars down below us.

The fire was keen, bright and eager. A steady breeze, a few wisps of smoke and the cool night air kept the insects at bay. We sat and watched the sun disappear, saw the stars come out, listened as a couple of coyotes tried to get a sing-song going, and finally turned in when the last of the light had gone. Perfect. In the morning, as the sun came up over the range, we brewed our coffee, packed up and hiked back to the red house.

Thursday 30 June - evening

We are in south central Nebraska – or, more accurately, in a tiny little house in a field on the edge of Red Cloud, just a hop skip and a jump from the Kansas line. We are in a single L-shaped space that serves as living room, bedroom and kitchen, plus a separate bathroom.

We're making our way to Lincoln, from where A flies home. We arrived last night just as it was getting dark. The stars were out, fireflies were spiraling above the grass, the temperature had dropped from the hundred mark, where it had hovered all day, to 89, and this morning I have a sense of being a born-again Cather fan.

176

She was the first Great Plains writer I encountered. It was here in Red Cloud that I gave my first and only academic paper in 1993, where I met Frank and Charlotte Wright, who wrote down Caroline Sandoz' address on a piece of paper and sent me on to the Sandhills.

Getting on our way was an adventure in itself. Mercy was at the top of the hill, and the trail was still impassable. We took the wheelbarrow, loaded up A's back-pack, my suitcase and the box of groceries and set off up the hot scarred trail, weaving our way between the crevices like some re-enactment of Mormons on their way to Utah.

Our stay in this renovated 'little house on the prairie' has been a delight. Our host, Ardis Yost – her husband is related to the late Nellie Snyder Yost, a biographer of Buffalo Bill - has made the place very comfortable and gave us a very warm welcome. She even baked some banana bread for us.

As well as fixing up the house, the Yosts have restored a one-room tin school house, which stands on the same grassy plot. Ardis was a teacher for many years. She taught her first class in 1949, and the way she has re-furbished this place seems to reflect her experience. The room is well stocked, not just with the usual desks and chairs, but with encyclopedias, atlases, text books and readers.

At the far end, on the right of the room, is a large photograph of Willa Cather. The Yosts are devotees, and the first question I was asked when I called to book the house was, 'Are you here for Cather?' I had to admit that while I used to be very interested in her work I have since become more involved with Mari Sandoz. It turns out that the Yosts' son, John, is a leading light in the Cather Foundation. I would say director, but I'm not sure of the title. Anyway, he lives and works in New York City, in banking or finance, and doubles up as the head honcho.

We spent much of the day in Red Cloud. We took a guided tour of the Cather childhood home, and one or two of the many buildings that feature in her work. They have been beautifully restored, the highlight for me being the attic room in Willa's childhood home. She moved up there when she was about twelve, leaving her brothers on the floor below. Its walls are still decorated in part by the paper she put up as a teenaged girl.

Last time I was here was 1994, on my cross-Nebraska bike ride. The Cather Foundation has moved on by leaps and bounds. They've taken over the opera-house, and set up a handsome office, shop, gallery and exhibition space, as well as renovating and restoring the theatre. All this in a town of 1,300 inhabitants. It makes me wonder what the Sandoz people could do in a college town like Chadron if they had the will.

'That danged guy from the Government'

Friday 1 July

I'm sitting in the lobby at the Cornhusker Hotel, about ready to hit the road west. This morning, at nine o'clock, I went with A to the airport, had a cup of coffee, and said goodbye. It's going to take a time to get used to being alone again. But... I've done it once and I'll do it again.

Yesterday we looked around the capitol building. It's just a short walk from here, but with the temperature reaching 102, and a strong wind blowing, any kind of walking was hard work. I always find the capitol building an inspiration. It's not just the architecture, which creates a sense of towering ambition when seen from the outside, with an interior space not unlike what you'd find in a European cathedral; it's also the way the art, sculpture and inscriptions celebrate aspirations and values that seem uniquely American.

THE SALVATION OF THE STATE IS WATCHFULNESS IN THE CITIZEN. You could say that we ought all to be mindful of that; it's hardly controversial, whereas the epigraph that runs along the wall above the judges' seats in the supreme court made me wonder how many appellants have sat and pondered these words while the learned judges listened to the arguments for and against them: EYES AND EARS ARE POOR WITNESSES WHEN THE SOUL IS BARBAROUS. That last seems a remarkable word to use in such sober surroundings.

On days like yesterday you soon find yourself scurrying for shelter. By late afternoon we were back in our room showering, and didn't venture out until the evening, when the temperature had dropped to a more bearable 93. We took a stroll over to the Haymarket district, by the old railroad depot, where warehouses and workshops dating from the last century have been re-invented as coffee-shops, galleries and eating-places. We lounged a while in Michael Forsberg's photographic gallery. There we were, surrounded by his gorgeous images of Plains and Sandhills scenes, and I found myself unwilling to take them in. I think I was feeling a little bit proprietorial. I am now familiar with those plants, these animals, that particular cloud formation. And I have my own images – many hundreds by now. Few of them will ever hold a candle to his masterful pieces, but they speak to me now in a way that somebody else's never will.

We ate in an Indian restaurant and walked back to the hotel. And then it was morning, and time for leave-taking. See you in three months. It feels an awful long time.

Monday 4 July

I walked up the path to the front door of the red house, carrying a bag full of dirty washing, to find a three-foot long bull-snake gliding across the doorstep and wrapping

180

itself around the dustbin. I chased it away with the broom and watched it disappear into the cellar. The laundry can wait till tomorrow.

Leaving Lincoln was hard. I have to admit I was feeling pretty sorry for myself.

After I'd left A at the airport I drove back to the Cornhusker, checked out, and headed for Interstate 80, the road that gives most people their first and only impression of Nebraska. It's easy to see why they think it's flat, dull and empty.

I drove towards the sun for an hour and a half, maybe less, before I ran out of steam; and that was a pity, because I don't think it was the smartest thing to stop at that point, not on the Highway 2 Business Loop in Grand Island. Weary and feeling very lonesome indeed, I pulled in at the first motel I saw. I'd checked in, paid for the room and unpacked the car when I realized that there were flies all over the window-sill – half of them alive – and a patina of dirt over just about every surface, crumbs of food on top of the fridge.

Today, however, I felt considerably better. I did some grocery shopping and headed out on Highway 2. Within an hour or so the cornfields had given way to rolling cattle country. Three or four hours later as I drove up Highway 61 from Hyannis, passing four vehicles in 60 miles, I finally felt myself relax.

Kitty took me and my supplies down to the red house in her truck. You don't take rented sedans down here. On the way we met her father, who was almost through re-grading the road. It looked nice and flat, but it's still very soft in places.

The house was as I left it, but the weeds – mostly sunflowers – have grown about a foot in five days. And

181

the good news is that the vegetable plot has also come on. I picked enough lettuce leaves to make a bowl of salad for my supper. I was starting to feel almost cheerful until, on my way back to the house, I spotted a several-days-old footprint in the sand. A's.

Tuesday 5 July

I sense a chaotic few days coming up. But, for the moment at least, there is a calm at the centre of it all. I have driven to Chadron and am staying at the Olde Main Street Inn where my hostess, Jeannie, has put me in the Mari Sandoz Suite, which feels like an honor and a privilege. It's very comfortable, and spacious. I have a bedroom, a sitting room, a bathroom, and there's even a fridge-freezer and stove. Most important, there's a bed that gave me seven solid hours of deep, delicious unconsciousness. On the wall is a copy of one of my favorite photos of my heroine. She's caught in profile, from the waist up, sitting at a desk typing, her face relaxed, her hair shining, a smile playing around her lips. I am reminded of what a University of Nebraska academic once told me, that in New York there was always some fellow chasing after her. And I recall a long letter I found in the archive in Lincoln years ago, from a guy she had been friendly with. This was 1927, and he was on his way to Miami, by car, writing from Kansas City. He addresses her as 'Dearest' and signs off 'Goodnight sweetheart'. It was four months since she had told him – I'm reading between the lines here - that there was no future in their relationship, close as they might be, and he was still grieving. He was planning to camp out, re-read all her letters to him, and burn them. But the night is rainy. Instead he's sheltering in the

Public Library. He imagines that he has lit a fire under trees, by a river, and that, as it dies, she appears from across the water and dances for him. He goes on for fifteen long pages, and his pain is palpable throughout.

Yesterday, the Fourth, was hot. 97 when I left home and drove past the ranch house. By the time I hit Chadron at seven o'clock the skies had blackened; rain was falling; the temperature had dropped 30 degrees. At the Olde Main there was quite a gathering of Jeannie's friends and quite a collection of fireworks. The rain eased off, the temperature recovered, the mosquitoes yawned and stretched and swooped on us as we set off bottle rockets, firecrackers, and sparklers. The *piece de resistance* was a device done up to resemble Osama Bin Laden, which fizzed and popped and spewed out fire, but was finally killed off with a couple of sharp cracks. I was tempted to say it seemed a little tasteless, but then I recalled how we Brits burn an effigy of Guy Fawkes every November 5th. All he did was plant a load of gunpowder under the Houses of Parliament – something we all feel like doing from time to time.

Wednesday 6 July

I'm back from Chadron, but have already booked a room at the Olde Main for Friday and Saturday, and paid for it. I know I am going over budget, but I don't want to go home in October and kick myself – as I have so many times in the past – for letting good opportunities go. The Fur Trade Days weekend is well worth a visit.

I spent a few hours in the Sandoz Heritage Center archive before I left. I found a few useful bits of information but am more and more coming to the conclusion that a scholarly book on Mari Sandoz is best

183

written by what I used to be twenty years ago, a scholar. I'm more of a fan these days, and besides, I have only ninety days in which to produce something. I'm counting on my passion for her work, my new familiarity with the Sandhills, and the story of how I got here, to feed into what I write.

Thursday 7 July

I spent most of today on the computer. I had a lot of correspondence to catch up on, sorting out over a hundred photographs from various sources for the Old Jules Trail website and composing text to go with them. All of that meant that I only got out a couple of times. In the morning I put in an hour mowing the grass and spraying against insects; in the afternoon I went up on the hill to call A, and to watch the progress of some very dark clouds. The radio was warning of severe thunderstorms and I was fretting about my vegetables, still in recovery. My luck held: we had some lightning and thunder, the temperature dropped twenty degrees, and it rained heavily for half an hour or so but, mercifully, no damage – although I suspect that my insecticide was washed away, to judge from the number of bugs that swarmed around me just now when I went to check on things.

Up at the ranch things seem fairly quiet just now. Matt has got the rest of his hay crop cut, baled and stacked, and yesterday the 130 acres under the center pivot was being sprayed with herbicide by a guy from the farm co-op.

Friday 8 July

I used to think I was quite a dab hand at plant recognition. At home, for years I would go on walks with an *Oxford Book of Wild Flowers* in my pocket and I could generally identify most of the plants I saw in my part of England. Here in the Sandhills I'm finding it rather harder than I thought. I've tried blaming the books, which tend to highlight the flowering parts more than the foliage, but I suspect the problem is that I can no longer be bothered to sit and study the plants the way I used to. There's also the insect problem. Last night I could barely stay still for as long as it took to snap a photograph before I had to scamper away from a cloud of whining, whirring, biting demons.

There's a new species of bug around, and a surprising one. Every time I go out on the range these days I have dozens of large dragonflies droning around me. I suppose they are emerging from down by the water. I would never have expected to find them up on the dry grasslands. The good news is that they eat mosquitoes.

The biggest disappointment just now are the soapweeds. A week or two ago they were all sending up vigorous spikes of flower-bud, and I was looking forward to seeing their creamy white blooms: they really are spectacular. But they've all disappeared, snapped off. I know that cattle browse on them, but Matt's beasts are a long way away in another pasture. I can only presume it's the deer – although last night I saw a porcupine scurrying away from a squashed, flowerless yucca.

Saturday 9 July

Chadron. The sun is out, the parade has gone by, it's cool under the linden trees, and I've cured my headache

185

and my woes with a very American remedy: a breakfast of strong coffee and sweet cinnamon rolls, an early lunch of hot dogs (which they're *giving away* over the road here) and Pabst on tap. I'm sitting on a hay-bale in Jeannie's yard. The cowboy band that's about to start up is of special interest to me as it features Jerry, the 6 foot 5 brand inspector. Some years ago he was playing the Olde Main Street Inn and invited me to a branding next morning. I had to decline - I had an earlier appointment – but it was incidents like that which persuaded me to try and fix up a six-month stay out here. He tells me he'll be at Gordon livestock auction Tuesday, and that they serve a free barbecue lunch - so that's another date.

This is a festival weekend in Chadron, their Fur Trade Days, which celebrate the French trader the town was named after. Last night we had an excellent band out here, playing a mixed bag of rock classics with an ever-shifting line-up, two impressive singers, and a mean old guitarist. One member of the band was George, who teaches music at Gordon High School and is married to Jeannie's daughter. With him getting his kids up to play bass guitar, drums and one or two other instruments, and Jeannie's mother looking on, the Goetzinger clan were represented by no less than four generations. Not your average rock gig.

It wasn't a huge turn-out, being nearly all family and friends, plus a few college kids. So the atmosphere was intimate and I got the chance to meet guys like Tony, a biker from Denver who knew Jeannie way back when, and Tom, a 64-year-old fitness freak, youth worker and part-time Revolutionary War fighter. He's out at the black powder camp on the edge of town today – so called because they use the traditional black powder, as opposed to the smokeless stuff.

Between sets I had a chance to talk with Jerry about his work as a brand inspector, a job he's been doing for thirty-five years. When any cattle are taken to the saleroom, or to an abattoir, or moved from ranch to ranch, they must be inspected to ensure that they carry the owner's registered brand. The owner pays 75 cents per animal, and that income pays the wages of the eighty inspectors in the western part of the state. Back east, with much smaller farms, they don't have to brand. In busy times Jerry will put in a 60, 70 or even 80-hour week, balanced against times like this when there is little movement and he maybe only works 20 hours.

Among the pleasures of spending two nights in town was having the time to have a chin-wag with a local writer, Ed Hughes (pen name Poe Ballantine). The fact is that when you're a specialist there are times when you really do hunger for the chance to converse with one of your own kind and talk the language you both understand. I admire his writing, as does Jeannie, who sells his books over the counter and has a portrait of him behind the bar.

I spent a part of the afternoon east of town at the black powder camp. The people out there take what they do pretty seriously, putting on the fringed buckskin, the moccasins and coonskin caps and generally trying to dress as authentic representatives of their particular period, and to use the right equipment: big old iron cooking-pots and long shiny knives. They put up heavy canvas tents supported by stout wooden poles. Some were just sitting stirring the coals of small fires; others were dozing in the shade on beds covered with tanned hides, or coarse woven blankets, while one or two were selling craft items: axes, bead necklaces, wristbands, or items in cloth or hide. I spent some time with a mountain man and craftsman called Badger Buckley. He makes moccasins, among other things. I took his card. Maybe I'll buy some to take home.

They had a beautiful spot to camp, a shallow wooded canyon with a lush grassy floor about eight miles south of Highway 20, with a cool spring coming out of the hillside in one corner. At the far end of the canyon the muzzle-loaders were lining up for target shooting – and I discovered when it was too late that I'd unwittingly missed a great opportunity. This morning, over coffee, Tom, who had been out there with the piece he'd built himself, casually said to me, 'You should've come and found me; I would've let you fire a few rounds.'

I really felt a bit sorry for myself this morning. I met some great people over the weekend, heard some excellent music, and I still haven't got used to being without A. I'm just not ready to resume my solitary life just yet.

Tuesday 12 July

First thing this morning I headed for Merriman to get a pair of shock absorbers fitted to the car. I bounced and lurched my way up the soft sandy undulations that used to be a road, arriving at the top of the hill feeling I was ready to take on a bucking bronco – or that I already had. By the time I got to the highway I'd relaxed, and remembered that my wallet was still on the kitchen table. Nobody at the garage turned a hair. 'Just pay us next time you're coming through,' I was told. 'Hey, we know you ain't going far in that old thing.' So, I'm about $100 poorer – or will be when I pay them – and Mercy now bucks as before, but doesn't bang at the front end the way she used to.

It was interesting to sit in the garage for an hour or so. There's a coffee machine, a table and a pack of cards. I picked them up and played Patience for a while. The twelve-year-old boy who's having to hang around there during the long school vacation while his dad works told me he was bored – but not bored enough to take up my suggestion that he sweep the forecourt. I thought of teaching him a card game or two, but then got distracted by the old dog, who sidles up to everybody in turn to have her silky soft head ruffled. Odd people drop in for gas, or for coffee and a chat – like the elderly man who sat a while, looked me up and down several times and finally asked, 'Are you a Snyder?' He was a perfectly pleasant gent, but something about the way he was eyeing me made me glad I wasn't.

The weather was what we'd call close, or muggy. It was humid, and overcast, and the radio kept talking of storms. Back at the red house I kept an eye on things and wondered how I might protect my garden, where this morning the first bloom has opened up on the zucchini squash. While I was out there I realized that the dragon-fly population is really exploding. Pretty creatures, about two and half inches in length. They were everywhere – although so were their supposed prey, the danged skeeters. Thankfully, I have my tube of Anti-Itch cream (extra strength) which does pretty much what it says on the packaging.

By early evening the radio warnings were more frequent and more unsettling. We had severe storm and tornado warnings, and Cherry county was getting mentioned. I could hear rumbles in the distance, and was aware that the sky was darkening. Then came an alert to say that a tornado was making its way north from Mullen. I checked the map, saw that it was too far west to affect us and went up onto the range to see what I could see. There were some inky clouds to the west, and rain was clearly falling out that way, but it was moving swiftly south.

Wednesday 13 July

64 degrees, damp and cloudy. This is the second cool day in a row, and it's wonderful. It feels like home. And what good luck to go to Gordon yesterday and not fry. Remember that my jalopy, for all its two new tyres and shock absorbers, that glint of chrome where I cleaned the fenders, has no air conditioning. What I have that works is the heat ON and the heat OFF buttons, something a pioneer would have died for in winter, but not a lot of help in summertime.

At the livestock market I bumped into Matt, and Kitty's dad, as well as his cousin and his cousin's son, who ranch up-river from here. I tried to follow what the auctioneer was saying. I caught a 'dollar' here and a 'seventy-five' there, but otherwise very little. When I wandered into the ring they were selling the beasts singly. In there with them was a guy with a paddle, whose job it was to usher each lot in and see it out through the other gate. He seemed to have it pretty easy – or so I thought until a sizeable heifer put her head down and charged, whereupon he slipped behind his little barricade with the grace of a ballet-dancer. No, make that a matador. Next minute the lots were coming in dozens, and I decided, yep, he can have that job.

I sat and watched for a while, then realized that

everyone else was tucking in to plates of beef and beans and some very dark, gooey chocolate brownies. Of course: the free grub. I was down those stairs 'quicker than Grant took Richmond', as an old friend from southern Illinois used to say. After I'd cleaned my plate I took a walk outside. Way out the back, in amongst the various pens, a couple of horseback riders were lining up successive lots, to-ing and fro-ing at a leisurely pace, looking very much like men at ease with themselves.

I didn't stay till the very end. I was worried about getting out of the parking lot, which was muddy and crowded – and the sun was threatening to come out. Besides, I'd got what I came for - my free grub.

Thursday 14 July

Self-discipline. Even at my age I struggle with it from time to time. I realized yesterday that it was a week or so since I'd done the thing I most like to do: go for a hike. I mean more than just a stroll up to the top to watch the clouds, or the sunset, or to make a phone call. A combination of factors have kept me from it. I have been to Chadron – twice. I am still adjusting to being alone. It's been hot. The insects are more and more of a nuisance. And I've been getting plain lazy, as people do in July and August – although not in England, where the temperature rarely gets much above 70 and we have a long history of keeping busy lest we freeze to death.

But yesterday was pleasantly cool, and breezy; and I'd run out of excuses. I put on my boots, shoved a drink into the back-pack and set off down Champagne Creek, to which I am claiming naming rights. In fact, I may well plant a British flag along its headwaters and set up a small republic. I've never seen anybody else down there, so who's going to complain?

The whole place has been scoured by the run-off from the rains, with deep gouges leading to the start of the creek. I have to say I felt a little uneasy walking between three- and four-foot high embankments, with the grasses and soapweeds brushing my sides, but the fact is I've not set eyes on a snake since I bought those boots, apart from the one on the door-step the other day.

Just as everywhere else, this place was swarming with dragon-flies. I worked my way slowly downstream. The bed has changed in character, being broader than it was a month ago, and full of sand. Where it disgorges into the river there was a low, rippled mound of the stuff forming, with tiny rocks being washed down all the time. I amused myself for some time by digging out handfuls and diverting the flow. I soon got carried away and was halfway through building a dam of fallen timber, with visions of an island, a flag and a small fortified dwelling... when I realized it was two-thirty and I'd promised A I'd be in position to receive a call at three.

Friday 15 July

Some time today I have to summon up the energy to clean and tidy. I have another visitor coming on Sunday, just for a day or two: Don Green, former Dean of Humanities at Chadron State College. He's on a long drive from his home in Florida, connecting up with various friends and members of his family.

I barely left the house yesterday, just a quiet stroll amongst the jungle of sunflowers that have recently started sprouting. They're all around the house and already four or five feet tall. Matt says he may come by and mow them before long, but warns that that'll encourage the sand-burs. Meanwhile I take pleasure in cutting a few down with a casual swing of the scythe.

The vegetable garden is – dare I say it – thriving. I am eating lettuce every night with my dinner, there are three or four zucchini starting to plump up, and I have thinned out the beetroot to the point where I can see them starting to swell at the base. No flowers on the tomatoes yet, but I'm seeing more and more French beans appearing. For the second night in a row we have had half an inch or so of rain. I can't remember the last time I watered.

In theory I am now entering a period of sustained productive work. I really would rather laze about, drink beer and take the odd dip in the river.

Saturday 16 July

Yesterday was a quiet day. I took a short walk, did some washing, and wrote – mostly in the morning. It was hot, around 85 degrees, and with little or no breeze the bugs were out in force. More troubling than the biting things right now are the grasshoppers, which are assembling in numbers that will soon give them plague status and waxing fat, largely on a diet of sunflower foliage as far as I can see. As I walked they were scurrying in droves from my path. How long before they acquire a taste for domestic produce, I wonder?

My walk took me through the sunflowers, up the track towards the spot where I make phone calls, generally sheltering under a particular cedar tree. Some weeks ago when A was here, we became intrigued by the cedars. We couldn't understand how there came to be both purple and green fruits on the branches – and a lot of purple ones on the ground. When we read up on them we discovered that the fruits are formed one year and don't ripen properly until the next. It's a two-year cycle.

Sunday 17 July

0835h. It's just touching 80 degrees out there, and they're forecasting 100, with the media's beloved 'heat index' reaching 120. I might be cooler than I am had I not just spent an hour vacuuming and cleaning; and having the oven on doesn't help. But… the place was looking pretty squalid, and I was out of bread. I'm still doing five or six loaves at a time and they're lasting me up to three weeks. They'll be out in a few minutes, thank goodness.

Yesterday I was up at five-thirty and on the road a little after six. With a bit of cloud cover the weather was more or less tolerable on the outward journey. I got to Valentine in time to grab a breakfast and then saunter round to the venue where the River City Writers were gathered to hear Duane Gudgel talk about marketing – which was the main attraction for me. He focused on self-publishing, on the basis that if you have a publisher they will sort out all that on your behalf.

I must have been too busy digesting my breakfast, because I didn't manage to gather my thoughts in response to that assumption, and now I wish I had done. I've had experience of self-publishing (one book, a long time ago, on the subject of Britain's best supported and most hated soccer team, Manchester United) and of working with publishers. My advice would be, do *not* bank on support; get out and promote yourself and your product. With vigor.

Some years ago I ghosted an autobiography, *Brim Full of Passion*, for a cricketer. He was not a big name, but he

194

was special: he grew up in inner-city Birmingham of Kashmiri immigrant parents and was the first British-born Asian to play the game professionally in the U.K. He's now a very high-ranking administrator and promoter of the game through schools. In 2006 – or was it 2007? - the book was selected by the English cricket fans' bible, *Wisden*, as their Cricket Book of the Year. We were jubilant. But not for long. Within months it had disappeared without trace. I have twice had royalty payments of less than £1.00 (from which my agents dutifully and unflinchingly deducted their 15% take). The reason for this failure? A small publisher with little or no sales force, no promotional budget, and little real enthusiasm for the book. Personable and articulate as Wasim is, he was tied up with his full-time job and unavailable for promotional work. My point is that even if you publish with a mainstream company you should be out there hustling. Ask anybody in the world of books. Publishers, agents, booksellers, they all want visible, available, pro-active authors.

And now a first, something I've always wanted to say without a trace of irony: Meanwhile, *back at the ranch…* I am under siege. Grasshoppers: suddenly they are fatter, more numerous, bolder, and are investigating the vegetable garden. I'm afraid I am going to have to spray around the house again today.

Monday 18 July

Insect repellent is all very well, but it is, when it comes right down to it, repellent. And I am smothered in the stuff. My visitor – Don Green, friend, confidant, *bon vivant* and cowboy pantheist – tells me that mosquitoes don't bother him, and never have. So we stayed outside from about four thirty, when he arrived, until nine thirty. We drank beer, ate barbecued steaks and baked potatoes, traded stories – some of them true – and finally toasted our friendship with Irish whiskey while the bats darted in and out of the roof, a few stray fireflies twirled about under the trees, and the mosquitoes fed on my blood.

I can't remember when I first met Don. It must have been in 1993 or '96, on one of my earliest visits to the Sandhills. We seemed to get along from the start, and at one time he was trying to arrange for me to come over and teach a course or two at the college in Chadron, but that foundered on the usual reef: budgetary considerations. In 2000, I think it was, he took me on my first trip around the Old Jules Trail. In 2004, when I was Writer in Residence in the Kerouac House in Orlando, Florida, we met up again. He had retired and moved down there. Later he had me do a little research into his family ancestors in Durham. He was trying to trace one Christopher Davis, born in the city in 1615, who served as interpreter to Peter Stuyvesant in his negotiations with the Iroquois over purchases of lands along the Hudson river. That was in the 1650s. Apparently the two men loathed each other. Davis couldn't even sign his own name, but he spoke a number of native languages and so was indispensable. No wonder Don is so keen to trace him. I couldn't find what he was after in the local records, so the search continues, and Don is planning a trip to dig a little deeper, perhaps next year.

It's not eight o'clock (a.m.) yet, but it's already 80 degrees. The odd thing is, it feels cool out there. That's either a reflection of how hot it was yesterday, or how stifling this house is. However, I am excited by the news that Matt has ordered the material for a new roof and has

196

rounded up a posse of friends to help put it in place, some time over the next month or two.

I'm not sure what we'll do today, but I'm sure we'll be talking. Don is excellent company, has a vast store of knowledge on the subject of America's past, and his own, and tells a good story. He has traveled in Europe, has lived in Ireland and brings to his studies of history the crucial ingredient of humanity – an understanding of people and what makes them tick.

Tuesday 19 July

Almost ten at night and the house is still like an oven. Don has gone to bed and I've been rampaging round with my fly swatter. We are suddenly being pestered by what look like plain old house flies, except that they suck blood.

Don and I have had a pretty lazy day. This morning he wanted to take me out to breakfast, but when we got down to Merriman we were reminded – by the large CLOSED sign in the window - that the Sand Café doesn't open Mondays. I was reminded of Lola's place in Buffalo Gap, Texas (pop. 499) which I stumbled upon in 2001 – the year I drove up the 100th meridian from Laredo clear through to the Canadian border, and back. Lola closed on Mondays but left a key for her regulars so that they could come in, make coffee (25 cents in the jar, thankyou) and chew the fat with the mailman. They made me very welcome – and the mailman drew me a map showing me how to get around Abilene, which, in his opinion, was to be avoided at all costs. However, there was no key at the Sand Café, so we drove to Gordon and breakfasted there.

Don has a fund of stories about his family, and the

history of the American West. His folk migrated through the Cumberland Gap in the wake of Daniel Boone. He had great-uncles who were cattle drovers, coming up the long trail from Texas to Montana, and gunfighters. And of course he knows a huge amount about Mari Sandoz, having come to Chadron in 1990 with the aim of establishing a dedicated Center at the college.

I had a question for Don. I was sure – I *am* sure – that some years ago when I was researching in Mari's papers at the University of Nebraska, Lincoln, I came across a reference to Old Jules having shot a man in Switzerland, possibly a brother. Had I imagined it? Did Don know anything about it? Yes, he said, he too understood that Jules had shot a man – although he didn't think it was a brother. And then he added, 'I always figured he must have done. Think about it.' And he went on to point out that the purported reason for Jules' argument with the family was his demand for a higher allowance from his father. How could he live the life of a scholar and a gentleman if he had to do his own laundry? Does this tally, Don asked, with a man who left the country, crossed the Atlantic, and traveled into an uninhabited region where there was no law? Don's point was that most people who went this far west were on the run, from a woman, from debtors, or from the law. We know that Jules was an excellent shot, and that he was prepared to defend himself at the point of a gun.

Well, more to chew on. And that's the pleasure of having a visit from a guy like Don, and why I'll miss him when he moves on today.

Wednesday 20 July

Amongst the things I sought when I planned this

enterprise was to gain a few insights into what the pioneer farmers of this region faced. I have, of course, to use my imagination. I have a refrigerator, electric light, running water in the house. I can get to a grocery store within an hour and buy whatever I fancy. I have a screen door – even though it required a deal of pioneer ingenuity on my part to erect it. And I am glad of all these things – more so, in the case of groceries, since the grasshoppers got into my lettuces yesterday. They are also making rapid progress through the beets, but prefer so far to leave the tomatoes alone.

So, next time I look through the *Little House* books – and who knows, that may be when I read them to my grandchildren – I will be able to say, of the locust plague and the hailstorms that wrecked the Wilders' hopes, 'Yep, they wiped out my garden too.' In fairness, this grasshopper problem is localized. Up at the center pivot, where the next crop is already starting to poke through the stubble, there are fewer of them.

I had hopes of producing some work during the day but in the end the heat got the better of me. All I did was complete some email correspondence, and re-arrange things so that I now sleep in the living-room. On Kitty's advice, I took a hammer and a couple of wrenches to one of the old wooden windows at the south end of the room and managed, after a lot of heaving and grunting, to prize it open. So, last night, when the wind got up and the lightning flashed (there wasn't even a sniff of rain) I wallowed in a blissfully cool through-draught.

The joy of being here in the heat of summer, of course, is the river. I spent some time in it yesterday. Just walked down there in my plastic sandals and shorts and sat in the water - occasionally lying down - until I'd cooled off.

So far I haven't felt too lonely. I've been absorbing some of the many, many stories Don told me, and doubtless jumbling them up in my memory. The way he switches from academic discourse on the history of the fur trade, or his Dutch ancestors (the Schoonovers), his Welsh ones (Roberts), and back to earthy accounts of growing up on a cattle-ranch - and let's not even get started on the love-life of a seventy-five-year-old… well, I guess this is how novelists work: let it all sink in, stir it around and see what comes out.

I have little experience of writing fiction, and I don't think I've ever had any real impulse to make up stories. What I always wanted to do, from childhood, was to tell my own story and have people listen. I could never make them do that – I was never noisy enough, or assertive enough – and so I wrote my stories down. Most of what I composed as a young writer was transparently autobiographical. Later I learned the joy of writing up other people's stories. It began in my early years as a builder's laborer, office gopher, gardener, parcels porter, freight train guard, rural rat-catcher, immigration officer and so on, when it seemed the world was full of people with infinitely more colourful pasts than I would ever have. Imagine a fourteen-year-old public schoolboy working in a steam laundry and overhearing the following conversation between two ancient crones (who were younger then than I am now).

'Course, we never `ad no contraception did we, Else?'

'Back in them days? No, Vi, we never did.'

'Mind, we knew what to do, didn't we?'

'Course we did, Vi. Make `em laugh.'

'That was it, girl. Make `em laugh. Popped out like a

bleeding cork, didn't it?'

I should point out that when I speak of a public school I mean a private one. It's an idiosyncrasy of British usage. And then I must add that I grew up in public housing (same meaning as the American phrase) but that, being considered extraordinarily bright, and having no mother at home, I was granted a scholarship to attend a boys' boarding school. I still thank my brother (he now lives in Kentucky) for getting me the vacation job in the laundry, where he worked. That experience was the beginning of my re-acquaintance with a world – a world of common people, you might say – from which boarding school seemed to have abducted me, a world I desperately wanted to know.

And now, I suppose, I am someone with a past of my own. And today I must continue with that part of it which deals with my fifty-year interest in the American west.

Thursday 21 July

I sometimes wonder why we ever bother making plans. Yesterday morning I made my way up to the house to do the usual online stuff: checking on emails, catching up on sports news. I'd grabbed a cup of coffee and gone up there early, while it was still tolerably cool. Hadn't washed, hadn't eaten, had hardly really dressed. All I had on my mind was getting back down here and starting to write. So I was taken aback when the phone rang and I heard my contact from the National Resource Conservation Service in Valentine asking me if I'd got his message yesterday. What message was that, I asked. That they were doing a survey of the ranch and did I want to come along? Sure, I said, and when is this? We'll be there in about thirty minutes.

I made it okay. Showered, changed, ate, packed some lunch in a bag and was waiting for them as they turned in off the highway.

What these people do – I'm going to call them L and C – is to survey a ranch, using satellite photographs as a basis. Their initial task is to map it – that is, to pinpoint what the photograph may not show: fence lines, wells, gates and windmills. (I really don't like that word windmill; those things don't mill anything. I prefer to call them wind-pumps; but then I have been called a pedant in my time....) They locate these features very precisely with a hand-held gizmo, about the size of an early mobile phone, which communicates with a satellite to get the co-ordinates. They are accurate to within three feet or so.

The day's work consists mainly of driving along every fence-line and logging the position at every junction or bend. Around the center pivot that means quite a few stops. On a particularly steep or difficult stretch it means getting out and walking.

While L was doing this, and getting a stiff arm from holding the sensor out over fence-posts, C was in the back seat of the pick-up making notes on the condition of the various sections of pasture, the state of the grasses and forbs, the amount of bare soil, and so on, giving them grades of fair, good, or poor, then comparing her assessment with L's. They rarely differed by more than half a grade point. She would also be tracing lines on her own map, showing where good pasture turned to fair, fair to poor and so on. In addition she would photograph certain features.

L was everything I could have hoped for in terms of answering my questions in full, and then throwing in a whole stack of related information. In my experience any expert, whatever the field, any person who is really absorbed in a subject and knowledgeable on it, is a joy to listen to. And this guy had that one extra thing going for him: he clearly loves what he does.

So I learned a lot – and probably forgot even more. I learned that in this part of the world there are four seasons: calving, branding, hunting and winter. I learned to identify such grasses as downy brome, needle and thread, and switchgrass – and how to differentiate between that and sand bluestem by its 'hairy arm-pit' – a patch of short hairs in the joint between stem and leaf. I also learned that all the tree growth along the river, which looks so natural to me, simply isn't. Until the settlers came, prairie fires would sweep through regularly, burning off the brush.

L has a wonderful job. He must be in his early thirties. He grew up around here and probably never imagined he would find such a perfect job on his door-step. His biggest problem is the fact that he works for the government, and people in this part of the world hate the government with a passion, so his first task is to overcome that prejudice. But it's a small price to pay when you get to spend days like we had out on the open range, then park your vehicle on a promontory overlooking a great loop of the Niobrara, and sit and eat your lunch as a hawk cries down below you, the cicadas sing and the buzzards swoop above your head.

One of the main advantages to the rancher of working with this agency is the expert advice they are given. After a survey such as this, for example, L will compute the ideal number of AUMs (Animal Unit Months) each section of pasture will support. And he might recommend the installation of another well, a fence, or a pipeline to bring water out into a dry spot, these partially funded by tax-payers' dollars. I had assumed that with the river running through it, this ranch had few water problems, but L pointed out that when cattle find a water source they tend to hang out nearby, and over-graze. They consume – this staggered me – some forty to fifty gallons a day. So if a rancher can get a number of alternative sources – and divide up some of the huge pastures into smaller lots – they can better assure that the entire range is evenly grazed. The big pastures, he said, are a hangover from the days when a rancher liked to ride his land on horseback and not have to stop to open gates. They're no longer appropriate.

At one point we passed one of Matt's lick-tubs – in fact we ran into it, dragged it under the front fender and squashed it. 'I like to see that,' L said, when we'd extricated it. 'Putting a lick-tub well away from the water source. It encourages the cattle to move.'

L's assistant C must be nineteen or so. She's a student at the University of Nebraska in Lincoln. I believe she said her course was in grazing and range management. I may have got the wording of that wrong, but you get the idea. She grew up on a ranch just across Highway 61, is planning to return to it when she marries, and eventually take it over. At some stage during the day we were at a wind-pump and she was measuring its diameter. L was saying that this was an ideal hang-out for a rattler, with plenty of cover under the weeds, and C remarked that she was bitten – twice – when she was four years old, and almost died. She was rushed to hospital, given one of the two serums available, and turned out to be allergic to it. It took her an awfully long time to recover – several weeks. I have to say I felt reassured when L said that she was the only person he'd ever met who'd been bitten by a rattler.

As well as taking note of what was under their feet, L and C were keeping an eye on things from a more distant perspective, pointing across the river to an area a mile or so away, where there was a subtle change in colour from one side of a fence to another which might have been caused by over-grazing. L told me that after a hailstorm you can often trace, from a distance, the precise line of its passage by the way the grasses have been cut back.

Our day lasted about six hours. We covered that part of the ranch that lies south of the river, so they'll be back in a few days to look at the north side, and have invited me to join them once more.

Friday 22 July

Today started out nice and cool - 62 degrees at six o'clock, with a fair breeze. Later it got up to the low 90s again, but in the early evening the sky darkened, the thunder rumbled and we had a sprinkling of rain. It was barely enough to settle the dust, but that brief hour of fresher air gave me the energy I'd been lacking all afternoon.

I don't think most people realize just how tiring creative effort can be. I experience something akin to actual physical pain after I've written for any length of time, especially if there is an emotional content, or if it's very important to me - or indeed if it's going well. So this afternoon, as I took a break in the reclining chair, I nodded off for over an hour. Now, of course, eleven at night, I'm wide awake, listening to the insects pinging off the lights, or smacking into the screens. Earlier I sat outside and lit a fire, drank a cold beer and listened as the coyotes started up their yipping and yowling. But it was all a bit half-hearted: I got the impression they were struggling to get a quorum.

I plucked up my courage this evening and ventured into the vegetable garden. I didn't really want to be in there, seeing the wasteland that the grasshoppers have created this week, but there were a few green beans - my first and, I dare say, last – which I ate, cold, with sliced tomato. Very tasty, and all the more poignant for that. After dinner I went up on the range and watched as a shower passed away to the east, leaving a beautiful double rainbow.

Saturday 23 July

This morning I am bathed by a cool, refreshing breeze. It is only 68 degrees out there, and it's cloudy – but then it is only a little after seven o'clock. I'm enjoying it while I can. I've just slept for nine hours, which didn't really surprise me. Yesterday was a full one. The NRCS guy, L, left me a message late on Thursday to say he was coming through to complete the ranch survey. We were out for another six hours, just the two of us this time, bouncing around the sandhills in broiling sun, and the flow of information picked up where it had left off on Wednesday afternoon.

It wasn't just plant ID, or range management techniques. It may have been my own fault for asking, but I also got an explanation of the old survey system, and how, in the period of westward expansion, Government land was divided up into Ranges and Townships. I must admit that I had puzzled over that for years, so I welcomed L's brief lecture. Several times I have been confronted by old ledgers in which are recorded some settler's claim, and I've always been unable to interpret what I saw. Only last month I was staring at one which showed the extent of the old Spade ranch. All I knew was that a Section was a square mile, a township site six miles by six. What I now know is that from a certain longitudinal baseline – and here, for once, L wasn't sure of his facts – the land was measured and surveyed in Ranges heading from east to west, and townships heading south to north. Within each township ("Twp" on the map) were 36 numbered sections. Numbers 16 and 36 were deeded to the state of Nebraska. Now, I'd heard of school sections, and presumed that they were lands set aside to house a grade school. I was wrong. They were to provide the income which would fund the universities. There is in fact a school section right here on Matt & Kitty's place, more or less alongside the cemetery. It is leased from the state, and the lease is auctioned afresh every few years. In practice, of course, there will only ever be one bidder, because no outsider could guarantee access to that piece of land. I apologize. I am starting to sound like L, who surely has a career as a teacher or TV presenter waiting for him when he gets tired of his present job.

As we rode around I was surprised to see how the colour of the pasture in certain areas had changed, even since a week or so ago. Suddenly it's looking almost like winter, a sweep of pale tan dotted with the greyish-white heads of the annual wild buckwheat, or umbrella plant. What has happened is that the cool season grasses have set seed and ripened, and one of L's concerns was to see how the warm season grasses were coming along. Along the way he had more to say about his particular *bete noire*, the invasive cedar tree. He pointed out what I had observed, that the female cedar is laden with berries, masses of them, that birds will scatter them widely, and that once you have one tree making that much fruit in an open field, you can soon have dozens, hundreds, of young ones sprouting. He says that he can see the day when, although 'fire is a dirty word out here', it might be used to control them, the way it used to.

I could go on – and on – but that would mean delving into a jumble of half-remembered facts and, quite likely, getting some of them wrong. The last thing I want to do is misrepresent my guide, who gave me a superb introduction to this complex business of range management. Not bad for someone who knows he's only one small mistake away from being 'that danged guy from the Government'.

Besides, I have to report another incident from yesterday's outing that has hit me where it hurts. We were sitting on a knoll, overlooking a loop of the river, perhaps two hundred feet below us. Somewhere down in the trees cattle were bawling, but we could still hear the ripple of water over rocks. I had just devoured a chunk of bread and three or four slices of deer sausage – one of the last remnants of the grub the turkey hunters left me, way back in April – and got out an apple. Took a huge bite and felt something go ping! It was a front tooth, off my dental plate. The dentist in Gordon doesn't open Saturdays, so I'll be going over there Monday morning.

Sunday 24 July

I was lying on my back in the river, looking up at a flawless sky. Sunflowers nodded on the grassy bank, vivid blue dragonflies darted to and fro above the sparkling water. On the bank lay my clothes, with my straw hat perched on my walking-pole. This was what I always hoped it would be like. This was the first time in a while that I'd put on my boots and gone for any kind of a hike, but conditions seemed perfect. The insects weren't particularly troublesome, the temperature just pleasantly warm, and a stiff breeze was blowing. Walking was a real pleasure once more. I hadn't gone very far before I dived down one of the canyons, places I've been avoiding during the hot weather, and followed the creek slowly down towards the river.

After lozicking in the river for half an hour or so – 'lozicking' is a word we use in Yorkshire; I suspect that its nearest American equivalent would be 'lollygagging' – I put my clothes on, strapped my boots around my neck and crossed to the north bank. From there it was a short walk across ungrazed pasture back to the house, cutting short what would have been a long circular walk had I re-traced my steps. On my way home I found a plant whose appearance I have been dreading. I remember it all too well from previous visits to this part of the world. It was the first of the sand-burs, whose vicious little seed-heads cling to your clothing and stab your fingers when you try to pull them off. They have been particularly successful in colonizing the area outside the red house – and finding their way inside.

As I approached the river again I was delighted to see an old friend – and surprised that it should flower so late here. The elder is very widespread at home and flowers in June. Some people consider it a pest. It is renowned, amongst other things for being almost impossible to kill – or to burn. But I don't know why you would want to do such a thing. It's a truly remarkable tree. Its leaves have a pungent, unpleasant smell - although to tell the truth I like it, and always pinch one and sniff it as I pass. I still marvel that the same plant can produce a flower with such a gorgeous scent, and flavor. I've never yet made wine – or the more popular champagne - from elder-flowers. But for many years when my kids were young we made a cordial. The recipe came from Sweden. As I recall, it involves steeping the flowers in a pail of water for a few days, boiling up the liquor with sugar and lemon, bottling it, and sealing it. It would last all summer. Pour an ounce or two into a glass, add cold water, ice - or even better, carbonated water - and you've got a delicious, refreshing drink.

Matt came by last night and was talking seriously about this upcoming roof job. I took it as a hint that I should do what I said I'd do, and slap some red paint on the bare patches at the front of the house. Maybe it'll take my mind off the wasteland that was once my vegetable patch.

Monday 25 July

I slept like a dead man. I suppose a night-cap of Irish whiskey will have helped, and then of course there's the fact that I'd sat and watched the first half of *Lonesome Dove*. More likely, though, it was the busy afternoon I spent, armed with scythe, wire brush and paint-roller. Some years ago somebody started painting the garage here, and ran out of paint – or time, or desire. Whatever the case, they left a large patch of bare grey cement-block wall that's been bugging me since I got here. So I got to work. With a large step-ladder and a roller on a long pole I reckoned I might just about be able to reach the top of the grey patch, way up towards the ridge. I had a few shaky moments up there on the step-ladder, and I've splashed a few spots of red paint down my expensive hiking trousers, but the job is done.

I also did a test patch on the house. The worn concrete sucked the paint in like a sponge. It is, of course, getting on for ninety years old. It may be that it'll eat up two or three coats. In any case it needs a good hosing-down and a vigorous wire-brushing before I start on it. One thing worries me about this job. There's a little metal bird-box outside, which hangs from the eaves within a couple of feet of my front door. I thought it was there for fun, someone having painted 'WELCOME' on it. To my great surprise I find that it is now occupied. I think it's a wren. It looks like a wren, although it has a longer tail than the ones we have at home. I'd seen it darting to and fro, but it was only when I watched it fly in with a twig in its mouth, drop the twig, and fly down to retrieve it, that I was convinced. There – I just went to the door and it flew off to the tree.

Watching *Lonesome Dove* last night was a surprise pleasure. I tried to read the book many, many years ago and somehow never got on with it. I am a big fan – or used to be – of Larry McMurtry's early fictions, in particular *Horsemen, Pass By*, which became the movie *Hud*. I also enjoyed *The Last Picture-Show*, which was filmed by Peter Bogdanovich and gave an early role to one of the few current actors whose work I still enjoy, Jeff Bridges. I suppose it's an age thing: when you're young your movie heroes can be father figures, or the big brothers you wish you had. Then you get older and find it harder and harder to take the youngsters seriously. As to McMurtry's early works - and I'd include *Desert Rose* and *Leaving Cheyenne* among the ones I liked - I have a suspicion that I wouldn't enjoy them as much now. They had a bitter edge to them. I recently re-watched *Last Picture-Show* and found it quite dismal in mood, and peopled entirely by victims and losers. But then I recall finding *The Graduate* terribly funny when I was eighteen or nineteen, whereas now I can't watch it without dwelling on the tragedy that was Mrs. Robinson's story.

However, *Lonesome Dove*. Marvelous. How often do you find a movie-maker who dares to take so long to get his story under way, who allows the camera to linger, the dialogue to proceed at such a slow pace, in fragments, with thoughtful pauses – the way it sometimes does in real life? Can't wait to see part two, most likely tonight.

Tuesday 26 July

The dentist wore blue jeans, held up by a leather belt with a broad silver buckle. I was reminded briefly that Doc Holliday was also of the dental persuasion, but dismissed the thought. This guy was all smiles as he explained that my plate would have to be mailed off to a lab and ought to be ready by the end of the week.

I had a number of other calls to make in Gordon, among them a trip to the hardware store to collect food for Kitty's ducks, paint and sealer for the house. And a brush. They had the stuff all ready for me, piled on a little trolley.

By the time I got back here it was some time after four o'clock and I was thinking sundowners – by which I mean beer, corn chips and salsa. So I sat and looked at the cans of paint, surveyed the front of the house, and came to the conclusion that come tomorrow I might as well crack on with the job. Having made that decision, I opened a can of the Pabst Blue Ribbon that Don left here. It assuaged my thirst. I can say that much for it. But not a lot else.

Lonesome Dove continued at its own thoughtful pace. I knew it was a two-DVD movie; but I hadn't realized that it consisted of four ninety-minute parts. I remember now that in the book I got to about p. 80 and they were still debating whether or not to take the damned herd up to Montana, and here we are three hours in and they've only crossed two rivers on their way north. But I'm enjoying this. I can see that it's one of those stories which, after I've got to the end, will stay with me, the kind that you don't want to end, because you're enjoying the company of the main characters. The settings seem more real than in any western I've ever seen, the characters more plausible.

Wednesday 27 July

I think I'm in what they used to call the dog days of summer. It got up to 95 yesterday and seems to be heading the same way today, but I think we've lost the humidity which made it so uncomfortable last week. If the heat's having any effect on me, other than inducing a kind of lethargy, it's on my appetite, which is certainly diminishing at the moment. Anyway, dog days or not, I put in some good work yesterday - my contribution to the old place's refurbishment.

When those guys made their concrete block mould back in the 1920s they must have congratulated themselves on the rustic, coarse stone look. Yes, but… trying to persuade thick red paint into every nook and cranny, every little hole, required ever more vigorous brush-strokes, and every time I thought I'd got a block covered I'd stand back and spot several bare spots on the underside. By the end of the day my clothes and arms were thoroughly splattered with the stuff. But... the house is now unequivocally red, at least at the front. There is, of course, a downside. The trouble with having restored the façade is that the lamentable state of the woodwork is now highlighted.

The grasshopper situation continues to bother me. They are still increasing in numbers, and waxing fat. They're lazing about on the fence rail, the outside chairs, the path, like soldiers who have won a major victory and are waiting for orders. They really are striking creatures to look at. If they were on our side, as it were, I am sure we would celebrate them in art.

I got to the end of *Lonesome Dove* last night. I can't recall the last time I was so involved in a movie and its cast of characters, or when I was so sorry to be parting company with them, and I've been trying to figure out why. It must have something to do with the age of the principals, but mostly I think it's about the re-creation of so many western settings which looked so real, and the fact that so much of the action took pace on the cattle trail. Those guys were for the most part dirty, sweaty, unshaven, lean-looking individuals. They looked as if they really had been working those cattle – and from time to time they sat down and ate from plates of grub that were suitably plain and unappetizing. The amount of violence was troubling to me, and perhaps overdone – although each act of savagery was in itself perfectly plausible. But... great cast, terrific locations, and some superb dialogue. I wouldn't be surprised to find myself watching it all over again in a few weeks.

Today I ought to take Mercy down to Merriman. There is a hideous banging and clanking sound coming from underneath, and I dread to think what it might be. If I were a betting man, my money would be on a broken leaf spring, but the honest truth is I don't really want to know. I just want that old thing to keep going for ten more weeks.

The electricity supply has flickered off, and back on, twice while I've been typing this, dark clouds are sweeping in from the northeast – and here comes the rain.

Saturday 30 July

Now, insects. It's a pity they aren't edible; or should I say palatable? I know that some people really enjoy a fried grasshopper as an *hors d'oeuvres*. And an ant is supposed to be highly nutritious, but so is tripe for that matter. I thought that with a screen door, and screened windows I'd be free of bugs in the house. And, to be fair, I am managing to keep most of the big ones out. But with no blinds or drapes the windows attracts huge numbers of bugs each night, clouds of them, a surprising number of which get through the finely woven mesh. Every morning I have to wipe up a layer of them from around the kitchen sink, for example. No, I correct myself. Every morning I *could* wipe up a layer. Instead I look at them, pull a face and carry on filling my kettle. If I've left a dirty plate in the sink – and I often do, because the dribble of water from the taps means that it takes five or ten minutes to fill the bowl - I'll usually find a fly or a moth glued to the leftover bolognese sauce, or salad dressing, generally on its back. There is also a species of tiny creature, invisible to my eye, which gets in and bites me. And there are the moths, the stray hornets, the inoffensive little black beetles which crawl in through the gaps, the steady stream of house-flies, less energetic than the ones back home, and easier to swat. Added to all this are the noises – of cicadas chirruping, mosquitoes whining, the thud of a determined beetle against the glass, the ping as a moth hits the lampshade. Last night, watching the decaff version of *Lonesome Dove* (*Return To…*) I had to stop the action two or three times in order to work out whether a particular noise was on-screen or in the house.

Then the bat arrived. It's not the first one that's dropped by, and I suspect it got in through the attic and decided to have a look downstairs. The last one spent several days trying to get out and I still don't know whether it lived or died. It wasn't easy getting to sleep with the occasional flutter of wings disturbing the peace that descends once the lights are out, although there was a pleasant stirring of the air as it swooped past my face from time to time.

It looks as though today is going to be a hot one. Eight thirty and it's already eighty degrees out there. I suspect I shall gravitate towards that river before long.

Sunday 31 July

Yesterday I started digging amongst my papers again. One of the things I've been looking forward to doing while I'm out here is reading through the stack of journals from my previous western trips. I have various files, folders and notebooks dating from 1980. Some of those were epic journeys, or seemed so at the time. There was the train ride from Detroit to L.A., a couple of 5,000-mile road trips across the Plains and the Rockies, the bike ride across Nebraska – and the later journeys, which I've been thinking about this morning. They

216

include that journey up the Hundredth Meridian and back, a four-week drive along the entire Lewis & Clark Trail from St Louis, Missouri, to Astoria on the Pacific coast, and the several weeks I spent in 2006 following the veteran rodeo riders around Utah and Nevada.

The shocking thing is how little sense some of my notes make. There are passages I am having trouble actually reading. Some of them, I know, were written by a camp-fire, or on the road, many of them scribbled hurriedly while someone was talking to me. But there are also many passages which, even when I've deciphered the scrawl, seem to describe people or places, incidents or events of which I have no recollection. They make no sense.

Still, there are some great stories, and a few hidden gems. For example, my note from the Museum of the Rockies, somewhere up in Montana. This was in 2005, when I was selling a number of travel pieces to *American Cowboy*. Like most of life's lucky breaks it came about out of the blue. I was at home, scratching around for paying propositions. I'd just spent a five-month winter season working in the sugar-beet factory, and had followed that up with a four-month stint researching and writing the history of a businessmen's club. And then I got an email from this travel editor up in Sheridan, Wyoming. She'd come across me on the Net and thought I might be just the kind of contributor they were looking for.

Yes, the gem… in the Museum of the Rockies. They had a temporary exhibit called 'Hope in Hard Times', about the work of the various Federal agencies during the New Deal period, and how it affected Montana's ranchers and farmers. The Fort Peck Dam on the Missouri river was just one of the government programs that brought relief – and work – to a region hard hit by economic depression and a devastating drought. It was quite an exhibit. There were some terrific photographs by Margaret Bourke-White, and written records of the hardships faced on the land, including a telegram sent by the Governor to Washington some time in the mid-1930s:

THIS IS THE WORST CATASTROPHE THAT HAS EVER HAPPENED IN THIS PART OF MONTANA…. DROUGHT AND GRASSHOPPERS AND HEAT HAVE ELIMINATED ALL POSSIBILITY OF AGRICULTURAL INCOME HERE THIS YEAR, PEOPLE FACING ABSOLUTE DESTITUTION STOP.

In among the exhibits was a photograph of a grasshopper trap. It was really quite simple, consisting of a metal barrier a foot high which ran along the bottom of a fence, forming a barrier to the insects' progress. There was a picture of them piled up, many inches deep, ready to be sprayed with poison. I wish I'd come across this entry earlier. I might have run a little experiment down here.

I shall plod on with the journals. I have only skimmed through them so far. The parts that most interest me just now are the extensive interviews with representatives of Native peoples we met along the Lewis and Clark Trail in 2004. I made this trip with an old school-friend who lives in Ohio. We recorded conversations with leaders from a whole roster of tribes: the Ponca, the Lakota, the Mandan-Hidatsa, the Nez Perce, the Chinook, and got some provocative views on the meaning of the Lewis & Clark expedition and the Louisiana Purchase. In some ways these are no longer topical – the bicentennial is

218

long past – but in other ways they are as relevant as ever. So yesterday was quite a reflective day. It was also hot, getting up to 94 degrees, although late in the afternoon it looked very much as though a storm was brewing. It was, but it tracked eastwards of here. I spent the better part of an hour up on the hill watching the clouds build, fade, build again and pass right on by. At one point I could even smell the rain. It was quite tantalizing, but at least I had a strong wind to cool me. That was what kept me up there so long - that and the remarkable 'amen rays' on the eastern horizon. I'd never seen these before. With the sun low to the west a perfect fan of light-rays seemed to emanate from a point below the western horizon, as if presaging the rising sun. It was eerie, awe-inspiring, remarkable.

Eight-thirty a.m., and while I've been writing this the temperature has risen 15 degrees, to 80.4. It's going to be another hot one.

I think I am required to drink beer

Monday 1 August

No question about it: this heat is debilitating. Yesterday it was 97; today they're forecasting 100 – with added humidity. It's not yet seven o'clock and the thermometer is registering 74.

It's all relative, though. When I walked out to make a phone call yesterday there was enough wind to keep me fairly comfortable. I generally feel worse indoors, as when sitting here at the kitchen table with the sweat running down over my ribs – or my bare arms slipping and sliding on the wet table, a problem I've solved for the moment by laying a towel between me and the keyboard. More unpleasant is the feel of warm upholstery against my bare back every time I slump in the recliner. However, a few days ago I brought an oscillating fan from upstairs. That helps.

So does the river. I went down there yesterday evening – ran down, in fact, before the deer flies could get me properly in their sights – and spent a happy half-hour cooling off, cheering on the massed ranks of dragon-flies as they roamed the skies like a fleet of helicopters, seeking out mosquitoes.

When I came back I read some more of my old

journals. I was skimming through the record of my bike-ride across Nebraska. I'd got as far as North Platte and the temperature was up in the mid-90s. This was mid-September. I spent two nights there, camping in an RV park on the edge of town, just over the fence from the marshalling yards. I needed a rest day, and was particularly interested in looking at the old Buffalo Bill ranch-house. I wanted to find out whether they had any records that related to his voyages to Europe – and my great-great uncle, the ship's captain.

However, there was another museum at North Platte that caught my attention – and I really wish I could remember what it's called. They have a number of restored buildings from earlier times: a Union Pacific depot, a caboose, a school house, a Lutheran church, a two-storey log house dating from 1899, an army post, also of logs, built in the 1860s at Fort McPherson, and a whole street of little shops from the nineteenth century: barber's, dentist's and the like. There's also a wonderful exhibit on the North Platte canteen, an *ad hoc* sort of refreshment station set up in the early 1940s to offer drinks, food and cigarettes to servicemen, many thousands of whom came through by train, en route to the Pacific or European wars. Even as I wandered through the exhibit I met one or two veterans who had benefited from that hospitality, all laid on by volunteers at no charge.

The item that most captured my attention, however, had nothing to do with that. It was the unpublished memoir of one Cecil Calhoun, who homesteaded in a sod-house some 45 miles to the north of town, out in the Sandhills. I can't quite remember, but I think it was a typed, rather than a hand-written record. It's not a happy tale and, topically, it involves insect pests.

'Right here,' he says, 'the fable of the cowboy riding the range, his pony and faithful dog his companions, a guitar slung across his shoulder, a song on his lips that brought maidens swooning at his feet, must be shoved under the bed with the filthy underwear and fleas. There were no effective fly-killers; millions of these pests swarmed into the shacks & contested for every bite of corn flakes or fried potatoes. Who got the hog's share was a toss-up and many a fly lost as they landed in the milk glass or greasy skillet. At night the fleas and bed-bugs took over.... It became man against nature and many times we admitted defeat and taking a quilt would flee to some distant hillside to spend the night.'

He goes on to record that right into the late 1920s they were still using 'surface coal' (cow chips). It produced 'a quick heat that burned out in minutes and left a cold stove. In the spring the rainy season left the pile a sodden mass of garden fertilizer.'

One wet season, he writes, his wife and kids cut out pictures of a meal from *Good Housekeeping*, and laid them on the plates at dinner-time as a hint that he should get some stove-wood.

Things got worse as the Great Depression hit. In 1929 rye was fetching $1.96 a bushel. After the crash it was 21 cents.

In 1934 he gave it up and went west to look for better prospects. He took a grubstake of $50. Gas was 16 cents, a motel room $1, good meals a quarter. After a 2,000-mile trip he was back. He'd seen an opportunity in Twin Falls and decided to take it. He'd met a man willing to trade 40 acres of good land, with a dairy, a henhouse, 150 birds, some machinery and furniture, for their 1,280 acres in the Sandhills. Of this deal he writes, 'The man's wife said, Ray wants to try ranching and he might as well git it out of his system. They stayed ten months.'

Eloquent testimony – and it makes you wonder how many other stories like that are untold, or undiscovered.

Today looks like another day of damage limitation – by which I mean trying to stay comfortable. I suppose it would help if I didn't yield to the occasional impulse to attack the sand-burs. Trouble is, I hate them with a passion, and they are encroaching on the various paths I take across the yard. So I'm out there two or three times a day swinging my hoe and raising dust. All I really want is to be able to walk out and back without collecting several dozen of them on my boot-laces or trousers. But my goodness it's hot work.

Tuesday 2 August

Evening time, and relief at last, in the form of a cool wind, some threatening clouds and a few drops of rain. It's barely enough to settle the dust, but the temperature has dropped twenty degrees and suddenly I feel a little energy being rekindled.

It was a horribly uncomfortable afternoon, and since I climbed the hill to make a phone call the only exercise I've taken was going outside to make regular checks on the thermometer. It was in the upper nineties from about noon and kept on climbing, very slowly, to the point where I realized that I was going to be disappointed if it didn't reach three figures. It did, around five o'clock, peaking at 100.00 degrees precisely.

In the evening I listened to a number of audio recordings I made ten years ago. I'd come out to the Sandhills with a rather nice Sony tape recorder and a very expensive microphone. I'd borrowed both items from a BBC radio producer who was keen to make a half-hour documentary on Mari Sandoz with me. I spent some ninety minutes talking with Caroline Sandoz, and taped conversations with a number of academics, as well as Don Cunningham, editor of *Nebraskaland* magazine and an authority on the ecology of the Sandhills. Listening to him yesterday I noted that he spoke of some 700 plant species being found in the area, and it occurred to me to figure out – when I've nothing better to do – how many flowers, grasses and trees I have seen, or at least photographed. My one success yesterday, and it came after I'd flipped through both books several times and done a lot of muttering, was in ascertaining that the sticky little customer I'd come across behind the garage is the aptly named Curlycup Gumweed.

It was a bittersweet business, listening to my ten-year-old recordings. There's some good material there. I have an hour and a half with Helen Stauffer, Mari's biographer, a session with my late visitor Don Green, recorded at the grave-site with a meadowlark providing an atmospheric background, and an impromptu chat with a 90-year-old lady of Czech extraction whose father sent her to Rushville one summer afternoon in 1935 to buy *Old Jules*. He hardly spoke English, but he devoured the book in one weekend. He'd known Mari's father and declared it an accurate and fair record. The bitter part is that the documentary I'd planned never got made. Not for the first time, or the last, I had a producer sold on an idea – only for it to fall foul of the commissioning process.

This time yesterday it was about 84 degrees out there. It's just 70 right now. I shall celebrate by driving to

Gordon and stocking up on groceries.

Wednesday 3 August

Bliss. I woke up at 0615h feeling… cold. It's 59 outside, and I have put a sweater on. I think that's the coolest morning in four or five weeks.

Yesterday I baked. I'm not referring to the weather, rather to affairs in the kitchen. Last weekend, Kitty told me she was going to Chadron and asked whether I wanted her to pick up any groceries. Sure, I said. Bananas. 'How many?' she asked. 'A few,' I said. 'Maybe six.' Next day when I went up to the house she came out with six *bunches* of bananas. 'Well yeah,' she said, 'I did think it seemed a lot – but then I figured it was good that you were eating so much fruit.' I sent home for a recipe, assembled the ingredients, multiplied everything by three, and produced enough banana bread to satisfy my sweet tooth for the next couple of weeks.

Talking of teeth, I lost half an upper left molar yesterday. This was before I even looked at the banana bread. It seems as though another visit to my good friend Gordon Dental is on the cards.

I've now skimmed through just about all the travel journals I brought with me. I've been finding a number of interesting threads, in particular my familial connection with Frederick W Cody, plainsman, scout, Indian fighter and showman, better known as Buffalo Bill, which has been on my mind since I first got to know Nebraska.

I come from good stock. I number amongst my ancestors ship's captains, a Fellow of the Royal Geographical Society, the inventor of the hydraulic lift, a Clerk of Works in St Paul's Cathedral, and a more or less forgotten great-uncle who died in jail in the First World War as a conscientious objector. I mentioned, way back at the beginning, the objects I was familiar with fifty years ago, among them those autographed photos of Annie Oakley and Buffalo Bill, and that I was always led to believe that our great-great uncle, Captain John Wiltshire, captained the *State of Nebraska*, the ship which brought Cody's first Wild West show to the U.K. for a tour that started in April 1887 and lasted right through until the following spring. I even put out a press release to that effect when I set out on my trans-Nebraska bike ride. I was bitterly disappointed when I later read, in the archive of the London *Times*, that the master of the ship was one Captain Braes.

I often muse on the fact that while I call myself a historian, a biographer and so on, I have never had a very good grasp of my own family tree. It is my sister who did all the painstaking work of piecing it together, searching parish records, visiting Somerset House, prowling through old graveyards and calling on total strangers in villages the length and breadth of England as she traced our people back into the early eighteenth century.

I still have little more than a vague outline of all this in my head. I knew from an early age that I had at least one member of the family lost at sea, and I often wonder whether there's a connection to my own deep-seated fear of drowning. My father loved sea travel. He did all his sailing during the war. When I was very young he often talked about the thrill of standing at the stern of his troop-ship as they crossed the Bay of Biscay in a storm, looking up at an angle of 45 degrees (he said) to the prow. But the story I wanted to tell is of my great-grandfather, who married Capt. Wiltshire's sister. When he left home his wife was pregnant with their first child – my grandmother, who would raise me from the age of three until I was ten. Some months later, she was pushing the new baby down the street in the pram when a figure stepped out from behind a hedge, bent over to look at the child, smiled at her and disappeared. It was my great-grandfather. Several weeks later came the news that his ship had gone down with all hands several days out from a New Zealand port. For many years, my father would talk about a letter his mother always treasured. The mother of the cabin boy, who went down with the ship, had written to my great-grandmother telling her what a comfort it was to know that her son served under such a wonderfully kind and decent captain. I never saw that letter. I suspect it went the same way as the autographed photos of Cody and Oakley.

The point of all this is that I have had news from my sister. She has dug up a biography of Annie Oakley, in which she found the following passage:

'Shortly before Christmas, 1893, Annie Oakley and Frank Butler moved into their new house at 304 Grant Avenue [in Nutley, New Jersey].... Less than a week after moving in, the Butlers had dinner guests, an event that was duly noted in the social columns of the local newspapers. Invited were J. M. Brown, manager of the Atlantic Transport Company of New York; Louis E. Cooke of the Barnum and Bailey Show; and a Mr. and Mrs. Cannon of Newark. Mr. Cannon was a noted one-armed sportsman. *Also invited was Captain Wiltshire of the steamship* Mohawk, *which had carried the Wild West home from Europe the year before.*' There: captain. Very satisfying. And no wonder we had that signed photo of Little Miss Sure-

Shot on the mantelpiece when we were young.

My sister adds a poignant note about our great-great grandfather, William Royan, the one who 'appeared' to look at his baby daughter in 1882. Both he and Capt. Wiltshire, his wife's brother, had been raised on sailing-ships. The pair decided they would each make one last voyage under sail and then take lower positions on the 'new fangled' steamships. When he heard that William's ship had gone down, Uncle John bought a house to provide a home for his sister and the new baby, as well as a base for himself when he was ashore.

Friday 5 August

I am starting to become aware of the number of days remaining before I take off for home - it's only 60 - and I am watching my stocks of food. My aim will be to run them down to the point where I don't have to waste anything. There are still two massive turkey legs to deal with, for example. Yesterday I came over all reckless and poured a large pack of pinto beans into a pot. Result? Enough *chile con carne* to provide eight dinners.

Saturday 6 August

I've mentioned, many times, the rough track I have to drive up to get from here to the ranch house. Since the time it got washed away that journey has been a landmark moment of every day, and as the sand settles I count every successful trip as a minor miracle – although it's a lot of fun, bouncing through the soft spots that seem to get a little deeper each time I make the trip.

It's now mid-evening, and dark. I am starving, but do not know what to eat. I mentioned a couple of days ago that half a tooth popped out. The jagged edge of what remains is lacerating the side of my tongue, making eating a very painful business. On Wednesday, when I called my buddy Gordon Dental, I got a recorded message saying the place was closed until Monday. Let's hope I haven't starved to death by then.

To add to my woes, I have just discovered that sandbur season is truly upon us. I have been walking around the house barefoot the last few weeks – and now I'm paying for it. I seem to have carried in a dozen or so on the soles of my sandals and deposited them on the carpet. I suspect it's time to institute the 'no shoes beyond the front door' rule.

Sunday 7 August

It's been a while since I mentioned the condition of the pasture. The warm-season grasses are well and truly established now and all along the trail the sunflowers are in bloom. It makes for a picturesque drive up towards the house every morning. Today it had started out grey and cool, but by the time I made the return journey the skies were clearing rapidly. It occurred to me that I've hardly seen a cow in the last three or four weeks and have no idea where they are. I'm actually expecting Matt to shift some of his herd down this way before long – although the later it happens the better it'll suit me. I suspect that they'll bring a new wave of insects with them when they do appear.

Tonight I watched the last of the DVDs that I collected from Matt's bunkhouse. They're just about all westerns. I have now watched *Lonesome Dove* or its derivatives on eleven successive nights. In my opinion nothing that followed the original got close to it in terms of story, character, acting or dialogue. I guess the producers were milking the cow till it ran dry, and I wish they hadn't. The original epic was a masterpiece, the rest a massive disappointment.

Monday 8 August

I wonder whether this is just a temporary change in the weather, or a more seasonal shift. It got down to 57 degrees this morning, and I awoke at six o'clock feeling so cold that I had to drag a blanket across the bed for the first time since the end of June. Most likely it was the thunderstorm, which hit just about sundown last night, and dragged the temperature down from around 86 to 61 in twenty minutes. It looks as though we may have had something approaching a half inch of rain.

Wednesday 10 August

The little fire on which I cooked my steak is slowly dying. I've just dumped a load of dead sand-burs on it to spread a little smoke around and disperse the insects.

I've had a quiet day, but had an excellent walk over the hills this afternoon. Didn't get very far, but I had a moment of great excitement. I have finally found a genuine ancient artifact, a spear-head in pale yellow stone, its edges clearly worked by human hand. I stumbled across it quite by accident when I was picking my way down a draw that had recently been flushed by rain. It may be a common or garden piece, and it may well have been crafted by an apprentice or a child, but I shall treasure it. Its shape suggests that it dates from the Clovis period and is therefore 10-12,000 years old, information I obtained from a book about the Sandhills that lives down here.

Friday 12 August

There's a tornado watch in effect for our part of the state as I write this but it's calm out there, with a clear blue sky, the sun still plainly visible as it sinks towards the top of the bluffs. I realize that I've never described the bluffs. They overlook this whole curve of the river. In places they are sheer, bare limestone, in others a series of steep slopes covered with cedars or grasses. They always obscure the sun during that last hour or so of daylight.

Yesterday I went to town and had a haircut, spent an hour at the dentist and came out $280 lighter, but an awful lot more comfortable. So I was in a better frame of mind to enjoy the storm, which has almost taken out the road and has finally persuaded me that the day of the vegetable garden has passed. I can't see even the valiant tomatoes recovering from this. We had hail, thunder, torrential rain, high winds, and a temperature drop of thirty degrees. These storms are so dramatic, so unpredictable. I don't want to see anybody, or their property, come to grief, but for purely selfish reasons – namely, a desire to feed my unquenchable appetite for extreme weather - the more the better.

At around midnight, just after I'd fallen asleep, I was awoken by another storm which raged for well over an hour. I was soon re-arranging buckets upstairs and down and pressing my washing-up bowl into service as water splashed into the living room about a foot from where I have my bed. Meanwhile a bat swooped around the house in manic circles, the lightning flashed almost continuously, and the thunder came in a series of bangs that rattled the windows. Fortunately, the electricity supply was uninterrupted. Flicked on and off a few times, but kept going.

By the time I got back to bed it was two thirty, and I was reflecting on a good decision yesterday when I left Mercy at the top of the hill. That trail was rough yesterday; I suspect it will be impassable this morning.

Sunday 14 August

Wednesday night's storm, with the addition of a couple more showers on Thursday and Friday, brought around two and a half inches of rain. I've lost count of the running total, but I would bet that we've had close to an average year's moisture (around eighteen inches) in the four months or so since I arrived. Among the beneficiaries are Kitty's ducks, whose little pond has spilled over onto the track I drive along en route to the house.

I ventured down-river yesterday, on this side. It's the first time I've been that way for three or four weeks, and it was pretty hard going, such is the extent to which the weeds – mostly sunflowers or their relatives - have choked the paths. I had to go slowly and carefully, beating a path with my stick, just in case any stray snakes were lurking. Looking through my books, I see that there are quite a number of plants that grow as tall as the sunflower, and have similar arrangements of yellow petals radiating from the centre, and the differences are fairly subtle to the inexpert eye. There's the blanket-flower, there's Golden Glow, sixteen separate species of the sunflower, and there's the Jerusalem artichoke.

After crashing through the weeds for some way I managed to climb onto higher ground and enjoy the breeze. After the flurry of storms the weather these last couple of days has been gorgeous; bright sun, never too hot, and always cool in the mornings.

I celebrated by cooking a steak over a fire of cedar-wood. After I'd eaten I repeated the dead sand-bur procedure in the hope of smoking oute the insects.

The grasshoppers continue to plague me. When I walk outside now the sound they make as they hop away from me, in droves, is like a heavy rain falling on the ground. I'm not sure what they're doing in the yard, because they seem to have eaten everything worth having, and I have stripped the vegetable plot bare of what little they left. They seem to have entered that decadent phase which, history tells us, ultimately blights all successful societies. I have seen odd ones fighting, even feasting on the dead bodies of their relatives. Mostly they are among the weeds, up in the trees, basking on the newly painted front of the house, or lounging along the hitching-rail, soaking the sunshine into their sleek bodies, and occasionally engaging in acts of procreation, always the smaller of the two crouching on the larger one's back. Meanwhile, their relatives the crickets are infesting the house.

Tuesday 16 August

Crickets, I discover, have more than one way of annoying you. They hide themselves away in dark corners and sing. They gather in the sink, looking like cockroaches, and greet you as you fill the kettle, bleary-eyed, at six o'clock. They creep into bed with you and refuse to lie still. Or they sneak into your scrunched-up plastic laundry bag and spend the whole night scrabbling and fidgeting as they try to find a way out. I had no idea what it was that kept waking me up until five this morning when I got my torch and made a systematic search of the room.

The rain – and the irrigation – has brought on the millet crop under the CPI. I am intrigued. I always thought millet was a broad-leaved plant. Apparently not. It looks like a very vigorous wheat.

Yesterday I turned my attention to the remains of the turkey I inherited back in April. I have made three large hot-pots. A hot-pot is pretty much like a pie but with layers of cooked potato on top rather than a pastry crust. They've turned out well, as has the gallon or so of vegetable and tomato soup I made from the boiled-up carcass. I suspect that a hoarding urge is overtaking me. I checked the contents of the freezer as I packed the soup away, and saw that I have enough prepared meals to feed me on thirty of my remaining fifty days.

Thursday 18 August

I'm spending more time watching the clouds than I have done since I was a ten-year-old boy. For the moment I seem to have time on my hands. I'm writing at a steady pace, I'm not leaving the ranch more than once every eight or nine days, and I expect there's still a little way to go before it cools down appreciably. So I can indulge myself, go up onto the range and watch the storms develop – which they are doing every day just now.

I was around eight or nine when I caught the weather bug. We had the *Daily Telegraph* delivered to the door every morning, and I got used to looking at the front and back pages as my grandmother sat at the breakfast table reading it. I always knew when she was almost through because she'd pour herself a final cup of tea and turn to study the columns of births, marriages and deaths – what she liked to call the 'hatches, matches and dispatches'.

She was always looking for anyone bearing her maiden name, which was an unusual one, Royan. While she studied the back page I now had exposed to me the front, and the only thing of any interest to me there, down in the bottom right-hand corner, was the weather forecast. It took me some time to decode the isobars, cold fronts and warm fronts that patterned the map of the U.K., to understand what high and low pressure meant. I was aided by the gift, one Christmas, of *The Observer's Book of Weather*.

That book was like a bible to me. It explained all the jargon, and how forecasts were arrived at; but most of all it described all kinds of meteorological phenomena. Not just the fog and rain and autumn winds that I was used to, the names of all the different clouds I'd seen, but the extremes I'd heard grown-ups talking about: the legendary snows of 1947 and subsequent summer heat, the Christmas of 1927 when my father splashed his way to church in heavy rain and emerged an hour or two later to find everything white; the appearance of the Northern Lights as far south as Malta in the mid-1930s; week-long fogs that paralyzed London in the `50s, the flash flood that wiped out Lynton and Lynmouth in 1953. Tragic, yes, but to a ten-year-old boy exciting. I longed for excitement. And just once in a while I got it. The great thunderstorm of September 5 1958 that washed away my garden, the severe winter of 1963, colder even than `47 with a snow that came on Boxing Day and lay on our sports field at school until March 13, and one brief, glorious spell of freezing rain. Not quite as dramatic as in Robert Frost's poem 'Birches', but something at least to write in my diary.

So maybe that explains why I am content to stand up

there in the wind for thirty, forty, fifty minutes just watching these wonderful Plains clouds pile up higher and higher. Yesterday they were all to the west, and passing us by, taking their rain and a rumoured tornado into Hooker County, away to the south, but near enough for me to capture a few moments on film as a vigorous up-draught spewed a broiling mass of white into the clear blue sky.

Earlier I'd got out the ladder and tools and completed a little job I'd started on Tuesday, painting the two windows and doorway at the front of the house. I can't claim to have made the neatest job, but I think it's an improvement. There is still work to be done around the attic window, but I am having second thoughts about getting up on that roof. I simply don't like the idea of it, especially with nobody else around.

Sunday 21 August

On Friday I was up on the range, talking on the phone, when a white pick-up came trundling towards me, and stopped fifty yards away. Out leaped a manic golden retriever pup, followed by my neighbor Ken Jackson. He wanted to know (a) was I planning on visiting the Sheridan County Fair on Saturday, and (b) would I like a ride with him? If so, would I get myself to his place at six next morning.

I set the alarm for 0430, got up, dressed, grabbed a flashlight and walked the half mile to the car with thunder rolling around the eastern horizon and large rain drops pitter-pattering into the sand. By six I was at Ken's place, and by seven we were parked in Gordon, standing in line for the Tri-State Cowboys' breakfast and annual get-together.

236

I suppose it was a little ambitious to hope for beans, bacon and coffee served from the beautifully restored chuck-wagon, all spruced up for the parade along Main Street. While I tucked into biscuits and gravy served from hot trays outside the museum, the head honcho made various announcements, and then read a list of names: cowboys who'd ridden into the sunset over the past year. I counted 35, plus 14 cowgirls. They're a dying generation. There was applause for a centenarian, who stood and took a bow, then Ken got up and read a poem that took a swipe at Californians who come north to try the cowboy life – and then attempt to change it. After he'd read he introduced to the crowd some character who'd traveled 5000 miles to be with us in western Nebraska. Yes, take a bow Mister Alan Wilkinson. Then it was time for the Parade, which started under leaden skies – for which I was glad, having left my hat at home.

There was the usual succession of fire-trucks, ambulances, police cars and other chrome-bedecked vehicles, plus the marching bands, and in between each one youngsters scampered across the road to pick up the candies thrown out by the crews. The day went kind pear-shaped after that. I enjoyed a couple of Fat Tires over lunch, then headed for the library. It was closed. So, back to the bar to see if I could catch up with Ken and his family. Nope: they'd gone. But Jerry the brand inspector was there and it seemed only neighborly to buy him a beer – and, later, to accept one in return. By the time I got to the rodeo ground the sun was out, and I was ready for a nap. I still had ten hours to go.

Monday 22 August

I enjoyed the rodeo, as much for what took place in

front of me as for the memories it brought back of my time with the senior pro circuit in Utah and Nevada. I met some great characters down there, ranging from millionaire ranchers to Hollywood stuntmen to a bunch of highway workers on a two-week vacation from Wyoming. There were guys, and women, aged fifty, sixty, seventy and beyond, people who loved rodeo-ing so much they weren't about to give it up just because of what it said on their odometers. 'No rocking-chairs' is their motto. Mostly they were lithe and fit, but what was apparent was that they generally looked more elegant on their horses than afoot; and I got used to shaking hands with guys and finding they had a finger or two missing, due to some roping accident. Some of those people, the ones who could afford to, were on the road almost continuously from April to October, racking up points towards a coveted world championship. Others dropped in and out as they were able. Some were retired, some were young enough to have pre-school children with them. Walking down to the fairgrounds in Wells or Wendover, or Panguitch, Utah, strolling amongst the horse-boxes and trailers, pausing to sit on a hay-bale and chew the fat over a can of beer, was like being in a small town on the edge of town. They were very much a community, and within it they were safe. They embraced many different types of people. There were the churchy ones who invited me to Sunday worship on the bleachers, there were the committed party animals who stayed up late telling stories – and lies - and there were plenty who belonged in both camps. But they all lived by their version of the cowboy code, and on Saturday night in Wells, Nevada, when the rodeo sponsor threw a party and barbecue for them all, well, of course everybody showed up, wives, visiting writers and all, even though it was at Donna's Place, a licensed brothel across the railroad tracks. The only embarrassing part of that episode was when I had to ask the manager of the motel I was staying in how to get there.

I learned a lot about the rodeo that trip: the terminology, the culture, some of the skills and dangers involved. I learned about the rivalry between headers and heelers, heard the jokes about bull-riders and their supposed dumbness, and saw practical, self-reliant people working as a community, engaged in intense rivalry but always willing to applaud a competitor and help him out if needed.

When today's rodeo was through I linked up with Ken and his wife again. They ushered me into the pick-up and set off to visit friends of his, farmers who grow wheat and corn on the better land south of town. We sat and drank beer and ate chips, and after a couple more beers out came the whiskey. I tried to decline; mixing drinks is fatal for me, but of course they were being hospitable and I didn't want to appear unappreciative. They were great company, and very solicitous. 'Hey, that beer of yours is getting warm, lemme fetch you a cold one.' By the time the sun went down and we piled back in the pick-up, I had a serious headache coming on. Not the ideal preparation for an hour of stand-up comedy and a hard-rocking country band. I forget who the singer was, but I remember that he had three names, looked about nineteen, and was blessed with the sort of rich, deep voice which, if you heard it on record, you'd assume belonged to a grizzled fifty-year-old. The girls up front loved him, and he was in his element, signing autographs by the dozen as he sang.

We got back to Ken's place some time after eleven. A huge red half moon was just breaking the eastern horizon. I thanked him for a great day out, pointed Mercy out onto the highway, headed south and took the dirt road back here. Well, almost here, because I'm still not risking the drive down the series of gullies and wash-outs that used to be the road. As I picked my way carefully down the sandy track, flashlight bobbing, I realized my headache had gone. I fell into bed at a little after midnight and slept like a dead man.

Wednesday 24 August

Back in the eighteenth century the French traveler Hector St Jean de Crevecoeur remarked upon the effect of the wilderness on the new breed of American pioneer. 'I must tell you,' he wrote home, 'that it is with men as it is with the plants and animals that grow and live in the plains... their actions are regulated by the wildness of the neighborhood.'

I'll be brutally honest. I wanted to get a feel for the pioneer experience and I'm getting it. These are trying days. It's very hot and there's very little wind. It's sapping my energy, keeping me indoors and making every little job seem like hard work. The most demanding task I undertook yesterday was going round the house killing crickets. Those lucky enough to land in the sink I remove in a cup and throw into the yard. I'm not sure whether that's out of sentiment or a desire to keep the sink clean. But outside the sight of swarms of fat grasshoppers, sunning themselves on the hitching rail, hopping onto my legs and T-shirt as I do my rounds, perching on the trunk of the tree around my thermometer to stare at me every time I check the temperature... it's had an unpleasant effect on me. From time to time I take my stick and see how many I can beat to death before they take flight. And what I don't like is that I'm rather enjoying it.

The temperature did drop substantially overnight. Having reached 99 yesterday afternoon it was down to 55 first thing this morning. But it's climbing rapidly once more.

Some time ago, when A was here, we were surprised to see what we thought were lots of little frogs hopping about in the grass down by Leander Creek. I'm still seeing them, even in the parched vegetation up on the hills; and around the yard here. Yesterday a couple emerged from the remains of my zucchini patch and tried to get in the house. They're tiny toads, barely an inch in length. I presume they eat insects, so I murmur friendly greetings to them.

The hills around here are changing colour. Great swathes of the thinner, sandier land are now full of sunflowers. They're not the eight-foot-high giants you see growing in rows in irrigated fields, or even down here by the river. Most of them are barely a couple of feet tall, many less than half that. I came across quite a few clumps of goldenrod that were similarly stunted.

I've been watching the yucca. We've now reached the time of year when slender curlicues of fibre are unfurling themselves from the viciously sharp leaves, and you can see how the Native peoples got the idea of teasing out the threads and making a coarse cloth. The longer I stay here the more I marvel at the ability of the original inhabitants to survive this - and the many harsher environments further south and west. To have to stalk your prey in this kind of heat, to have to sit motionless

241

with insects buzzing around your head and biting you, to travel any distance without a drink, to confront all the many dangers and discomforts of this land on a daily basis… they must have been hard and stoical people. But I suppose they would have had one great advantage over the pioneers who came out here, namely a wealth of folk knowledge, gleaned over thousands of years, of how to live in this environment, what plants or animals to eat, what ones to avoid, where to find medicinal aids; and of course they would have had a second, inestimable advantage, that they were born here. They knew no other way of living. The temptation for a visitor is to find oneself comparing the place with home rather too often, and feeling the difference.

They're forecasting a little relief today. 90 degrees. I hope they're right.

Thursday 25 August

I was up at the ranch this morning, the dogs had stopped barking and I was busy online when a grader pulled into the yard. Out got a fellow I'll call Clint. Works for the county, looks after 492 miles of highway. 'How d'you mean, you look after it?' I asked him. 'Oh, I dump gravel, and level it, plough snow, that kinda thing.' He'd dropped by to straighten out the road down to the red house, mainly because tomorrow he's bringing the gang to put the new roof on the red house. I'm going to have to straighten a few things out myself – tidy away my clothes, books, papers, clean up the kitchen table – because they'll be sleeping here.

Friday 26 August

Tip of the day: if you fall to your knees – be it in

exhaustion, surrender or prayer – try not to fall on a patch of sand-burs. It was bad enough having to abandon the vehicle in the sand; I could have done without pulling all those nasty little stickers out of my flesh. I got stuck a total of four times, backing up again and again until I could get enough speed to plough through the deep, soft, dry sand to the top. Mercy may have four-wheel drive, but she has highway tyres, and not much tread on any of them. And, yes, I guess I'm not very good at driving off-road.

Still, it gave the roofers a good laugh. They'd arrived early and started ripping the curled-up, weather-beaten shingles off the roof on the south side and replacing them with a layer of tar-paper. The north is sound enough for the sheets of tin to go straight on top. I have to say I am in awe of the way these guys just run up their ladders, step onto the roof and clamber all over it with their shovels, claw hammers and bags of nails. Days like this I'm glad to be what I am. Working up there when it's 93 in the shade, and most likely around 120 in the sun? You can have it. I did a fair amount of outdoor work when I was younger – gardening, shunting trains about, killing vermin, working on building sites - but most of the time the major discomfort was the cold and wet. By far the hottest job I ever had was indoors, melting fifty-six pound blocks of cocoa-butter in vats at a chocolate factory.

So far I've only got half the gang here. The rest will arrive tonight. I've pitched my tent up in the hills, and will retreat at bedtime. All I need to remember is to check it for snakes before I bed down. But before that, I think I am required to drink a bit of beer.

Sunday 28 August

There were some pretty sore heads this morning, and the front yard looked like a frat house on a Sunday morning – littered with crushed beer cans, cigarette packets and the odd shoe. I came down at about six-thirty to find one of the lads shuffling around in his shorts drinking beer, another slumped on the toilet floor, the rest still fast asleep in beds, bunks and chairs. People have lost socks, shoes, one wallet, and several tools. Somebody left the bathroom light on all night and a few thousand insects swarmed in through the screen to die on the counter.

Once they'd shaken off the hangovers, the guys got going and worked right through the heat of the day. With the roof stripped down to bare boards – which are in remarkably good condition – they were soon ready to fit the corrugated sheets of steel. They talk of tin roofs, but it's steel they use, ten-foot lengths of it. One gang measured, marked and cut the appropriate lengths, another was on the roof fixing with power drills, while two other lads ferried the cut sheets to them.

By sundown, the south side was done, and they'd made a start on the north. Matt and Kitty showed up with a tray of steaks, and we all relaxed around a fire.

One of the guys had been up to make a phone call. On the way back he'd killed a porcupine.

'You shoot it?'

'No. Stabbed it with an arrow. It just stood there, so I pulled it out and stabbed it again.' The guy then puffed out his cheeks and exhaled though almost closed lips. 'It kinda went *pawwffff*...' He grinned and said, 'So I stuck it again. Went *pawwffff* again and went down.'

The conversation turned to the prospects for hunting.

'Might go kill us some goats Monday.'

'Goats?' I asked. 'You hunt goats?'

'He means antelope,' somebody said.

'Oh, like pronghorns?'

'That's right.'

Another couple of guys were talking about their weapons, using terms unfamiliar to me, things that had to do with calibre, range, how lethal certain types of ammo are, and how best to adjust your sights.

'Well, we could always go out the prairie dog town.'

'Yeah, that'd be fun. I could shoot them mothers all day long and not get bored.'

I was reminded of a guy I was drinking beer with in the Virginian Hotel, up in Medicine Bow, Wyoming. I remember him pointing across the railroad tracks and saying, 'Well, I need to be up early. Gonna go out and kill a few prairie dogs. That old gun o' mine ain't been shooting straight'

Just then another guy came back from the top. He'd been up making a phone call. They'd found a rattler, four feet long and killed it – more or less. It was in a cooler in the back of the truck, writhing slowly, a deep gash across its body, blood all around it.

'That's some fucker ya got there.'

'Sure is.' He pointed to the rattle. 'Eight beads and a button. Must be four, four and a half years old.' The guy picked it up, one hand towards the tail, the other just behind the head, and stretched it out. 'Got a measure?'

Somebody unclipped a metal tape from his belt.

'Forty-nine inches. Got a knife?'

He cut the snake's head off, inserted the blade under the skin and ran it down towards the tail. 'I'll keep this,' he said. 'Who's gonna eat it?'

'Put her in my truck. There's a cooler in back.'

I admit it, I wasn't comfortable. But later on I thought it over. Number one, these were nice guys. I mean friendly, considerate, welcoming to me, generous. But they seemed to take such relish in killing. So where did that leave me? I eat meat. I inflict death by poisoning on animals that get in my way: rats, mice, insect pests such as roaches, grasshoppers, crickets, ants, wasps. Yesterday I watched a grasshopper that had got too near the area I'd sprayed with insecticide. It staggered, went into reverse, staggered, blundered its way about, was attacked by a fly, twice, staggered some more, and the last I saw of it, it was moving more and more slowly, barely able to support itself on its spastic legs. Took hours to die.

As for the porcupine, if I had one on my land and watched it stripping bark off my broad-leaved trees, would I tolerate it? I remember the time, years ago, when I kept chickens. One Sunday morning I found a cockerel – not one of mine – caught up in a coil of wire outside the coop. I tried to free. It lashed out at me, and got further entangled. I tried again, and soon saw there was no way I could release it. Very well, then, I'd kill it – but what with? I should've had a gun. Instead, I picked up a little hand axe and started flailing about. God knows how many blows I aimed at it, or how many I landed. I know I made a hideous mess of it before it finally died. There was no way I could cook it: it was beaten to a pulp.

So, if we're talking about a killer instinct, what's the difference between what I have done and what they do? I far prefer to eat wild meat, which has to be shot or trapped by someone. And why shouldn't they take pleasure in the skills and knowledge they have acquired, the same as I do in the way I can turn a slab of beef into

246

a *boeuf bourguignon*? Why not take pride in their weaponry, their technique, their equipment?

And what about our basic nature? It's a few generations since we in Britain hunted for our food. These guys have grandparents who would've died without their guns and traps. And if we have a killer instinct – which I have found inside myself - are we to congratulate ourselves that we've overcome it, or do we blame our neuroses on the fact that we've done that? I can't help but ponder the difference between my squeamishness, my professed love of Nature – or natural surroundings – and the way these people relate to their physical environment. I have spent a lot of my life trying to break away from the cerebral and become better acquainted with the elemental world. And here I am, in it.

As I made my way up the dark hillside to my tent I looked up at the stars. There was no moon, and the Milky Way was like a long streak of cloud, stretching from horizon to horizon. How many times have I sworn I'd prefer to die out here, watching that infinity of space, than in a hospital, being fed through a tube? And would an animal, given the choice, rather live out its days on a farm awaiting the truck ride to the slaughter-house, or be shot by a hunter before the wolves get it?

Monday 29 August

Peace has returned to the red house. The roofers have taken off. The old place looks like new, at least from the front. In some ways this whole enterprise has been like an old-fashioned barn-raising. We all know that the material costs of a job like this are only the tip of the iceberg. By my crude reckoning something like 170 man hours went into it. But after Matt and Kitty had shelled out for the roofing material, that's all it cost them. These guys were friends, or friends of friends. They came from all over the state. They included line-men, construction workers, highways guys, one nurse, bound by a common interest: hunting. And that's what they get in return, a chance to kill deer up here when the season comes around.

Tuesday 30 August

It's a cool, clear, quiet morning. At least, that's how it is outside. In here I am plagued by the trilling of the crickets. I see plenty of them on the floors and worktops, and can generally mash them with the fly-swatter. Treading on them is harder: they are pretty agile. But if they decide to start singing their love-songs to each other, they generally find a quiet little spot where they can't be seen. I've had one going at it since six o'clock, and it's now seven. Every time I get anywhere near where it's hiding it stops.

I always thought crickets were supposed to be friendly little things. Didn't Disney create a chirpy little fellow called Jiminy Cricket who sang uplifting songs? Ha! As of yesterday morning, I know the full sordid truth. I was out and about when I came across a dead rat. And there was a little cluster of these things, sucking the juices out of it. Anyway, my familiarity with the breed now tells me that Jiminy was a grasshopper.

Yesterday was a bit of a wash-out. Around noon it started raining, and carried on, more or less, until dark. We had about an inch, which will please Matt. The temperature never got above 74 all morning, and after lunch dropped to 63. For an hour or so it felt like a wet summer's day at home, with the rain falling gently. I even sat outside in my waterproofs for half an hour, savoring it. Then, after a few rumbles of thunder, it came on a bit heavier until, quite suddenly, around seven, the sky started to clear and we had yet another of these wonderful evening skies, a rippled sheet of grey all lit up with red highlights.

Wednesday 31 August

Up at the ranch-house Matt gave me something for the crickets. I sprayed all around the outside of the red house, and inside, along the base of the walls, each room in turn. Then I dismantled the vegetable plot. Rolled up the wire and piled up the posts and poles for firewood. I guess it was worth trying to grow a few things. I did, after all, get to eat some lettuce, a couple of servings of French beans, one or two zucchini and a plate of baby beets. There was a moment, back at the beginning of July, when it seemed I really was going to succeed.

The insect spray seems to have worked. A few odd crickets are still emerging; one or two have chirped, but not for long; and I got an uninterrupted night's sleep. The temperature got up to 89 yesterday, and they're forecasting 95 today, but somehow the heat doesn't seem as oppressive as it was a week or two ago. The mornings are cool, and of course the days are appreciably shorter now.

When I was cutting hay that time...

Thursday 1 September

I finally got back to work yesterday, and sweated horribly while doing so. The temperature had reached 97 by mid-afternoon. I lurked indoors most of the time, just making the one trip up to the house to do my emailing. Up at the center pivot, I noticed, the millet, which was planted around the 12th of July, is forming its seed-heads.

Friday 2 September

Wonderful: a cold morning. Almost nine o'clock and it's cloudy, damp and still only 63 degrees after another brief storm last night. Not much more than a sprinkle of rain but a lot of lightning. I sat outside in the dark and took something in excess of a hundred photographs. I got a couple that weren't bad.

Yesterday I commuted between the garden and the recliner. Outside, I continued to dismantle the vegetable plot, using the excess soil to bank up against the sides of the house so that any rain-water will drain away from the walls rather than into them.

Inside, I listened to some more of the tapes I made ten years ago – no, it was eleven – when I was trying to make that radio program about Mari Sandoz. I dug out the long interview I had with her sister Caroline, who was then ninety years old. We covered a lot of ground. She talked about the 'batteries' of guns that stood at their front door when she was a kid: rifles, shotguns, but no revolvers. She reminded me that not only was hunting a favorite pastime of her father, but that he traded in guns and took them in for repair. The yard outside the orchard place was littered with scrap metal, bits and pieces from his ongoing work. He also fixed clocks and watches, something Mari doesn't mention in her books, as far as I recall. But of course, it's important to remember that Mari left home and got married when Caroline was four.

I talked to Caroline about marriage. Mari, she said, told her that she knew, within two weeks, that she wouldn't stay with Wray Macumber. 'She didn't like being married. Flora got divorced too. I didn't like it either, but I wouldn't let it fail. But then you have to remember that they had no kids. I did – and they were bright, fun.' She added that when Mari won the prize for *Old Jules* in 1935 she wrote to her little sister and told her to get a divorce and she would pay for her to go to college. So was Mari a feminist? 'Yes, she thought men had it way too good in this world. But she was exasperated with women because of their weaknesses.' Marriage, she added, was a practical necessity back then. You had to have a partner to look after the place, and the livestock, with a visit to town taking two or three days. But some old maids managed, and some widows. They'd maybe have an arrangement with a bachelor outfit to look after each other's livestock. It was practical; love had nothing to do with it.

Of her father she had plenty to say. 'He had two

sides. Never learned to curb his temper – but he never had heart trouble either.' She went on to explain that expressing your temper was good for you. The only trouble was that he did it to excess, and damaged his liver. 'He was a very interesting man. Always had something to talk about, and if he didn't he'd go and read his books until he found something.' People, Caroline said, would come to the house and get him talking, knowing that once he started they'd be there for hours, and meanwhile Mother would be preparing the next meal. She was an excellent cook – and of course they were hanging on until the meal was served and they would be invited to eat with the family.

As to Mari's book about their father, 'It wasn't popular around here.' But people bought it, and would hide it under the mattress. They didn't want anyone to know they'd got it. 'It was a dirty book about a dirty old man.'

Again, one needs to be reminded of the age difference between the eldest and the youngest. 'I saw Mari maybe once every two or three years when she came home – and she and Papa would start arguing right away. I really didn't know her till I read her letters [after her death]. Then I knew what she was about.'

I asked her about the time Mari, smarting from yet another rejection of her work, decided to give it all up, and burned seventy short stories in a wash-tub, in the yard of her apartment on 12th Street in Lincoln. She laughed. 'She was so mad she had to do something. She had copies of all those things at publishers. There's only two I didn't find.'

Saturday 3 September

It was a little before five. The wind was strong, gusting and noisy. I'd had very little exercise yesterday, and I was sleeping badly. So I got up, which was no bad thing since I needed to bake bread. It's now seven forty-five, the bread's in the oven and outside it's 43 degrees, but gorgeous: clear blue sky, little wind, the sun climbing above the hills – and a gaggle of young turkeys just strolled into the yard, the first I've seen in a long time.

Today's excitement is the end of season party over at Ken Jackson's place. I believe the trouble starts at two, as Mark Twain might have said. I need to shave, dig out a clean shirt and nip to town to buy some beer.

Monday 5 September

I have no sore head. That's today's good news as far as I'm concerned. I like a drink, but I hate hangovers, so I have become very careful over the years. Mainly, I take great care not to mix my drinks; but I got off to a bad start yesterday. Arrived at the party with a couple of packs of American beer in cans and was pounced on by a young man who wanted to tell me about the cooler full of bottled English ale he'd brewed. So there I was, Mister Cautious, with a glass in each hand, engaged in earnest conversation about the ideal serving temperature for beer in our respective climates.

This guy had gone through college in Fort Collins, graduated with a degree in - well, I forget, but it had nothing at all to do with banking. So of course that's where he ended up – in a bank in Gordon, working for his uncle, who just happens to own the place. Clearly he got lucky. Not once, but twice, because along the way he found himself a charming young wife who hails from the

Ukraine. She works in a nursing home in Gordon where one of her charges is Caroline Sandoz. She insisted that I ought to call in and see her, and I think I will. I can't say that I'll do so without a degree of trepidation, but this is an opportunity not to be missed.

I got to talk to a lot of people at the party, and was surprised at how many I already knew. There was the guy from the body shop down town; his brother, fresh back from Scotland with a flat cap stuck on his head; one of the ranchers I'd been talking to at the State Fair a couple of weeks back, in company with the lady who sells me mouse bait; the gal from the gas station with her husband and baby daughter; the crop farmer from south of Gordon whose place I visited recently. We talked about their lives and travels, about mine, and we strayed into the two areas I was always told to avoid: politics and religion. Now that I'm barely four weeks away from leaving here, I felt free to say how relieved I am – hugely relieved – by the religious skepticism of most of the folk I've met.

As the sun went down the temperature plummeted. One or two g u e s t s started drifting home, and it was soon time to light up the big old stove in the barn where people were starting to gather. By this time I had succumbed – as one always seems to – to Ken's insistence that I try something from his collection of malt whiskies. I've grown very fond of malt in recent years. Well, you fall for a Scottish woman and what do you expect? As I sat and sipped – and sipped some more, and realized that this was going to take some time, it occurred to me that if for some reason I had to buy my host a Christmas present I would get him a measure for his drinks cabinet; maybe one made of some precious metal, that he'd be proud to use. But… good food, good drink, great company – and, as I say, no headache this morning.

Thursday 8 September

'You drive, and I'll tell you where to go.' Kitty's mother, Charlene, had offered to take me to Rapid, but didn't want to drive both ways. She has a large truck with manual transmission and a six-speed gear-box, so it took me a while to get adjusted.

I have a lot of dashing around to do over the next four weeks so I'm renting a car – and Rapid seemed to be the place to get one; that way I can drive myself to the airport on October 5 when I go home.

We went the scenic route, through the Pine Ridge reservation and past the Wounded Knee memorial. I've been that way once before, in `96. I was with a friend, a former news reporter who has none of my reticence, so we parked the car, got out and went to look at the monument, the graves. All I really remember of that brief visit is the contrast between a site which commemorates a landmark event in Native history and, say, any U.S. military cemetery you care to go to. To put it bluntly, Wounded Knee looks shoddy. But then you could say it was a pretty shoddy event that took place there. I couldn't wait to leave.

I got a few more pieces of the red house history jigsaw from Charlene. As far as I could make out, she was saying that pretty soon after Hedvig died in 1941 it was empty, which would tie in with what Frances told me on Memorial Day, about living here for a year or two after her grandmother died. Charlene and Kitty's dad moved in in 1966, and he fixed it up. 'I loved it down

255

there,' Charlene said. 'Would be there now if I'd had my way.' Kitty loved it too, and after they moved out in about '73, every time they drove past the end of the road, Kitty would be bouncing up and down in her seat shouting 'Red house, red house!' It was Charlene who started painting the walls of the garage. 'I'd nearly finished when he decided we were going to move,' she said. 'Now you know why there was that grey patch.'

So, apart from the odd hired man who lodged there during haying or calving, that was it. By Charlene's reckoning the house has been inhabited for no more than twenty-five years or so in its entire life.

I lucked out at the airport. I'd booked the cheapest smallest car that Alamo offer – and got upgraded to a nice, comfortable Ford Focus. Works every time. After a large Mexican lunch I bought some groceries and headed south. At Chadron I had a number of calls to make. First, Lariat Liquor for some beer, then the Bean Broker for coffee and what they call a fruit scone but I call a rock bun. My grandmother used to make them, and this was every bit as good as hers – only twice as big.

From there I headed across to the Olde Main Street Inn where Jeannie's mother pulled out the paper and showed me a story about a certain Yvonne Sandoz from Switzerland who's coming over shortly and will address audiences in Alliance and in Chadron. I booked myself a room there and then for Sunday night.

Friday 9 September

Last night I sat down and wrote a chart, listing my remaining days here and the various things I wish to do, or have to do. I'm going to be busier than of late. Allowing myself a day for cleaning the house and

256

packing, I have 23 days, 13 of which are already earmarked for trips out, or visits.

I've been going back through the interview with Caroline Sandoz again – the one I recorded in 2001. Naturally, I asked her quite a few questions about her father. She didn't need a lot of prompting. She spoke of him as 'very bright, very talented, but quite lazy.' He didn't believe in undertaking physical labour. That was for the lower classes. But he had a talent for picking good workers. He was an excellent linguist. He spoke German as well as his native French; he learned English, she said, in six months. From his vacation work as a postal clerk back home he had a fair knowledge of Spanish and Italian. 'He could swear magnificently,' she told me, 'in five languages.' As for the violence that Mari had suffered, by the time Caroline came along 'he'd simmered down.' He made threats, 'but I knew it was all bluff.'

Caroline remembered going out with her mother to pick cow-chips for the stove – and sneaking off to feast on prickly pear fruit. Mostly, she said, they'd get the chips from around the wells. Back at the place they'd stack them carefully, layering them like shingles so that the rain would run off. She had fond memories of this crude fuel. 'When you burned it, it smelled like hay.'

She spoke of his decision to move to the Sandhills. 'People thought he was crazy. But he was crazy like a fox. He got by in this world, and he got what he wanted.' It was quiet out there; her older brothers and sisters were away at school and Caroline would sit and watch the road to see if anyone came by – and hope they had kids with them. There were no trees at first, so although the wind blew much of the time there was none of that soughing or rustling. And sometimes it didn't blow. One time they had nine calm days in a row, and there was no water for the cattle.

For Caroline, what people tend to overlook when they read *Old Jules* is the role of her mother. 'She was my hero. She was my protector – protected me from myself. The last licking she gave me I was eleven years old.' She laughed. 'It was a double-header. She gave me one and I told her I didn't give a damn, and she gave me another.' Her mother, she added, was much more honest than her father. 'Mother's background was middle class; Papa was a little bit upper class, and he never let her forget it.' She added something that I hadn't realized, that her mother originally came out to an uncle down in Arkansas. It was later that she traveled up to Hay Springs to meet the man who never showed.

I asked her about her father's appearance. What would we have seen had we bumped into him in town? He never used a cane, she said, despite his limp. He used a gun. A rifle in town, a shotgun in the hills. And he wore his tan canvas coat with brown buttons, sometimes an old army coat. He'd visit the barber once a year, for the county fair. And they charged him double: once for the beard, once for the hair. She often wondered what visitors thought about him – like the top officials from Swift of Omaha, the meat packing company, who came out to hunt and stayed at their place.

She spoke of her father's medical knowledge. He'd trained three years to be a doctor, she said, so he knew some basics. Besides, everyone was pretty healthy. Despite their rugged lifestyle, there was only ever one serious accident: one of her brothers came off a sled and broke his collar-bone. The doctor came out on his old grey horse. They had a balanced diet, with plenty of fruit and vegetables to go with the meat. 'Papa was a good shot and Mama was a very good cook, so we ate well. And Grandpa had been a veterinarian, so we butchered our own animals.' It wasn't considered right for a girl to witness that, but she saw plenty, 'looking through the knot-hole in the corral.' Jules encouraged others to live the way they did. 'We'd have wagon loads of carrots and onions. He gave people raspberry, gooseberry plants or slips. He wanted them to grow things.'

In sum, Caroline painted a different picture from the one we get in her sister's book. But then she was talking about an older man, an older wife, and more settled times. Mari got the full force of her father's rage, and perhaps of her mother's bitterness; she got successive babies dumped on her bed when they were two weeks old, to feed, clean, dress, love and discipline while her mother resumed work in the fields. Caroline has happier memories – of the treats that would always be included in any order from the store. 'We'd get a hundred-pound sack of "nigger-toes" – Brazil nuts.' And she talked of the fun they had. 'We always got the board games out after supper, and we all joined in – except Mother, darning socks.' For years Papa played pinochle. 'He'd get very excited... he'd pound the table.' But of course, by this time Mari was in Lincoln.

Caroline took pains to emphasise that her father had made a success of his life. 'He came out [in `84] with nothing.' And here they were, with land, a farm, a store, and modern conveniences: a travelling cinema that would set up in the barn; a telephone, albeit one strung along the top of the fence-posts that anybody could listen in on – so long as the cows hadn't chewed on the wire. 'I got a lot of entertainment from the phone. I was eight years old and had to sell things in the store while the others were out in the fields. As soon as it rang I listened. Learned a lot of stuff. Five rings meant anybody could listen.' And they listened to everything. 'Papa talked French on the phone so he couldn't be understood. But when some of the neighbors talked Bohemian he'd get mad.'

Life for Caroline was much more social than it had been for Mari in the early days. They had regular dances in the barn. 'Papa couldn't dance, but all of us did. Mama was an excellent dancer. Some of the settlers made a living out of playing. Papa would have a collection for them at midnight and if there wasn't enough he'd top it up out of the store.' Caroline married a man who never danced, 'but he took me anyway. You always had the first and last dance with your partner – so he'd take a friend for me. I had fun.'

Saturday 10 September

You're all alone, it's two in the morning, a full moon is illuminating the elk's head on the wall, and the house is echoing, periodically, to a metallic clattering, with occasionally scrabbling thrown in. I don't mind admitting it: I was rattled. I tried burying my head under the blanket, tried getting up and hunting around with a flashlight. Nothing. Everything was still. Except that as soon as I'd got off to sleep it started up again. I think it was at the fourth attempt that I figured out what had happened. A mouse had got its tail caught and was frantically dashing around the kitchen, dragging a trap behind it, trying to take cover under the refrigerator, the

260

stove, the cabinet beside the sink – all the noisy things. Every time it dived towards the gap, the trap whacked against the fridge/stove/cabinet and held it back. I let it go – not out of compassion, rather for the sake of some peace and quiet – but still have half the tail as a trophy.

Yesterday I planned to paint the windows, but when I was up by the ranch house Matt phoned me. 'Since you're up here,' he said, 'I got a little job you might like.'

It wasn't a job. It was cutting hay, and it was fun, fun, fun – once I'd got the hang of driving the big yellow machine. Then I was off around that center pivot, laying waste to the millet while Matt started up a second machine. When you see these things from a distance, creeping around a field, it all looks so peaceful. They seem to make steady, effortless progress in beautifully straight lines, puttering along over a surface as true as a billiard-table. I had no idea how bumpy that field was, how much it rose and fell, nor how the machine would buck and sway as I wrestled with the steering-wheel and tried to get the broadest swathe possible with the fourteen-foot cutter. In places I was making an eight-foot cut, in others thirteen, but I did, eventually, get them a little more even. It's another of those 'not as easy as it looks' jobs. When Matt told me to hold my speed at about 5.5 mph I thought he was erring on the side of caution, but as I gripped the wheel with whitened knuckles on my first circuit I stole a glance at the speedo: 3.6. I slowly settled into a rhythm, making long semi-circular sweeps, first clockwise, then anti-clockwise, scaring up a couple of rabbits, a lot of birds and a solitary fawn.

We did half the circle between us. Matt's playing safe, leaving the second half until he's got the first lot ripened and baled – just in case the weather changes; so I should, in a few days' time, get to play again. It depends on my schedule, which is suddenly looking rather crowded.

Out on the range, the fall colors are starting to take over as the bunch-grass ripens a pinkish-brown, reminding me that I'll soon be on my way. September always makes me thoughtful. Even after 45 years I associate it with packing my trunk and going back to boarding-school. I am longing to be home, but I'm going to miss this horribly. And the more the weather settles into this glorious late summer groove, the harder it's going to be to take off.

Sunday 11 September

I was in Gordon yesterday, for their annual Willow Tree Festival. I went for the music. There was an Irish folk band, bluegrass, a singer-songwriter with guitar, and a pianist. This guy particularly intrigued me. He lives at Cody, a little place not much bigger than Merriman. I believe it has 149 inhabitants. He has a degree in Maths, he's a welder, and he played everything from a Chopin Polonaise through Elton John to an arrangement of a Metallica number. If I needed it, here was a further reminder that you should never, ever, dismiss a place as too small, too ugly, too drab to be of any interest. I'm not saying that Cody is any of those things, just that as you whizz along Highway 20 it would be easy to assume that there's nothing there. Back to what most Americans have told me over the years about the entire state of Nebraska. Flat, dusty, empty. It's simple laziness. Stop anywhere and engage with people and you will find gems. Sometimes it requires courage, sometimes persistence; and yes, sometimes the well is dry and you move on rather than drill another one. When I was at that party the other night an elderly rancher, in jeans and boots, with calloused hands, remarked in passing that he'd taken his degree at Yale, and then carried on with whatever he was saying before I could ask for more.

Among a number of familiar faces at the Festival I bumped into one of the people I'd met at Ken Jackson's last week, a lady who knows Caroline Sandoz and has agreed to accompany me if I go calling. The fact is, I am nervous about breezing in on someone I haven't seen for eleven years and whose memory, I am told, is gone.

Before I left town I called in at the hardware place and bought some grass-seed. Back here I took out the pitch-fork, scratched the newly-laid soil around the house, and sowed it. It's an annual mix which, I am assured, ought to germinate before the frosts come. I watered it well afterwards and will hope for the best.

Tomorrow, if things go to plan, I shall prepare these windows for painting. But that's asking a lot. It's been a while since anything went to plan.

Monday 12 September

The best place to be on a day like yesterday is down where the tall trees keep the sun off you and cool water runs over the rocks. Somewhere like Champagne Creek, for example. I went down there in a hopeful frame of mind. Packed a plastic tub and religiously checked out all the vines I'd seen earlier in the season. But if there were any grapes, the birds have had them. It wasn't a hopeless quest: two years ago A and I canoed the river a little lower down, below Valentine, and helped ourselves to great fistfuls of ripe sweet fruit – and some delicious wild plums. Luck of the draw, I guess.

Down at the river I took off my boots and spent a pleasant twenty minutes cooling off. As ever I got involved with moving sand to re-arrange the course of the little creek. I guess I really am ready to be a grandfather. By the time I get home I'll have three weeks to wait for the arrival of my daughter's baby – plus a year or two until it's old enough to help.

On the way back up I spent some time sitting and listening to the sounds in the valley. I had my eyes closed when it occurred to me that there's a substantial and noticeable difference between the gentle rushing noise the wind makes in the top of the pines compared to the rustling that underlies the sound as it blows through, say, the cottonwoods. Walking down there, hearing that sound and smelling the distinctive piney scent, gives me the distinct feeling of being some place that isn't the Sandhills. It reminded me of places further west, of very different experiences I've had in New Mexico, Colorado and Arizona.

Noticing those very different sounds, against a background noise of the creek cascading over the several falls, reminded me that it was only a few years ago that I realized how varied are the individual sounds that make up what we hear as a river flows past. We were sleeping out under the trees beside a tiny beck on the North York Moors, and as dawn broke I became aware that my ears had started to differentiate a number of separate 'plinks' and 'glops' and gurgles and splashes as the water ran over stones of different sizes. At a casual hearing it's simply generic 'river noise'; listen carefully and you can hear the individual instruments that create the symphony.

Today I'm heading for Ainsworth. I've been invited

to take a short trip with a couple of members of the Arent family who visited the red house on Memorial Day.

Wednesday 14 September

It's gloomy out there: cloudy, grey and 46 degrees – a chill reminder of what I face when I fly home in three weeks. Not that I don't like winter. I enjoy the four seasons; it's just that some years we only seem to get three, none of which could really be called summer.

I'm staying at the house of Keevin and Dottie Arent, a couple of miles south of Ainsworth (pop. around 1800). Keevin is the son of Phillip, the youngest of the eight Arent children who grew up in the red house, the only one to be born there. He bought a ranch up near Johnstown in 1936 and ran it for 37 years. Keevin has pulled out a copy of an article published some years ago that relates the details of a horrific multiple murder that took place in 1952 not a hop, skip and jump away from the red house. I'd heard mention of Blaine Ellis, and the incident at what was the Mensinger ranch, right beside Highway 61 on the river crossing, but until now didn't know the details. It seems to have stemmed from a falling-out over an argument in a bar which developed into a fist fight. Weeks after the event Ellis showed up at the place and shot dead his former friend George, and his wife Alleen, who was Keevin's cousin. Then, on the run, he killed another rancher before a posse of neighbors gunned him down. According to the newspaper report they fired a thousand shots at their quarry. The article Keevin showed me was written by Frances Walton, who had been a friend of Ellis and wrote that she had always found him kind and good-humored. She lodged with his family while she was in high school.

Thursday 15 September

Back at the red house, and it feels as if I'm back home, although even the north-east of England doesn't get it this bad in mid-September: 43 degrees and raining steadily. I've had to fish out the moleskins, turn on the heating, and then dance a jig of joy: there are no bugs in here, nor at the windows, nor at the screen door.

Keevin and Dottie looked after me as if they'd known me all their lives, and sent me home with a box of home-grown tomatoes and pears. Yesterday they pulled out a tape recording that Aunt Astrid made in 1966. She was the second oldest of the Arent children who grew up down here. The tape has corrected a few misunderstandings, although I'm still not a hundred per cent sure it answers all my questions about the history of this place. One thing that came up, which I don't think I'd registered previously, is that Holger Arent, Keevin's grandfather, was never fully fit. He'd lost the use of a lung after a bout of pneumonia, so he probably did well to survive some twenty Sandhills winters and live to the age of 59. Astrid was the second of the eight children who were, with one exception, born at two-yearly intervals. She came along in 1892, and would have had memories of the Omaha years, although on the tape she says nothing about those times other than referring to the fact that her father made furniture there for the family.

Astrid came out with her mother and five siblings in 1901. They were met at Merriman by her mother's brother Uncle Julius, who piled them onto his horse-drawn lumber wagon and took them south. Their father stayed in Omaha to try and rustle up some more cash. It took them two days, she said, to get to Grandma's sodhouse, which was down on the Snake river. The place had two rooms, one serving as a kitchen-diner-living-space, the other as a bedroom. Grandma, Astrid says, had come out to keep house for Julius. Her other son Peter was homesteading nearby but was married. She returned at least twice to Denmark, even though she had staked her own claim. Astrid doesn't say why.

That first winter was 'rough', but none of the family got ill, nor even had colds as far as Astrid remembers. If anyone did get sick locally, they would be looked after by Aunt Emilia, Peter's wife, who had worked as a nurse in the old country. The family were getting all their water from the windmill that fed the cattle tank, so presumably that would have been clean, and for a toilet they used 'the great outdoors'. They had some chickens, but lost several to a badger which Mother had to kill with a hand-axe. In summer they went barefoot and were always pulling prickly-pear spines out of their feet. They were out a lot. Julius had loaned them a pair of cows which in the summer took to the river-bank to brush the flies off themselves on the shrubs that grew down there. The kids had to go down to round them up, but it wasn't easy: they couldn't see above the tall reeds and willows.

The family lived on Grandma's place for three years. Herman was born there in 1902. By that time five of the children were ready for school. Past ready. As Astrid remarked, they hadn't seen a school or a church in all the time they'd been out there. So they moved with their one horse to Harlan, about ten miles up-river from the red house, where there was a post office and a schoolhouse nearby. Home was a one-room sodhouse; one end served as kitchen-diner, the other end for sleeping. This had been the home of the Lyons family, Hester and Jim, affectionately known as aunt and uncle but not actual relations. 'Uncle' Jim loaned them a second horse and a wagon, which made life a lot easier. Astrid says that when Keevin's father, Phillip, was born Aunt Hester took the other kids in for Christmas. She remembers her delight at the presents she received: pencils, paper, the first ribbons she'd ever had, and apples and popcorn, quite a thrill after their daily diet of potato and corn-mush.

After nine months, some time in 1904, they finally moved to their own homestead, here where I am staying. Astrid spoke of the difficulties of crossing the river, down near the present highway bridge: the steep hill they had to descend, and the climb up the other side. The river was shallow, but the current strong, and it would soon whisk you away if you weren't careful. Some time later they saw their first car on that hill – pioneers heading for the Black Hills. Her father towed them up it with his team, but the settlers 'didn't offer him a cent.' It was many years, she said, before they could afford a Model T and enjoy pushing that up the hill. Keevin told me that it was common practice to go up backwards. There was no fuel-pump, and the steep incline starved the engine of fuel if you tried it nose-first. They had to learn to deal with the sand, letting the air out of the tyres to get more traction. It worked, so long as you remembered to pack a bicycle-pump in the car.

Friday 16 September

I barely set foot outside yesterday. The temperature

hovered around the 44 mark all day and it rained more or less non-stop. Today has started out grey, cold and damp.

Still, it wasn't all bad. I needed some time to decipher and write up the notes I took on my trip to Ainsworth. I see that I forgot to mention that the murdered Alleen Mensinger was the daughter of Keevin's uncle, Lloyd 'Skinny' Jones. The family were called Johansen, and came from Norway, but their name was amended to Jones upon arrival in the U.S., or soon after. Keevin attended the funerals, which, he recalls, took place on a bitterly cold March day. The road to the cemetery at Ainsworth was covered with ice, and he remembers his mother anxiously gripping the seat as the driver of the car sped along. He seemed in a hurry, as did the undertaker. It turned out that they had another funeral the same day and were anxious not to be late. The murdered couple's child, he told me, was taken to Idaho and raised there.

There are a few more loose ends to clear up from Astrid's tape. Helga, the eldest of the Arent children, died in childbirth in her twenties. Her husband took the baby, Clydie, to Illinois, and started a new life. Martin never married, and is the only one of the offspring to be buried up at the cemetery here, having barely outlived his mother. Astrid also mentioned her mother having a breakdown and spending a full year in a sanatorium. The children, she said, were sent to an aunt; I am not sure that she said which one. She was living by a lake which was, if I heard correctly, her source of drinking water; either that or the children drank from it, the result being that Astrid got typhoid fever.

At some stage Uncle Julius and Aunt Kristina left the

area and moved to Florida, buying an orange grove. Every Christmas a crate of citrus fruits would arrive at the depot in Merriman. Uncle Pete and Aunt Emelia also moved, to California.

Astrid's tape is full of interesting details, but of course it raises almost as many questions as it answers. That's so often the way when people reminisce. She wasn't being interviewed: she sounded very much as though she were reading from a script she had put together, so nobody interrupted and asked her to expand, and she glossed over a number of interesting points. That's the nature of research: you're glad to find new pieces of the jigsaw, but you're often left to make the best sense you can of them.

Astrid did mention that she attended the Center schoolhouse, which stood by the cemetery here, through 6th grade, before going on to Merriman. Her three sisters, she said, all became teachers. Her reference to the schoolhouse reminded me that I've never recorded the story Kitty's father told me when I bumped into him up there one day. I may not have got this entirely correct, but the bare bones are that after it had stood empty for some years he bought the old place for $50, thinking to haul it to his ranch as a barn or workshop. But he couldn't move it, and after several tries was happy to trade it to a neighbor in exchange for a used dish-washer. This guy couldn't shift it either, so he persuaded a third party to take it off his hands for a few bales of hay. He thought he'd got a good deal – and so did Kitty's dad. The house stayed where it was, and they kept grinning smugly to themselves until a snow came – whereupon it disappeared overnight. The fellow had put skids under it and dragged it away to his place where it now serves as a hay-barn. While Kitty's dad was telling me that story, he glanced across at the cemetery and said, 'I've got my plot reserved. Cost me five dollars.'

Saturday 17 September

I had today all planned out: I would take a walk along Leander Creek to where it joins the Niobrara. But I awoke to grey skies, wind, and talk of rain on the radio. It was midday before it brightened up, so I put my boots on and set off across the hills. I was out for two hours, maybe more, but never got further than a mile or so from base. Having spent most of my life – certainly most of my hiking life - focused on a distant objective and always watching the time, I am finally getting the hang of wandering aimlessly, with no thought of getting anywhere. Perhaps one needs to learn such skills as one gets older.

I scratched around in what I thought were likely spots for ancient artifacts – high spots where the sand has been exposed and washed downhill. I found a few pieces of rock that bore signs of having been worked, and several pieces of fossilized bone, but nothing worth taking home. I came across a few prickly-pears bearing fruit. I'm very fond of the taste of the *tunas*, but was disappointed to find most of them small, damaged and seedy.

As I walked home I started to feel a little wistful. I have got used to wandering freely out here, undisturbed by other people, by noxious fumes or the distant noise of traffic; I'm going to miss that, and these great expanses of sky, mostly blue. I can find many of these freedoms at home, but they generally require planning, preparation, a car journey – and waterproof clothing.

I had some good news today from Rick Otto, the

271

superintendent at the Ashfall Fossil Beds, out near Ainsworth. I visited there when I was with Keevin and Dottie the other day and mentioned to him the fossilized bone that Phil found back in May. He suggested I send him a photo. 'It appears,' he writes, 'to be the lower portion of a shoulder-blade from an elephant. Considering the location it is probably from a gomphothere, one of the four-tuskers that are commonly found in Ogallala Formation sediment. A rough estimate on age would be 8 to 14 million years old.'

Monday 19 September

I am forced to conclude that if things went to plan life would be a dull old business. Originally I was coming to Chadron to hear Yvonne Sandoz' talk. Then I heard that it had been shifted to Crawford, 25 miles further west. Crawford doesn't look like much at all from the highway, nor indeed from the main drag, Wagon Wheel Road, but it has a beautiful city park with mature shade trees, well-watered grass, a fountain and the usual picnic tables. I've spent many a relaxed lunch-hour in such places, and camped in plenty of them; they are the great uncelebrated facility available to all travelers through the smalltown West.

I brewed up coffee on my spirit stove, sat and drank it in glorious late summer sunshine, then went to the meeting place to be greeted immediately by Yvonne, who introduced me to her cousin Joy, sitting alongside her. In profile she is the spit and image of Mari.

Yvonne's talk was interesting enough, but the important news from my point of view was that she was taking off directly to her cousin's place for two nights and would be repeating her talk in Chadron library on

Tuesday – so (a) my talk with her will have to wait, and (b) I needn't have dashed out there after all. I suspect that what's happening is that she's getting new invitations all the time and, because this is a vacation from her work as archivist to the city of Basel, and time is tight, she's going with the flow. She agreed that we would catch up on Tuesday night at Jeannie's place.

That means two more nights at the Olde Main, which is an unexpected expense but no hardship. One keeps such good company there. I have been given one of the suites on the third floor. Last night I slept like a dead man. But all that came after a bit of a detour. I arrived at the hotel to find Jeannie out, and I couldn't get her on the phone. That was when I hit on the idea of looking for Ed Hughes, *aka* the writer Poe Ballantine, who lives around the corner facing the railroad tracks. On the back of having to re-schedule half of this week and feeling somewhat rattled, I spent a delightful hour or so drinking his beer and chewing the fat about writing, writers, the literary establishment (we're agin `em) and certain other orthodoxies. Not only can this guy write – like Bukowski without the venom - but he's scrabbled a living as a cook, kitchen hand, handyman and so on in the back alleys of urban life; and so he speaks with the wisdom and understanding that an astute observer will gather along such a road. We seem to have a number of things in common.

Tuesday 20 September

Yesterday felt like a vacation day. It kicked off with tea and cinnamon rolls in the bar here, after which I strolled round to the Bean Broker where I had a meeting with Bob 'Badger' Buckley who had driven over from

Crawford to get his car fixed. He's another remarkable individual who has more or less made his living as a trapper, hunter and guide and can turn his hand to certain traditional crafts like flint-knapping, tanning (with brains, the Native way) and working in hides. He attends rendezvous around the region to trade, and sell his wares. I remember that some years ago when I traveled the Lewis & Clark Trail, from St Louis to Astoria, I met a number of 'mountain men' (re-enactors, that is) who made that their full-time occupation. I was meeting Bob to buy some moccasins to take home, but our meeting turned into an hour-long discussion – which is one of the pleasures, as I've said before, of smalltown life, and another reminder that these places are never what they appear to be on the surface. The longer you hang around the more you discover.

Jeannie's mother, Evva, is still in town; she spends the summers here and her winters in California, not far from Palm Springs. I was chatting with her yesterday afternoon, when two bikers arrived at the hotel. One of them had worked behind the bar for Evva when he was in college, forty years ago. Far from expecting to find his former boss at the bar drinking beer with a Limey, he admitted that he'd expected to find she had passed on – but at 85 or thereabouts she's certainly alive and kicking. The visit prompted Evva to dig out some old newspaper cuttings from the 1960s and '70s, including an advertisement for her latest innovation at the time, a go-go dancer – and an article about the public debate it stirred up.

The visitor reminisced for some time, on a variety of matters; what stuck in my mind was his recollection that Native visitors to town always felt safe at the Olde Main, and were well treated. He recalled that people would come in by truck on a Friday night to drink and party, but would generally sleep on the streets. More than once, when he was serving at the bar, somebody handed him a bundle of cash and ask him to look after it, lest he lose the week's wages in some drunken card game.

We were joined later by three bikers from Omaha and Lincoln – lawyers on a trip towards the Black Hills and the Devil's Tower, up in Wyoming. I think a writer could hang out at Jeannie's, never go anywhere else in town, and gather all kinds of material. It's an attractive prospect.

I am now ensconced in the Sandoz Center looking through the archived collection, and have just found Mari's death certificate. She departed this life at 3.05 pm on 10 March 1966. Tonight I will hear again Yvonne's talk at the public library, and with luck collar her for an hour or so in the Olde Main bar.

Wednesday 21 September

I've done it again: set out with a plan and watched it go up in smoke, simply because I will get talking to people. This morning it was Badger Buckley telling me about his background in martial arts, learning Japanese, and German and French, and travelling to Okinawa, and growing organic vegetables, and grapes, and making wine out at Crawford... and slipping me an ancient spear-point as a parting gift, along with the finished moccasins.

Later, over my hot tea, it was Yvonne Sandoz, clearly exhausted with all the jawing she's done over the past two weeks or so – not to mention shooting prairie dogs from the cab of a pick-up yesterday. Old Hector St Jean de Crevecoeur was dead right: take a mild-mannered, civilized European, stick 'er out on the Plains for a week or two, and what does she turn into? A killer. D.H. Lawrence made a similar observation, I seem to recall.

Friday 23 September

I'm writing this on Thursday evening as I wait for the spasms of cramp in my legs to calm down. It's my own fault, I suppose: I haven't done anything like as much walking as I'd like to the last few months, and I sort of rushed things today. There has always been a problem with going down Leander Creek. Nobody has been willing to go out on a limb and say how far it is to the confluence with the Niobrara. Unsurprising, really: I haven't met anybody who's done it on foot.

I wanted to set off early, and I managed that – even though I had to drive the first 3-400 yards with my head sticking out of the side window until I could get Mercy pointed at the sun and melt the frost off the windscreen. Up at the ranch I transferred to the hire car and drove out to the highway. I parked just short of the bridge that crosses the creek and was over the fence and on my way by 0800h. It was a simply perfect morning for hiking: a cloudless sky, no wind, and the temperature climbing through the 40s.

I was carrying a pack loaded with a gallon of water, a dry lunch, one of Matt's ready to eat Army meals, and my mug, coffee and trusty methylated spirit stove, 34 years old and going strong. Most people I've spoken to have said I should walk along the creek-bed – and then corrected themselves: they've never seen water in it this time of year before. I tried to follow the margins, but it turned out to be a little like the river up here: meandering, and flanked by draws with steep sides and dense tree cover. So I was forced ever further away from the water. Not that I minded: this was a beautiful walk, and I was enjoying it. I was stopped in my tracks twice: once by a snake, a harmless-looking thing, smooth and slender, with red streaks along its body. The second incident, however, had me quite excited. A sort of fawn-colored creature, quite a bit larger than a coyote, with a longer body, shorter hair and longer legs – shorter ears too - was walking along a low ridge about a hundred yards in front of me. It was only visible for about four or five seconds. It looked slightly menacing, so I called out to it, whereupon it slipped down the far side. I am trying to convince myself that it was a mountain lion, but the fact is my sighting was so brief that I can't be sure.

I was walking fast, but was still surprised when, after only two hours, I got to a point where I could actually see my destination about a mile away, the Niobrara just visible through the trees, the sunlight reflected off its rippling waters. I sat against a stout ponderosa pine and ate lunch, taking in the view. Then I dropped down to the flat delta of land that divided the two waterways, wading through thick growths of dead sunflowers and pig-weed, seven and eight feet tall.

I'd been told that there was an old settlement down there, and I soon found it, across the creek – a substantial but derelict barn and a log house. I'd heard Matt say it ought to be rescued, but one look told me it was beyond that. The logs were square and grey and starting to rot, and the chinking had crumbled. The roof would have been sound up to a few years ago by the look of it, but is missing quite a few shingles now. Inside there was an old bedstead with a torn-up mattress on it, in the kitchen an old forties-style fridge and beside it an enameled stove. On the wall hung a sieve, a frying-pan and a potato-masher. One or two of the windows still had glass in, but it would take a real enthusiast with money to burn to make the place right. At least most of it will return to the earth and nourish a later generation of plants and animals.

From there I walked on down to the flat V of land where the sparkling watercourses actually met. I brewed up some coffee and sat, basking in the noonday sun. Whoever had built that old cabin must have felt he'd found a little piece of heaven: a stretch of bottom land that grew sunflowers eight feet tall, plenty of timber, abundant water, good grazing. Just the problem of access. As far as I could see there was no easy way in, or out.

Rather than return the way I'd come – up down up down up, the scenic route – I sought out a two-track about half a mile further away from the creek. It made the route easier to follow, but I hadn't taken into account the heat, nor the fact that there wasn't a scrap of shade I might rest under; so, seven miles non-stop on loose sand. I was trudging along like some old hobo well before the highway came into view.

Saturday 24 September

I've just got back from Valentine, and the land registry, looking for a bit more information on the red house. The lady in the Deeds Office, Debbie, put herself at my disposal and spent the better part of two hours, either side of her lunchtime, pulling down huge ledgers containing records of land ownership and transactions. I gathered fragments of information, as I've been doing

278

for almost six months now. The first record pertaining to this piece of land that the red house sits on describes it as, 'the West half of the South Half of Section 34 [i.e., a quarter section, or 160 acres] in Township 33 North of Range 38 West of the Sixth Principal Meridian, Nebraska', and notes Holger Arent's receipt of his patent on 5 June 1911. As I understand the homestead laws, that would normally be available five years after the original claim was registered, and required proof of residence on the plot and improvements to it. On 4 September 1913, Holger received patent on a further 466.56 acres, so it's a fair assumption that he made a claim under the Kinkaid Act (1904), which allowed a total of 640 acres in these dry, western counties. I suspect that the odd figure involved has to do with it being river-side land.

It seems that Helga, the Arents' eldest child, also made a claim. She died in childbirth, in her twenties, which would explain the record I saw of her land being assigned to her heirs on 21 March 1916. As to Hedvig's brothers, the Petersens, who had come out here as early as the 1890s, their land was indeed along the Snake river. I saw no record of their acquisition, but there is a deed whereby Julius and his wife Kristina sold various parcels down there to a Carl Jorgensen. The contract was made in June 1914, the deed exchanged in October 1916. Presumably this was when they moved to Florida. The sum involved was $13,568. As to Peter, he and his wife Emilia sold two 40-acre parcels of land to a Hans Jensen in 1910 for $1920 - and again, that would likely be when they moved on, to California.

In 1948 five of the six surviving Arent offspring – Herman (and Effie, his wife), Phillip (and Louise, his wife), Otto, Margaret (now married to James Herrington) and Anna (married to Harley Collins) signed a document granting the tenancy of this place to Phil and Dorothy Wright. Helga and Martin were both dead by this time; Astrid was still alive, and, I believe, married to Hans Gammel, but was not a signatory. Ultimately, the land would pass to the current owner, Kitty's dad, in 1961. So far I have found out nothing about the Wrights.

In addition to all this I gleaned a couple of other scraps of information which interested me. Some time ago, when A and I hiked down to the place where the wagon train was burned by the Cavalry, I mentioned the old wooden home we came across, known locally as the Thayer place. The records show his full name as Alvin R Thayer. I also found the name of a settler on the plot where I saw the log house down on Leander Creek, James J Goodfellow – although I have since found a record of a Mrs Nicholls who lived down there. Perhaps the one followed the other. Finally, on the audio tape recorded by Astrid Arent, she spoke of the family staying with the Lyons for a few months before they finally came here in 1904. Lyons' place was in Lavaca Township, about eight or ten miles up-river from here, one mile north of the Harlan school and post office. Does this get me anywhere? Not really, but there's a satisfaction in seeing those names, and a pleasure in emailing the Arents to tell them what I've discovered. Some of these place-names, like Harlan, really did refer to nothing more than a post office, which in turn was named after the post-master. Old Jules was always keen to have a post office. He had three, I recall, and lost them all, such was his penchant for falling out with people. But so long as he had them his neighbors for miles around would have to call at his place for their mail, which would be addressed to the sender at Sandoz, Cherry County.

Sunday 25 September

Yesterday was a leisurely day. In the morning I spent a full hour up by the ranch listening to soccer commentary from home and even received a half-time text from a friend who was at the game I was listening to. People love to complain about modern technology; on days like today I love it. In the afternoon I wrote, and in the evening I went out and sat on a hilltop to watch the sun highlight the yellowing leaves and the pink of the bunch-grass before it slipped below the sharp outline of the distant hills.

Back home I looked through the photo-copies of documents that I took in the Sandoz archive. I suppose if I was looking for anything it was for a few more clues about Mari's character and personality. I knew, for example, that she was known to have a passing interest in aspects of spiritualism. And I came across some evidence, although nothing more than the superstitions of a woman who was desperate to be reassured that she was going to make it as a writer, sometime – and that, having made the breakthrough, she would continue to succeed. There were wish-lists, generally to do with her attempts to sell a piece of work, and sheets of paper on which she'd spelled out a title or a publisher's name in capitals, allotting each letter a number according to its place in the alphabet. It's a form of numerology, I suppose. M, for example, would be 13, and 1+3 would make 4, and she would add the numbers up to see what single digit she arrived at and, presumably, deduce the likely outcome. There was a letter from a graphologist, analyzing her handwriting and homing in on her 'practical mind and very strong will'. There is also evidence that she used playing cards to seek portents. Against the title of her story 'Foal of Heaven', which was out at *Harpers*, was the verdict 'improbable'; she had only drawn '2 aces in first 13 cards'.

I don't think there is any great significance in all this. If there was a secret to Mari's success it had nothing to do with such attempts to see into the future. It was simply the dedication, diligence and determination that saw her through her twenties and early thirties, and her willingness to shut out the world when she needed to – even if it meant pinning a very blunt note on her door to keep visitors away. 'Busy till July 1' read one of her hand-written cards. Later in life, as her health gave way, that red-hot determination hardened into an iron stoicism, particularly when the cancer that struck in the mid-1950s returned a decade later. There in the files is what appears to be a master copy, as if she planned to send standard replies to people enquiring after health, and so cut short the tedious business of explaining her circumstances to everyone individually. It reads, I am sorry that you had to hear of my illness. I am told, as was my sister, Mrs. Pifer, when she was at the hospital here, that there can be no positive answer for some time. Either I come out feet foremost, or I come out for some interval, return for more treatment, etc. There is no known cure, and no cause for grief – some people are struck by drunk drivers. Sincerely....'

Monday 26 September
I awoke at four-thirty yesterday from a dream about

282

skunks. I was telling someone to relax: 'We don't have skunks in England.' True, but we do have them in Nebraska, and the bedroom was filled with that pungent, unmistakable smell. Had one got into the basement? The house itself? It was daylight before I found the droppings outside the front door, and by then the air was breathable again. I think my visitor had just been marking out its territory – right under my bedroom window.

After a leisurely breakfast I took a little tour. I set off down Hwy 61, a lonely road with next to no radio reception and precious little to look at, just the constantly shifting colors of the fall grasses. I passed four vehicles in 57 miles and veered off the pavement just once, distracted by my thoughts. Turning west at Hyannis and heading along Hwy 2, I paused at Antioch, a scattering of buildings now but in the period 1916 to 1921 home to 2,000 souls and a thriving potash industry. Supplies from Europe being cut off due to the war, somebody discovered that the vital mineral could be extracted from the alkaline content of the lakes down there. In *Old Jules* Mari refers to those bodies of water as 'stinking as old setting eggs, the gray water edged with alkali-bleached tufts of grass.' But suddenly they were valuable, and people whom Old Jules had scorned for their stupidity in settling on such land were making a mint. Over those boom years there were five plants working round the clock. Then overseas supplies were restored, production came to a halt, and the buildings were left to decay. Interestingly, Merriman also had a potash plant, employing as many as 300 people at one time – until a fire burned it to the ground.

I stopped too at Ellsworth, again little more than a

handful of buildings around the junction with Hwy 27. This is where the old Spade Ranch had its headquarters, and the former company store is still there, now re- invented as Morgan's Cowpoke Haven. Unfortunately for me, it's closed on Sundays.

I was heading for Alliance, a large town by the standards of western Nebraska, having almost 9,000 inhabitants. I was looking for Old Jules' grave, which I'd never seen. I hadn't the faintest idea where he was buried, so I walked into the first gas station I came across and asked to be directed to the cemetery. The guy at the cash register was not from around these parts, but a customer came to my rescue. 'Which cemetery?' she asked. 'City or Catholic?' I couldn't imagine Old Jules resting easy amongst the Catholics. 'City,' I said, and then listened as the lady tried to explain how to get there. She soon realized it was a lost cause. 'Look,' she said, 'I'm not doing anything special. Follow me. I'm in that jeep.' She led me all the way to the cemetery, pointing out its directory, before accepting my thanks and driving off.

The directory, which looked like a cross between a mausoleum and an automated cash dispenser, was an electronic, touch-screen job. As soon as I keyed in 'Sandoz' up it came. Block 8, Section 5. I found Jules, Mary and Flora tucked in beside the Strasburgers, whose nephews Jules threatened when they came to talk about running a new phone line across his land. Mari it was who prevented bloodshed, striking the barrel of his raised gun to send the shot harmlessly over their heads.

Further along I found the thing I'd come to see. But what do you do at a grave consisting of no more than a loaf-shaped piece of stone set in the grass, and bearing the words 'Father. Jules A. Sandoz. In Loving Memory'? I read the words, and tried to imagine a conversation amongst the children, and Mary, about what they should put. Did the wording represent a resigned acceptance that that was what ought to be there, or did it come from the heart – and if so, from whose? And should I be standing over the man's remains thinking about that? It seemed inappropriate, intrusive.

I'll go out on a limb here and say a little about my own family, and add another layer to the many reasons why I am fascinated with Mari's story. My father was not a nice man – at least, not to his wife, whose fate was distressingly similar to Henriette's, nor to his children. There were times when he was violent, abusive and neglectful towards us. We feared him. He spoke about the good stock we came from but showed no ambition, ever, to lift himself out of the poor circumstances into which he had slumped - although he expected us to. Yet there is within us, as a brood, a residue of affection for some part of him, a regard for the qualities that came from our ancestors, through him, to us. And maybe that's something that intrigues me about Mari's relationship with her father, and why I stopped to think about those few words carved on the stone. Our father's grave is even simpler than Old Jules'. It is unmarked, unvisited, its precise location forgotten.

I drove home up Hwy 87, through Hay Springs and Rushville, completing a circular trip of 200-plus miles. If I can get to see Caroline this week I will have made all the pilgrimages I intended to make.

I mentioned earlier the many colors that mark the hills just now. There are pinks in the grass, and reds, yellows and greens. Sometimes they are mingled together; elsewhere there are separate broad splashes of a single hue, according to the type of land, the amount of moisture and so on. Where there are trees, other than cedars, there are spots of yellow emerging, here and there the vivid red of a grapevine. It's a glorious time of year, and it's going to be a real wrench to take my leave next week.

Tuesday 27 September

There are times when you realize something is bugging you, but you just don't know what it is. Occasionally it niggles away at you for days, a sense of something not done, or that needs fixing – except that the feeling is so vague that you can't pinpoint it. You wake up, as I did this morning, feeling out of sorts and wishing you knew why.

I drank my tea and went out to check the temperature: 56 and rising fast. The sunlight was coming in, almost horizontally, shining on the bare earth that I'd piled up against the side of the house some weeks ago now, and seeded. That's when I realized what was troubling me. I'd been waiting for the grass to come up, and it hadn't. Until this morning. There it was, emerging like a slightly threadbare emerald carpet. Over the past couple of weeks I have watched wave after wave of fat, greedy grasshoppers crawl all over that bare earth; and I'd convinced myself that they were eating the seeds, as well as any emerging shoots, and that my efforts had been wasted. I sowed the seed in the hope that I might walk away from here in a week's time with fresh green sward in place against the newly painted façade. I had a clear picture of it in my mind – red against green, with the white of my newly painted door and windows - and the idea that I'd failed was getting to me. So, fingers crossed.

Yesterday I drove Mercy to town to put some gas in the tank, and while I was down there I embarked on something of a farewell tour. I realized that I'd yet to take any photos of Merriman, other than from the air – and since I'm already booked in to give a talk on my adventures to the University of the Third Age next spring I want to be able to show a British audience what a town of 118 people looks like. I've also been gathering one or two bits and pieces of information about Merriman's history. It was born in 1885 as the Fremont, Elkhorn and Missouri Valley railroad pushed west, and it was named after one of that company's officials. By the turn of the century it had four stores, three hotels and a pool-hall, a butcher's, two barber shops, a bank, two restaurants, a drug-store and a blacksmith, two doctors and a couple of lumber-yards. It was a major cattle shipping depot in the early 1900s, used by the Spade ranch, amongst others. It saw more cattle, it has been said, than any other town between Omaha to the east and Casper, Wyoming, to the west. The town was also, in the early days, an important trading-post for the Indian reservation to the north, and thrived on the trade of the Kinkaiders who poured into the Sandhills after 1904 to take up the free land released from the cattleman's grasp.

While I was down there I called in on someone I'd met at one of the parties I've been to. I found Will doing what proprietors of small businesses always end up doing, sweeping the place out. He has a body-shop tucked away in an alley off Main Street. We talked about a number of things, and he was soon telling me about his adventures in London and his thoughts on the beer they serve there, and how he got shouted at by drunken louts for being a ******* Yank… but I was only half listening. Something that was hanging on his wall had caught my eye. A canoe, I thought. I was wrong. It's the rotted hull of an old sailing-boat, made of steel, with lead in the joints. That, my friend explained, was brought to the Sandhills by an English nobleman who bought a place just north and east of the highway, back in the 1890s. He had a lake on his land, fancied the idea of sailing on it, and had this craft, along with several others, shipped out. Will salvaged it from a blow-out. So what happened to my fellow-countryman (who, I have since learned, was probably a Captain Fuller.)? It seems he had a rather good racket going on, a sort of dude-ranch where he fetched in Englishmen who wanted a taste of adventure, put them to work on the spread and charged them for the privilege. It all went to pot when he took off to California one time and left the inmates in charge of the asylum, so to speak. There was a blizzard, and they had the bright idea of bringing the cattle in off the range – right into the stack-yard, where they climbed all over the winter's supply of feed and pretty much destroyed it.

As I drove home I was thinking about this, and the stories I've yet to hear; and wondering, not for the first time, why anybody ever bothers to write fiction.

Wednesday 28 September

I am starting to dash around from task to task, one eye on the calendar, one on the weather. As I write, my desk is a disaster area, the floor is dotted with sand-burs, the sills are dotted with squashed flies. Outside there are signs of the changing season – new ones, daily, that I'd like to see, absorb and record. But I only have five days left and quite a list of things to do.

Yesterday I ran into Kitty's dad for the first time in an age. I was walking down the hill to the red house, my laptop slung over my shoulder, my camera, as ever, in my left hand, when he came by on his ATV. He was interested in my recent researches into the history of the red house, and told me that the Wrights, who took it on after the Arents left in 1948, were struck by tragedy. Mr Wright was taking his young daughter up the hill, not very far from where I was standing, on the old road that preceded this one. The scar of it is still there, in the hillside. He had a problem with the vehicle, stopped to jack it up and managed to roll it over on top of himself. By the time help was summoned he was dead.

Following this, the property passed to another Wright family, not related. I don't know whether these people lived here, but am assuming that the first Wrights would have done. It seems that my attempt at a history of the red house is destined to be re-written every time I get into a conversation about it. Kitty's dad told me that when the place was up for sale in 1961 another party was all set to buy, but couldn't agree over a couple of hay-stacks that were on the land. The prospective purchasers wanted them included, the vendors didn't. Negotiations stalled, and that's how the land ended up in his hands.

In the afternoon I went to Gordon to meet up with the lady who had agreed to accompany me to see Caroline. She greeted me with a bag of plump ripe tomatoes from her yard. Mari Sandoz' last surviving sibling was asleep, and although she seemed to waken after a few minutes she wasn't really focused. Down the corridor we found Tanya, the young Ukrainian woman I met at the party some weeks ago. She got a response. Squatted down, put her hand on the old lady's knee, and addressed her, loudly and clearly, with a smile on her face and love in her voice. May we all be so well treated as we approach the end. Caroline did perk up a little, more so when we showed her the books I'd brought, the ones she'd produced about Mari's life and signed for me fifteen years ago, but she didn't speak. Tanya suggested I return another day, before lunch, which she tells me is one of Caroline's better times.

On the way home I paused at the crossroads in Merriman, then swung north. Among the ranchers whose acquaintance I've made these past few months was L. He'd told me to call in some time at his place, a few miles north of town. Big house, he said. Can't miss it. I encountered a familiar scene as I drove into the yard: sheets of tin lying about the place, a ladder against the side of the house, and a guy on his knees with a pair of cutters in one hand, a pencil in the other. He was re-roofing. L was walking towards me, frowning, trying to figure out who the hell he knew who would be driving a car with Montana plates.

We sat for a good hour, more like two, drinking beer and chewing the fat. I wasn't surprised at the way the conversation ranged from the economics of ranching to near-death experiences, from women to foreign travel, from the people he met on the streets of New York to the old Native man he knew as a boy who one night strung out a water-snake on a wire fence and summoned up rain in a dry spell. I think that's why I'd called in: this guy is always good for a provocative view on life, and a story. And he paid me a compliment, one I will remember with pride. Twice he told me he was real sorry to see me go home, because he admired me for what I was doing. What, I said, lazing around in a hunting lodge all summer? 'No,' he said, 'for coming out to the Sandhills. You don't want a ranch, you don't want a cow, you don't want a fence, you just seem to like being here.' I think I saw what he meant. And then he gave me a warning. 'Some time after you get back home,' he said, 'you'll hear them calling to you, these hills, and you'll wish you could be back.' Matt has hinted at that too, and this morning Kitty showed me the poems she wrote when he was in Afghanistan, expressing the very same thing. We shall see. As I've said before, I am more than ready to be home, but I know, as surely as I know anything, that I am going to miss this place hugely.

I drove back here with a couple of small books L has loaned me, a collection of reminiscences written by his grandfather. 'Drop `em off at the station before you go,' he said. He meant the gas station.

Friday 30 September

I had a feeling it would be like this towards the end. The weather has conspired to make it very, very difficult to think about leaving. The air is as clear as could be, the warmth of the late summer sun is balanced by a gentle breeze which brings a freshness I haven't felt for weeks, and the colors out there are simply stunning.

This afternoon I walked out onto the center pivot, partly for the pure pleasure of walking through the stubble, a thing I always look forward to at home, but also to satisfy my curiosity as to the precise size of those bales. Each cylinder is about five feet wide, and would be a little more than that in height if you stood it up. I doubt that those dimensions are of the slightest interest to a living soul in western Nebraska, but when I get home and show my pictures, and talk about what I've seen here, I want to sound as though I know what I'm on about.

I ended up walking down-river a little way. It felt a rather as though I was starting on a long round of goodbyes - to certain trees, certain grasses, to a whole landscape that's given me company and beauty these last few months. I dare say I'll come this way again. I don't seem to be able to avoid it. This is, if I remember correctly, my twelfth visit to Nebraska.

A last supper

Monday 3 October

I must have been nine, because we'd certainly got our first television. I was in primary school, and it was morning assembly. My mate and I were having a whispered conversation about the latest *Lone Ranger* episode when I saw the headmaster peering at me through a crowd of heads. I'd like to blame what followed on my strict upbringing, which was based on Bible teaching, with special emphasis on fire, brimstone and the awfulness of sins such as bearing false witness; but perhaps I was just stupid. I thought that if I stopped talking it would be like pretending I hadn't been; and that, surely, would be a little like lying, a deliberate deception. So I carried on, and when the headmaster finally reared over me with a face like thunder I was hit by something that seemed awfully like a fusillade of fire and brimstone. I tried to explain, but couldn't make him see the sense of it, that I had carried on talking in order *not* to deceive him. I think I've been trying to explain some of my actions to the world ever since – and maybe that's why I write. However, I am going to resist the temptation to launch into a lengthy rationale about what I've been up to these past six months. When it comes, it'll be brief.

The sun is easing its way stealthily down towards the top of the bluffs. I've just scrunched up a few of the dried sunflower stalks from the yard, broken a couple of down branches for kindling and fetched an armful of the logs that are stacked up beside the garage. Checked them for snakes, naturally. They're very dry and quite light. They'll burn rapidly. In a few minutes I'll put a match to the fire, then go and prepare that 12-ounce rib-eye steak I bought yesterday. There are one or two potatoes left at the bottom of the fridge, one last fat tomato grown by my friend in Gordon. I have the makings of a decent supper.

I came here six months ago with the intention of learning more about Mari Sandoz and maybe writing a book about her. I soon became more interested in my immediate surroundings: the ranch, the folk around me, the community of plants that thrive on this dry, sandy soil. I think I perfectly understand Mari's attachment to the region now, as well as her reasons for having to leave. I doubt that I've contributed a great deal to Sandoz scholarship, but maybe I'll persuade a few people to read her works. I've learned a lot here, and tried to record the best of it, but the truth is I still feel massively ignorant around my neighbours. I still struggle, for example, to differentiate between a white-tail and a mule deer at any distance, although I suspect that I know more flowers and grasses than some of the cowboys I've encountered. I hope I've done a decent job – not so much of describing the Sandhills as evoking them. The *spirit* of the place: that's what I've been after.

I have, too, become attached to the red house. That is surely evident. I have lived here longer, I think, than all but a handful of people since the Arents sold up, which was not long before I was born. I have helped, in a small way, to improve the old place – and that has been a privilege. So I feel it's okay to put it in the title and thus stake a minor claim to it. I hope too that I've given Nebraska a bit of a boost. I've been wanting to do that ever since that cowboy at Bushnell damned it as 'de-so-late' – although, like most Sandhillers, I'm uneasy about letting people in the wider world know just what a great area this is. Still, it survived the migrations of the 1880s and `90s, and the land-hungry Kinkaiders. It could surely survive the odd visitor looking for this particular stretch of the Niobrara.

The sun has just now disappeared, the hills opposite are flushed pink, and through the rustle of the cottonwood leaves I can make out the rippling of the Niobrara as it heads east, doing what it's done day after day, year after year for all the generations of people who have lived down here, in tipis, in caves, in soddies and in this little red house. The Running Water. It's an appropriate name.

My fire has been blazing for some time now and is slowly reducing to a bed of red coals. I've just cracked my last bottle of Fat Tire. Soon as I've drunk that I'll throw the steak on the grille.

Looking Back

The odd thing about leaving next day was that, as I climbed into Mercy one last time and set off along the two-track, I didn't look back. Sure, I glanced in the wing-mirror and saw the little house, brand new roof gleaming, freshly-painted concrete blocks glowing blood red in the afternoon sun. And sure, I thought about stopping, about getting out for one last, lingering look. But then the thought came to me, unbidden, fully formed and already shaped into the words that best describe my feelings about the entire trip. *I have drunk my fill.*

That was it. I had drunk my fill. I had done what I hoped to do, satisfied a craving to know and be part of something that has always meant so much to me, something vast and truly mythical. The American West. Yes, I understand - because I have traveled in all seventeen trans-Mississippi states over thirty years and more - I understand that there is no single 'West', any more than there is a single 'American Dream'. There are the Rocky Mountains, there is the Great Basin, and the Texas Hill Country, the dreary Oklahoma Panhandle, the Upper Missouri country. There is too New Mexico, with its white deserts and snowy peaks, its Alpine meadows and red mesas. There is even California, enclosing within it landscapes of every kind, and I have seen all of those places during a dozen extended road trips, and there are the damp woods of the Pacific northwest; but this place - the Sandhills of Nebraska - is where I chose most often to stop the car, light my fire and unroll my bed. This was the place where I chose to dig a little deeper, put down a few temporary roots and imbibe the very spirit of the place. And now, after six months, the cup was indeed empty, my thirst quenched, my hunger satisfied. And so I put my foot down one last time and charged up that rutted, bumpy old track towards the ranch-house, where I would transfer to my clean, air-conditioned hire car, drive to Rapid and start the long journey home.

A little more than four months have elapsed as I write this post-script. I wasn't sure what I'd think when I re-read the narrative I'd created, those last days down by the Niobrara. Would it make sense? I hope so, because in the end, I don't feel inclined to change a great deal. I've been busy adjusting to life back in England, and picking up my other work. But my time in cattle country is always there, in my head. I regularly browse through my hundreds of photographs and every week or two select a fresh one for a screen-saver. Mostly it'll be two-thirds sky, one-third grass - and the sky is generally dominated by a towering thunder-cloud, or illuminated by a setting sun. Sometimes the grass is dotted with black cattle, other times it's soapweed or sunflowers. I remember voices, make notes to myself to check whether I've included them in the narrative - and generally find that I have. And already I dream of further adventures, perhaps with those rodeo riders I knew briefly down in Utah; perhaps in New Mexico, the other place that has a hand on my heart; maybe up in North

Dakota - which, like Nebraska, was nowhere near as drab as they say it is.

Now imagine a period of silence as I look out the window at an English winter sky - grey clouds slipping over red-tiled roofs, low sun peeping through the gaps - and then decide that no, right now I have nothing more to add. Believe me when I say that I have gone over this account several times and decided that the preceding 90,000 words have told the story the best way I can.

Durham, England
February 2012